Spirit on the Move

Religious Cultures of African
and African Diaspora People

—

Series editors:
JACOB K. OLUPONA, Harvard University
DIANNE M. STEWART, Emory University, and
TERRENCE L. JOHNSON, Georgetown University

—

The book series examines the religious, cultural, and political expressions of African, African American, and African Caribbean traditions. Through transnational, cross-cultural, and multidisciplinary approaches to the study of religion, the series investigates the epistemic boundaries of continental and diasporic religious practices and thought and explores the diverse and distinct ways African-derived religions inform culture and politics. The series aims to establish a forum for imagining the centrality of Black religions in the formation of the "New World."

Edited by JUDITH CASSELBERRY &
ELIZABETH A. PRITCHARD

SPIRIT
— *on the* —
MOVE

Black Women and Pentecostalism
in Africa and the Diaspora

Duke University Press | *Durham and London* | 2019

© 2019 Duke University Press
All rights reserved
Designed by Julienne Alexander
Typeset in Franklin Gothic and Arno Pro by Graphic Composition, Inc., Bogart, GA

Library of Congress Cataloging-in-Publication Data
Names: Casselberry, Judith, [date] editor. | Pritchard, Elizabeth A. (Elizabeth Ann), editor.
Title: Spirit on the move : Black women and Pentecostalism in Africa and the diaspora / Judith Casselberry and Elizabeth A. Pritchard, editors.
Description: Durham : Duke University Press, 2019. | Series: Religious cultures of African and African diaspora people | Includes bibliographical references and index. Identifiers:
LCCN 2018032578 (print)
LCCN 2018042518 (ebook)
ISBN 9781478002116 (ebook)
ISBN 9781478000136 (hardcover)
ISBN 9781478000327 (pbk.)
Subjects: LCSH: Pentecostalism. | Women, Black—Religious life. | Pentecostal churches. | African diaspora. Classification: LCC BR1644.3 (ebook) | LCC BR1644.3 .S65 2019 (print) | DDC 270.8/3082—dc23
LC record available at https://lccn.loc.gov/2018032578

Cover art: Photograph by Laura Premack.

We dedicate this volume to the women and
religious communities whose vision and labor
made it possible and whose steadfastness
continues to fire our imaginations.

CONTENTS

Acknowledgments ix

Introduction — Elizabeth A. Pritchard 1

PART I: SAVING RACE

1 — VOICES OF GOD: *Blackness and Gender in a Brazilian Black Gospel Music Scene* — John Burdick 27

2 — RACE, GENDER, AND CHRISTIAN DIASPORA: *New Pentecostal Intersectionalities and Haiti* — Elizabeth McAlister 44

PART II: SCRUTINIZING AND SANCTIFYING THE BODY

3 — WOMEN AND THE AFRO-BRAZILIAN PENTECOSTAL WAR IN MOZAMBIQUE — Linda van de Kamp 67

4 — "DRESSED AS BECOMETH HOLINESS": *Gender, Race, and the Body in a Storefront Sanctified Church* — Deidre Helen Crumbley 89

PART III: SONIC POWER

5 — WEST AFRICAN AND CARIBBEAN WOMEN EVANGELISTS: *The Wailing Women Worldwide Intercessors* — Paula Aymer 109

6 — "THE KINGDOM IN THE MIDST": *Sounding Bodies, Aesthetic Labor, and the End Times* — Judith Casselberry 128

PART IV: MODELING THE STATE

7 — A CRITICAL APPROACH TO CONCEPTS OF "POWER" AND "AGENCY" IN GHANA'S CHARISMATIC (OR NEO-PENTECOSTAL) CHURCHES — Jane Soothill 151

8 — BLESS US WITH CHILDREN: *Pregnancy, Prosperity, and Pragmatism in Nigeria's Christ Apostolic Church* — Laura Premack 180

References 197

Contributors 221

Index 225

ACKNOWLEDGMENTS

We would like to take this opportunity to thank Bowdoin College—specifically, our former dean, Cristle Collins Judd, for funding the symposium from which these essays are drawn. We thank, too, our colleagues whose work does not appear in this volume but who contributed enormously to the symposium, whether by planning, presenting, or responding to papers: Melvin L. Butler, professor of ethnomusicology, Frost School of Music, University of Miami; Alex Dauge-Roth, professor of French and Francophone language and literature, Bates College; Marla F. Frederick, professor of African American studies and religion at Harvard University; Cheryl Townsend Gilkes, John D. and Catherine T. MacArthur Professor of Sociology and African American Studies at Colby College; David Gordon, professor of African history at Bowdoin College; and Yolanda Pierce, dean of Howard University School of Divinity. We remain grateful to Emily Hricko, who judiciously and cheerfully organized the many details of the symposium, and to David Israel, who artfully and expertly built and managed the symposium website. We also recognize the financial support and professional endorsement supplied by Olufemi Vaughan, former chair of Africana studies, Bowdoin College, and now Alfred Sargent Lee '41 and Mary Farley Ames Lee Professor of Black Studies at Amherst College, and Jorunn Buckley, former chair of and now professor emeritus of religion, Bowdoin College.

INTRODUCTION

ELIZABETH A. PRITCHARD

In the past two decades, scholarly attention to Pentecostalism has increased significantly in an effort to address this fastest-growing sector of contemporary Christianity. At the turn of the twenty-first century, followers of Pentecostal Christianity number 345 million to 523 million, with an estimated 9 million conversions annually. Overwhelmingly, growth is evidenced outside of the West, with women constituting 75 percent of the membership (Anderson 2004: 11; Robbins 2004: 117). Amid this astonishing growth, Pentecostal belief and practice continues to reflect variety, complexity, and even paradox. Pentecostals eschew worldly affairs, categories, and structures, yet they are also known to be avid participants in political elections and citizenship campaigns.[1] Some Pentecostal churches embrace sober and simple lifestyles; still others accumulate significant wealth, as well as extensive and diverse media holdings. Pentecostal gender discipline suggests a revamping of patriarchal domestic relationships yet empowers women with spiritual authority and prompts men to forgo significant gender prerogatives.

Given this explosive growth, obvious appeal to women, and global reach, the moment seemed exactly right for academics to gather together to reflect on these trends. The essays in this volume are drawn from a symposium held at Bowdoin College that brought together leading and emerging scholars in Africana, religious, and feminist studies, as well as history, anthropology, sociology, and ethnomusicology, to discuss

Pentecostalism's appeal to Black women in settings as wide-ranging as Brazil, Ghana, Grenada, Haiti, Mozambique, Nigeria, Rwanda, the United States, and Zambia. The variety of these contexts showcases Pentecostalism's reach, as well as its adaptability to specific cultural and political formations.[2] Although missionary entanglements with US churches continue, local agentive processes of religious appropriation and transformation have been present from the start (Corten and Marshall-Fratani 2001: 16). The flows of Pentecostal people and ideas scramble colonial "center-periphery" templates; they crisscross lines between former colonies and establish South-South relations. Indeed, this diversity is also reflected in the fact that not all of the authors use the term "Pentecostal." Some use "evangelical" or "Neo-Pentecostal," the latter referring to more recent trends emphasizing "health and wealth," spiritual warfare and deliverance, and the extensive use of media. Others use the designations "spirit-filled" or "sanctified." "Pentecostal" is perhaps best understood, then, as signaling a "family resemblance" among convictions and practices. This resemblance largely pertains to "the working of gifts of the spirit" (Anderson 2004: 13), which include healing, prophesizing, and speaking in tongues.[3]

The primary rationale for a volume focused on Black women and Pentecostalism in diaspora is a sense that, although Black women constitute a substantial proportion of the world's Pentecostals, there has been a dearth of explorations of their experiences, theologies, and innovations in diverse contexts. In addition to fleshing out the complex subjectivities of Black women, then, the contributors to this volume place them at the center of scholarship on Pentecostalism to explore the interosculation of gender and race, as well as class, religion, and nation. This aim reflects the insights and commitments of intersectionality theory, as coined by Kimberlé Williams Crenshaw (1989) and reflected in Black feminist sources dating to the nineteenth century.[4] According to various contributors to this theory, people experience structural inequalities, as well as sources of identification, as simultaneous, miscible, or interlocking rather than as discrete categories. Intersectionality analyses challenge the presumption that one form of domination or identification is more foundational or explanatory than another; they also contest monolithic readings of identity that deny intragroup differences. However, it is only very recently that theorists of intersectionality have considered addressing religion (see Goldschmidt and McAlister 2004; Singh 2015). Some of this neglect is certainly attributable to a presumption of secularity whereby religion is regarded as an axis of oppression necessitating resistance on the part of fully emancipated subjects. At the same time, the reluctance to engage with religion reveals the gender-, class-, and race-based aspects of conventional understandings of religion and secularity. As Gayatri Spivak (2012: 396) suggests, "The separation of Church and State and the separation of the public and the private are too race- and class-specific and indeed gender-specific to hold up a just world." Similarly, Marie Griffith (1997: 205), writing about secular feminists' lack of engagement with spirit-filled women's movements, has noted that "general hostility toward religious and cultural 'backwardness' is fueled by interests that are profoundly class-based."

The second rationale for this volume is our conviction that taking into account Black women's diasporic dislocations sheds new light on the political implications of Pentecostalism. These dislocations challenge modern secular pretensions of clearly delimited subjects, nations, and religions. They belie the presumption that all the world's inhabitants are citizens whose bodies and interests are equally and sufficiently claimed and protected by sovereign states and their vaunted "rule of law." Black women across the globe—variously disenfranchised and displaced or disaffected by racism, misogyny, corruption, civil war, neoliberal privatization, poverty, and climate change—continue to cultivate diverse modes of mobilization and to enter fraught negotiations with the media sensations afforded by globalization. Spirit work signifies and expresses their *struggle*, not just in cosmologies, churches, individuals, and households, but within and among nation-states and their migrant corridors. To this end, we insist that a major appeal of Pentecostalism to Black women worldwide consists in its being the proximate and preeminent opportunity for these women to engage what Lauren Berlant (1997: 81), albeit in a different context, refers to as "undead desires to form a live relation to power." For instance, accounting for her shift from a Baptist to a Pentecostal congregation, Mrs. W., whom Arthur Fauset describes as "a middle-aged colored woman," declared that she needed "more power."[5] This lived engagement with the Pentecostal "gift of power" undoubtedly reflects the specificities of particular contexts, yet it betrays a consistent and resolute focus on detecting and dispelling disabling power and cultivating enabling power (Hardesty 1999: 49).

The massive growth of a transnational religious population enamored with power was not supposed to happen. In the modern secular context, power was to be centralized and monopolized by "states," while "religions," never really privatized, were nonetheless downgraded to various edifying projects of meaning making, self-fashioning, and cultural heritage. State and religion were to be fully extricated and confined to their respective jurisdictions; possessive spirits were to be sent packing; liminal and festive orgies were to be curtailed; and boundaries were to be installed all around to prevent the indiscriminate mixing that would confound the aspirations of rational actors, nation-states, and capitalist markets.[6] According to Charles Taylor, rational actors or secular subjects are not "enchanted" but "buffered." Taylor's buffered self is in contrast to the purported "premodern self" who was susceptible to random flows of power and influence, both spiritual and demonic. He writes:

> Modern Westerners have a clear and firm boundary between mind and world, even mind and body. . . . For the modern, buffered self, the possibility exists of taking a distance, disengaging, from everything outside the mind. . . . As a bounded self, I see the boundary as a buffer, such that the things beyond don't need to "get to me," to use the contemporary expression. That's the sense of my use of the term "buffered" here. *This self can see itself as invulnerable, as master of the meanings that things have for it.* (Taylor 2011: 40–41, emphasis added; see also Taylor 2007: 300–301; Taylor 2011: 39–42)

Taylor's (2007: 423) description of buffered subjects is incongruent with his acknowledgment of the "penetration" everywhere of electronic media. Moreover, we are not convinced that modernity affords inviolable boundaries, feelings of invulnerability, or mastery of meanings. Indeed, where or who is the modern West in the constantly shifting context that is the postcolonial diaspora, with its transnational circuits of migration and media? We repudiate conceptions of modern subjectivity that are uninformed and undifferentiated with regard to class, race, gender, sexuality, and nation.

The essays gathered here highlight how Pentecostals forge "connections [that] chafe against the realpolitik of geopolitical mappings" and make "hemispheric linkages within the deepest epistemic and affective logics of empire and violence." In doing so, they draw attention to "shared cosmologies of suffering which bring together [for instance] displaced mothers" (Chatterjee 2009, quoted in Swarr and Nagar 2010: 46). These connections reflect how Pentecostals' affective attachments alternately mediate, mirror, and remedy the injustices, deprivations, and opportunities posed by the diasporic dislocations of modernity. Black women's bodies, in particular, continue to be points of production for the antagonisms of civil war, neoliberal capitalist exploitation, and racist stigmatization. Thus, we insist that even the personal and domestic settings for the labors of spirit power—dress and comportment, housekeeping and parenting, infidelity and abuse, fertility and death—are to be understood against the backdrop of the inequities and conflicts produced by state formation and failure. This insistence is a reflection of one of the lessons of intersectionality: that sources and practices of identity are inextricably linked to, and thus reflect and respond to, political and economic structures.

In contrast to Taylor's account of modern subjects, Pentecostals imagine "spirit" not as a safely contained, distant, or transcendent divinity, but as a power pulsing through and linking individuals. Spirit power is not a sacred trust, then, but "a reservoir of signs at the disposal of individuals" who have no need of or access to extensive and costly credentialing systems. In spirit-filled practice, religion as an embodied "chain of memory" entailing calendric ritual observance has given way to more expressive and ephemeral performances tied to the social and political changes wrought by neoliberal capitalist modes of production (Hervieu-Lèger 2000: 168; see also Hervieu-Lèger 2000: 59, 137, 172–73). These characteristics of Pentecostalism evidence John Modern's version of secularism, whereby individuals are porous vessels subject to "forces . . . neither visible nor strictly corporeal" (Modern 2011: 34, 46). Such forces cannot be critically overcome or even entirely exorcised; they can only be caught and channeled through continually refashioned circuits of connectivity.

In shifting our attention from the racial, class, and gender assumptions and aspirations of the "modern West" to the diasporic contexts of postcolonial Africa, we find much that contradicts the conventional suppositions of the secular: religions are not confined to private or so-called sacred spaces, clearly marked congregations, or unidirectional flows from authorized people and hegemonic centers. These instances do not indicate the persistence of a premodern and enchanted Africa as against a secular modern West. Rather, they indicate the inadequacy of standard models of secularity and the need to rethink binary relations of state and religion, public and private, political and spiritual. We might consider, for instance, the extent to which religions—in a postcolonial diasporic context—have become secular or "worldly," circulating as signs, constituting various publics, and making up for state failure or neglect.

For instance, we suggest that Pentecostal gatherings can be seen as performances of what Michael Warner (2002: 26) calls "collective public intimacy." They tacitly contest bourgeois publics that are predicated on relative strangerhood and on distanciation from the body's particularities. Pentecostal media stage expressive publics that rely on affect rather than deliberation, textual mastery, or academic authority. Thus, Pentecostal publics appear to qualify as to what Warner (2002: 26) calls a counter-public—that is, a public that is in "tension with a larger public. . . . Discussion within such a public is understood to contravene the rules obtaining in the world at large, being structured by alternative dispositions or protocols, making different assumptions about what can be said or what goes without saying." Our focus on gender and race—specifically, our attention to the related, albeit diverse, perceptions, aspirations, and actions of Black women—highlights the extent to which Pentecostal churches and para-churches provide opportunities for marginalized people to speak and to do so in multitudinous ways. Pentecostal publics also qualify, then, as specific instantiations of what Nancy Fraser refers to as "subaltern counterpublics." For Fraser (1990: 67), these publics are "parallel discursive arenas where members of subordinated social groups invent and circulate counterdiscourses, which in turn permit them to formulate oppositional interpretations of their identities, interests, needs." Pentecostal worship services are hardly venues of escape; they are, as Ruth Marshall-Fratani (2001: 90) notes, evidence of "a conscious project of creating—modern, functional spaces and forms of association." These gatherings—which use media technology and eschew narrow boundaries of locality—are virtual worlds in which spiritual affiliation seeks to neutralize the antagonisms and anxieties of unbuffered selves.

We share with proponents of "lived religion" a focus on religion's role in contexts of dislocation and struggle: "The study of lived religion has attended with particular care to moments of conflict, dissonance, and displacement. . . . [It] has focused chiefly on people whose lives have been ruptured by social, political and historical circumstances, and such work highlights multiple creative uses of religion in the midst as well as the aftermath of those dynamic changes" (Griffith and Savage 2006: xvii). At the same time, we think that the contemporary flows of people and media are reshaping religion such that "lived religion" conjures an erstwhile stability or continuity that is not reflective of diasporic contexts. The transnational flows and forums of Pentecostal missionaries, migrants, and media celebrities resemble better what Peggy Levitt refers to as "religious assemblages." Levitt derives the idea of religious assemblages from philosophical theories predicated on the image of the rhizome (Deleuze and Guattari 1987: 21). In botany, a rhizome is a plant whose nodes or extensions behave as roots, allowing for extensive lateral growth. As a philosophical idea, it represents entities that are nonhierarchical in that they afford multiple entry points, affiliations, and offshoots, with no definitive origin or singular root. Levitt borrows this idea to convey religious affiliations that entail "contingent clustering" and myriad "sites of encounter" and that make for an "unruly, clumsy collection that is constantly on the move." Levitt is particularly concerned to capture the dynamism and opportunism of religious activity in a context of global movement. Although the movements may not be subject to control and resist centralization, they are constrained, and thus uneven. Levitt describes the process this way: "new overlays land on pockmarked geographies, enabling some things to travel easily while inhibiting others" (Levitt 2013: 160, 165, 169). Levitt's theory has affinities with Amit Rai's theory of "media assemblages." Rai challenges readers to think of media as the "contested production of sensation," rather than simply methods of information delivery or a series of representations that are finished products reflecting hierarchies of power. Accordingly, such contested productions are events or scenes of circulation of "a predictable but patterned trajectory of present conforming to past but open to future mutations." Rai's theory is useful to scholars of diasporic Pentecostals insofar as it captures the dynamism of spirit-filled stagings and directs attention to Pentecostal "ecologies of sensation"—that is, to the passionate attachments of various populations (Rai 2009: 2–3).

By way of illustration, consider the following scenes. The first two come from a praise and worship service at the Pentecostal Revival Church, a largely Ghanaian church in southern Amsterdam, the Netherlands, on

Pentecost, May 27, 2012.⁷ The service (in English, Dutch, and Akan/Twi) was held in a large performance hall, used regularly by the church. One of the special guests that day was the Evangel Concert Orchestra of Evangel University (Assemblies of God, Springfield, Missouri), which was wrapping up an extended tour through major European cities. Larry Dissmore, the director, explained that although their repertoire of African American spirituals would be unknown to the various residents of Europe, it was a particularly fitting gift from his American institution. (Dissmore did not, however, acknowledge the orchestra's overwhelmingly White membership.) He added that although the audience would not know the songs, they would find familiar their rhythms and laments. The large assembly listened politely as the orchestra and chorus performed the spirituals. When they finished, the Ghanaian pastor, Emmanuel Koney, announced to his American guests that now they were going to be treated to *true* African music and dance. At that point, the crowd roared with delight and jumped up to sing and dance in a decidedly joyous fashion.

Another special guest the same day was the Ghanaian actress Mercy Asiedu. She paid tribute to the authority of the minister, but then in song and dance playfully put him in his place, to the energetic affirmative responses of the women in the hall. Her mischievous energy and their supportive cheers lent tangible support to Diane Austin-Broos's (1997: 235) contention that patriarchy in large urban Pentecostal churches largely consists of "set pieces" that are "overtaken by the practice of women."⁸ Moreover, the impromptu performance served to confirm Nicole Toulis's (1997: 235) observation that within spirit-filled churches women use their expressive power to monopolize a service, despite being excluded from the role of "pastor."⁹ Indeed, Asiedu then proceeded to sing several songs from her gospel recordings, while the pastor wove in and out of rows upon rows of people, hawking her CDs.

The third scene is lifted from the fact and fiction that is Asiedu's celebrity. As she demonstrated at the church in Amsterdam, Asiedu is deft at riffing on gender expectations and performances; she has a wonderfully comic routine on YouTube in which she plays a rapper bossing around her male assistant and boldly challenging another female rapper to a song contest.¹⁰ Rather than simply competing against each other, however, the women combine their critical and comedic talents to putting the hapless male assistant through his paces. Asiedu is best known, however, as a television actress who is particularly adept at playing women who simmer and scheme at the limitations foisted on them by patriarchal relationships and dead-end jobs. Asiedu has a complex international media presence. She has been pressured to respond to rumors about infidelity with her co-stars on Ghanaian TV and in film, and she has been ridiculed for not mastering English. Yet she was also the recipient of an award at the USA-African Gospel and Movie Achievement Awards Night held at the Bronx location of the Apostolic Church International in March 2012, an event hosted by an agency dedicated to "rebranding" Africa.

These scenes show how Pentecostal religious assemblages unsettle boundaries of nation, gender, race, class, religion, and entertainment. More specifically, they raise a number of questions about the meaning of "Africa" in postcolonial diasporic contexts. Who may lay claim to the legacy of "African" culture or aesthetics? How is it that White American Pentecostals perform African American spirituals as emblematic of America for their European audiences? Why are some Pentecostals invested in staging performances of what is "authentically" African while others are "rebranding" Africa? For some Pentecostals, it is imperative to celebrate African music and dance that is unaligned with the particular brutalities of slavery in the Americas. For others, "Africa" signifies "traditional" religion that is variously figured as pagan, idolatrous, or demonic. What these instances indicate, however, is that Pentecostal invocations of "Africa" encapsulate political imaginaries that challenge, as well as reflect, hegemonic narratives centered on "the modern West."

These scenes also highlight the provisionality and tensions of Pentecostal gender performances in diasporic media. In some cases, the glamour of celebrity acts as a solvent on reified gender roles; in others, it attracts additional scrutiny of unconventional women. Who was the recipient of the award? Asiedu the gospel singer or Asiedu the YouTube rapper? Asiedu playing the scheming wife or Asiedu the beleaguered headliner of the Ghanaian gossip pages? Increasingly, the macro- and micro-movements and positionings of Pentecostal bodies are simultaneously lit up by the spectral presence of media assemblages. Consequently, having committed to wide-ranging media circuits, Pentecostals cannot presume to consistently control the messages relayed by the aggregate of their transnational ecologies of sensation.

In insisting on modern subjects as "buffered," Taylor ignores the political and economic inequalities and instabilities that make for a contemporary postcolonial context of people, data, and capital on the move.[11] Although the fact that people migrate to gain access to resources, to escape war and persecution, and to secure employment is not peculiar to modernity, the modern movements of people—one of the defining characteristics of what is termed "globalization"—are unprecedented in scope and intensity. Given these pressures, we resist the reading of "diaspora" as an archipelago of liminal spaces infused with nostalgia. Scholars must take care to avoid theories that rhetorically romanticize the movement of peoples as reflecting open-endedness and dynamism rather than idolatrous or dogmatic closure. Wallace Best (2005: 1) has remarked, "Blacks have long connected their freedom to the ability to move, to change place or spatial direction, recognizing that, as Ralph Ellison [1980: 133] put it, 'geography is fate.'"[12] Yet it is precisely by paying heed to race, gender, and class that one avoids a simple conflation of mobility and emancipation. The advantages afforded by insertion in transnational networks must be considered along with the uneven pressures, deprivations, and insecurities that compel and attend such movements. We salute our fellow theorists when they insist that religions are not "reified substances," but we are skeptical when religions are *generalized*, *catalogued*, and *defined* as "crossings" in keeping with "a cultural moment in which movement and relation seem important" (Tweed 2006: 22, 54, 59). Scholars need to be careful not to "naturalize" or de-historicize the movements of religious bodies—movements that vary historically as exile, crusade, expulsion, slavery, or circulating commodities in global capitalism.

Pippa Norris and Ronald Inglehart (2012) have argued that, as long as there is the existential insecurity and social and economic stratification that accompanies neoliberal capitalism (of which increasing migration and decreasing support for public safety nets are prime characteristics), there will be a need for religion. Pentecostals have developed these transnational assemblages alongside nation-states that are variously racist, punitive, negligent, depleted, or corrupt. Such contexts engender and exacerbate profound inequities within states and among states, prompting surplus populations to seek alternative structures of social and economic support, shared imaginaries of belonging and possibility, robust narratives of denunciation and exorcism, and markers of prestige and moral glamour (whether of privation or prosperity). Pentecostals' demands for and practices of spiritual, physical, and material well-being testify to their pragmatic detachment from and implicit critique of the state, as well as their efforts to supplement modern states' ongoing retreat from public services.

Having delineated the broader context that calls into question Taylor's description of modern secular subjects as invulnerable to multitudinous currents of power, we turn now to the question as to the dimensions and efficacies of Pentecostal power. The preoccupation with delimiting real and authentic power or agency from its fake and presumably atavistic sources and deluded claimants is a rarely acknowledged, though foundational, characteristic of secular modernity. Moreover, it is also central to the Pentecostal project. Webb Keane (2007: 54) observes that Pentecostals share with European colonialists and anthropologists a sense of "the moral danger of mislocated agency." Thus, an immanent critique of Pentecostal claims to offering "technologies for accessing power" is entirely appropriate (Meyer 2012: 107). Pentecostals supply implicit normative criteria for evaluating power in their touting self-overcoming, healing, victory, and prosperity. Their visions of salvation include bodily and material needs and the righting of relationship. This does not mean, however, that spirit power is incontestably a boon to the well-being of the women who cultivate a relationship to it, although this inconsistency is certainly not peculiar to spirt-filled technologies of power.

Power, whether understood as spiritual or material, is the production of effects in the world; power makes things happen. Power draws on and acts on various media, and its measure is always relative. Some people may gain power at the expense of others; some people are adept at sharing power. As we made clear at the start of this introduction, there are undoubtedly asymmetrical relationships of power in the world. The challenge is to illuminate these asymmetries, even as we draw attention to the varieties and transmutations of power. The question is not just *who* gets to wield power but what *kind* of power is wielded. Indeed, asymmetries of power are kept in place by a number of factors, including assumptions about the relative efficacy of various forms of power. For instance, the distinction between religion and state is frequently described in terms of their respective powers. John Locke argued that religion (he referred to "church") and state employ *persuasive* power; the state alone employs *punitive* power. For Joan Scott, the difference is, confusingly, both quantitative and qualitative; political power is both greater than and fundamentally different from religious power. She writes, "The relationship between the political and the religious is asymmetrical ... states have coercive power that *exceeds* any influence religion may have." She also makes a distinction, which she does not explain, between *political* power and *spiritual* power (Scott 2010: 96, 102). Scott's attempt to distinguish degrees and kinds of power hints at the challenge of doing justice to the various registers and relationships of power. Certainly, possession of wealth or armed force affords ample opportunity for effective action in the world; at the same time, it should not be assumed that these forms of power necessarily subsume or trump others. Scholars must consider the interrelations among different categories of power, how certain forms of power justify other forms of power as well as attract or cascade into one another—for instance, the ways in which political power seeks moral authorization and the fact that religious patronage systems may yield employment opportunities, as well as significant wealth and social and political status.

To study Pentecostals in general, and Black Pentecostal women in particular, requires, we suggest, sensitivity to the full range of power's frequencies: persuasive and coercive, material and spiritual, subtle and palpable, hidden and ostentatious, injurious and expansive, exploitative and accountable. Insofar as the communities we study recognize different categories of power, scholars must be wary of predetermining their distinctions or relationships. For instance, scholars ought not to dismiss spirit power as "soft" or "feminine" (much like religion in relation to the political or the state) and thus as lacking in reality or authority. Dorothy Hodgson (2005: x) describes the challenge as "how to reconcile the moral world with the material one, how to incorporate and analyze spiritual forms of power with political and economic ones, and how to understand the relationship of spirituality to the production, reproduction, and transformation of gender relations." In the context in which Hodgson raises this challenge, she talks about how Maasai women lamented their disenfranchisement from political and economic power even as they prided themselves as guardians of the moral order and their special relationship to the deity. Thus, the Maasai women distinguished these domains of power even as they criticized their loss of political and economic power as contradictory to their moral authority and to the moral order more generally. The Maasai women refused to downgrade moral authority in relation to political and economic power. Similarly, Pentecostal technologies for securing a "live relation to power" should not be dismissed as unrelated to political and economic contexts. Who is truly convinced of the efficacy, transparency, and justice of contemporary political fields such that Pentecostal struggles and remedies appear so obviously inadequate? Moreover, the Pentecostal claim that much of the world's problems and afflictions are attributable to spiritual malaise is not peculiar to Pentecostals. It has affinities with contemporary, albeit controversial, trends in US domestic and foreign policy. For instance, the rationalization of eliminating welfare provisions to break a purported "culture of dependency"; the provision of private faith-based initiatives to apply the "deep-redeeming power" of religion to intransigent social and economic inequities; and, internationally, the contention, on the part of neoconservative political economists, that development is a "state of mind" or attitude.

The implicit political theology of Pentecostals is that the spirit is no discriminator of persons. The conviction that "spirit goes where it listeth" is a harbinger of its egalitarian promise. As Maria W. Stewart claimed in 1832, "Just as God had given black people the gift of the Holy Spirit, surely they were owed their freedom and wages" (quoted in Cooper 2011: 72). In teaching that sin does not inhere in people, but that all people may be (indeed, must be) made new or born again, Pentecostals undercut justifications for hierarchical governing structures (including that of gender) and dislodge the stigmas of race and poverty.[13] As Cheryl Townsend Gilkes (2001: 47) astutely observes, "accommodation to racism is, in the context of the preaching of the Sanctified Church, an accommodation to sin." Of course, a capricious power is always available for corruption, and the lack of a *justification* for hierarchical structures does not necessarily mean that there will be no de facto hierarchical structure. Scholars must be careful to note the distinction between, on the one hand, the potentially subversive power of a democratization of charisma and, on the other, the institutionalization of political power that is constituted by and accountable to "the people." This distinction is crucial to Marshall-Fratani's study of Nigerian Pentecostalism. For her, Pentecostalism is a "political spirituality," the aim of which is renewal and an end to corruption through self-overcoming. The postcolonial social imaginary in Nigeria is one of disorder: of contending, predatory, violent, and hidden power. In this particular context, there is no authoritative way to detect where political, economic, or spiritual power comes from—whether it is divine or satanic. Consequently, spiritual warfare is *the* field of experience, it is the form of power. In her estimation, and again in the *context* she studies, Pentecostalism fails to create new modes of sociability predicated on trust, promise, and guarantee. Instead, it lends a pervasive sense of insecurity, volatility, and capriciousness to events and relationships (Marshall 2009: 18–27).

In a comment that bears repeating for the purposes of this volume, Toulis (1997: 215) admonishes her readers about the "need to put aside the preoccupation with visible office as power and a preconceived idea of who is a 'liberated Black woman.'" Given their restriction from various forms of official power, Black women have long had to take power where they could find or make it. Hence, they have had to be variously opportunistic, improvisational and pragmatic. As Gilkes (2001: 45) has written, "Within the Sanctified Church, black women have created for themselves a variety of roles, careers, and organizations with great influence but with variable access to structural authority." Such roles have included church mother, evangelist, exhorter, missionary, prayer band leader, deaconess, and teacher. One would be in error to suppose that such roles did not produce real power for these women, even if this power did not also entail the elimination of the gender, racial, class, and heteronormative privileges that constrain these same women's lives.

To attend a spirit-filled performance is to witness transformation: communal visceral memories shaken lose, reserved people gesticulating and shouting praise, singers tapping into and radiating ambient sound. This transformation draws from and inculcates a susceptibility to emotional reformation: enjoining exuberant clapping, training mournful weeping, imbuing dread and suspicion, or making alert and watchful. Such emotional reformation is simultaneously a mobilization: a willingness to stand apart, to call out, to set out, to get ready. Whereas we distinguish *feeling* powerful or empowered from *having* power, we would not dismiss the significance of the former, and we would insist on the need to be thoughtful as to the criteria we use to distinguish various kinds of power and their effects (see Becker 2005: 156). These more complicated renderings of power reflect key insights from Black feminist scholarship more broadly, including the significance of nonlinear and narrative knowledge that resists treatment as a "commodity to be extracted and traded" and the recognition that all subjects are simultaneously disciplined, as well as capacitated and resistant (May 2015: 20). In what follows, then, we invite readers to consider, critically, the multitudinous ways power pulses through Pentecostal performances: realigning gender and race, heralding the end of the world, linking hemispheres, electrifying singers and audiences, disciplining female workers, and anointing celebrities and politicians.

DESCRIPTION OF THE CHAPTERS

Whereas Pentecostal and evangelical churches have refrained from using the category of race while insisting on the equality of all people before God, in part I, "Saving Race," John Burdick and Elizabeth McAlister highlight the divergent ways "race" figures in these churches. Burdick interviews Brazilian gospel singers who not only identify as Black (*negro*), but who insist that their Blackness, albeit read differently from the points of view of women and men, is central to God's salvific action in the world. In the Haitian context, McAlister notes the ways in which race is disconnected from skin color and particular colonial histories of missionary work, yet festers in condemnations of demonic and idolatrous "African" traditions.

John Burdick's chapter, "Voices of God: Blackness and Gender in a Brazilian Black Gospel Music Scene," addresses surprising developments among evangelical Protestants who avidly embrace the gifts of the spirit, and especially spiritual warfare. As Burdick notes, these Christians have tended to downplay worldly identities such as race and to focus on the equality of all people before God. Relatedly, they have stressed the primacy of converting each individual soul rather than eradicating social and structural limitations to lived equality. In addition, celebrations of Black identity (or *negro*) have largely been the province of practitioners of Afro-Brazilian religion, which these evangelicals regard as the work of the devil. Nonetheless, Burdick has found that Afro-Brazilian evangelical singers of "Black gospel" have developed a Black identity politics that both pushes back against their religious tradition's hostility to Black identity politics and invites critique of the Brazilian state's myth of racial democracy. In addition, he carefully sifts through the ways in which gender inflects performers' understandings of human vulnerability to Satan and their respective roles in salvation history.[14]

Elizabeth McAlister's "Race, Gender, and Christian Diaspora: New Pentecostal Intersectionalities and Haiti," takes up the issue of evangelical/Pentecostal notions of Christian citizenship. The setting for her analysis is the contemporary prominence of the Revival/Third Wave/Spiritual Warfare movement in Haiti. In this case, transcendent Christian citizenship ("in this world, but not of it")—which relativizes all notions of national belonging, given the preeminence of membership in and ambassadorship on behalf of God's kingdom—is juxtaposed with a very specific reading of and prescription for Haiti's efforts at nation building. As McAlister carefully explicates, this juxtaposition belies a series of overlapping tensions. Rather than enjoining Christian membership in the City of Peace, this revival movement, begun by the American C. Peter Wagner from Fuller Seminary, envisions Christians as prayer warriors engaged in a spiritual warfare between the forces of good and evil. In this cosmology, Haitian Vodou is regarded as one of Satan's strongholds amid an extensive kingdom that includes all African ancestral and spirit traditions. Rather than providing consistent uplift in a context of multiple or perhaps chronic diaspora, then, Third Wave Christian citizenship contracts into a racialized, gendered, and heteronormative narrative of Haiti's struggle for nationhood.

What McAlister's analysis brings to light is the necessity of tracing the complicity of theological frameworks in racial constructions. The division of people into distinct races placed along a hierarchy of valuation is difficult to imagine in the absence of a theological framework, the terms of which encompass the extremes of good and evil. This is what makes McAlister's phrase "theo-geographies" so insightful and useful in a diasporic context. The diversity of spirit-filled people and their explicit avowals that *all* are God's people suggests that Pentecostalism is a truly postcolonial phenomenon. Nonetheless, as McAlister points out, leaders of the Third Wave may no longer correlate evil with dark skin, but they do correlate it with Haitians' stubborn attachment to their African history and culture. Thus, even if racialization is loosed from physiognomy, its insidious classifications can always adopt (or have already adopted) another guise: region, culture, desire, sex, or class.

Women's bodies are frequently the field of political and cultural production and contestation, and Black women's involvement with Pentecostalism is no exception. "Women and the Afro-Brazilian Pentecostal War in Mozambique," Linda van den Kamp's chapter in part II, "Scrutinizing and Sanctifying the Body," studies the ways in which Brazilian Pentecostalism in Mozambique enlists women's bodies in the aftermath of civil war and protracted political battles over traditionalist and progressive gender practices. In contrast, Deidre Helen Crumbley's "'Dressed as Becometh Holiness': Gender, Race, and the Body in a Storefront Sanctified Church" focuses on the ways in which the strict gendered dress codes of a Sanctified church founded and led by "Mother Brown" reflect Black women's desire to recoup a sense of control over and sacrality within their bodies.

Van de Kamp analyzes the ways in which spiritual warfare is made tangible in the lives of its female converts in Mozambique. The women attracted to Afro-Brazilian Pentecostalism are hoping to banish demons seeking revenge in the aftermath of Mozambique's violent fifteen-year civil war. These demons prevent women from marrying and conceiving. The spiritual obstacles to women enjoying positive and productive familial relationships reflects not only civil war traumas (including widespread rape), but also ongoing conflicts over women's appropriate roles and their obligations to extended kin, which have been exacerbated by women's increasing economic independence in urban areas and especially the capital, Maputo. In addition, post-civil-war nation building has led to debate and ambivalence regarding traditional culture and especially belief in and remedies for spirits. For the missionizing Brazilians, the project to free these women is part and parcel of their strenuous efforts to exorcise (forever) elements of African culture. These are the ongoing conflicts that lend poignancy to the spiritual warfare undergone by Pentecostal female converts. Moreover, they also account for van de Kamp's finding that Pentecostal women report increased tensions in their lives and eventual alienation from kin as a result of their involvement with the Afro-Brazilian churches. Far from curbing male privileges and establishing peaceable domestic partnerships, Pentecostalism in Mozambique appears to create recurrent cycles of stress, doubt, and anxiety in the women involved. Thus, rather than overcoming the spirits, the Afro-Brazilian churches succeed in convincing the women that they must engage in continuous struggle with the spirits without and inside—a situation that exacerbates a lack of trust but facilitates the ascetic individualism associated with market discipline.

Crumbley analyzes how considerations of race trouble the reading that Sanctified churches' dress codes serve to reflect and reinforce asymmetrical power relationships between men and women. In her study of a small Philadelphia church, Crumbley models a multifaceted understanding of Pentecostal fashions. As Crumbley notes, male saints were indistinguishable from their worldly counterparts, whereas female saints donned long skirts and head coverings for maximum coverage. Although women in this church are no longer restricted to wearing white for church services, they still do not cut their hair, and they still keep it covered in public. This raises interesting questions about the Pentecostal attribution of power and sexuality to Black women's hair, an attribution that is delightfully subversive in the American context of the perceived imperative for Black women to relax or straighten their hair (see Byrd and Tharps 2002; Craig 2002).

The case may bring to readers' minds that of Lizzie Robinson, the first overseer of the Women's Department of the Church of God in Christ (COGIC), who insisted that women could teach but not preach and that they must adhere to modest and almost uniform clothing (Butler 2007: 34–54, 80, 174n7). It is, of course, plausible to conclude that deflecting attention from their bodies and the erotic valence presumed to surround them has made it easier for Black women to claim leadership in churches and society.[15] One wonders, then, whether the rise in body-conscious, fashionable, and ornamental dress among some Pentecostal women has been offset by increasing emphasis on male headship and women's leadership role being circumscribed by the designation "pastor's wife." This suggests that Pentecostal women continue to perform a high-stakes balancing act. According to Bernice Martin, there is an "implicit deal" for women in Pentecostalism: "a substantive shift towards greater gender equality will be tolerated so long as women are not seen to be publicly exercising formal authority over men." Pentecostalism, she concludes, is a modernizing egalitarian impulse "albeit inside a formal patriarchal casing" (Martin 2001: 54–55).

Although many Pentecostal churches and spirit-filled ministries prohibit women from holding official leadership positions, their spiritual authority is central to the salvific work of these churches and ministries. In the particular cases under consideration in part III, "Sonic Power," women's wailing and singing, respectively, are deployed to reestablish a relationship with a God who seems to have forsaken the world or to have ignored the fervent prayers of the faithful. These paired essays reveal how women continually broaden the parameters and spaces of spirit-filled worship, as well as the productive tensions between discipline and spontaneity and the present world and the world to come.

Paula Aymer's research adds another circuit to the global tracks of Pentecostal prayer networks—this time a voluntary route of passage from Africa to the Caribbean. In her chapter, "West African and Caribbean Women Evangelists: The Wailing Women Worldwide Intercessors," Aymer analyzes the efforts of a worldwide interdenominational missionary organization, Waling Women Worldwide (WWW), which seeks to exploit conventional feminine characteristics even as it trains women to become ruthless masculinized warriors. She focuses in particular on a Nigerian band of evangelizing women's efforts to recruit women in Grenada. These women advocate constant intercessionary prayer in a style that is intensely emotional (sorrowful and fearful wailing). The key biblical text that justifies their efforts is Jeremiah 9:17: "Thus saith the Lord of hosts, consider ye and call the mourning women . . . and send for cunning women; that they may take up a wailing for us." (Coincidentally, this is the same biblical passage Lizzie Robinson used on her initial round through Tennessee, Arkansas, and Texas organizing Bible Bands [see Butler 2007: 45].)[16]

As Aymer notes, the success of this group of Nigerian women is rather surprising. In addition to significant class differences, the Nigerian women bring to Grenada an emphasis on a heteronormative nuclear family model that is at odds with the predominance of single motherhood in the Caribbean. Moreover, the WWW affirms an eschatological vision of a civil society in ruins and of a judgmental Father God who requires appeasing and softening. (Only the sound of wailing women can soften the heart of a stern and apparently disappointed figure.) This theology is in rather sharp contrast to the friendlier, more empathetic, and sometimes feminine Jesus that features in Pentecostal theology. This eschatological vision also requires training the Caribbean women to shift away from focusing on domestic relationships and recounting personal testimonies of salvation to concentrating on and interceding amid a *global* context of sin and terror.

Judith Casselberry moves beyond the hermeneutics of the Pentecostal body's surface to analyze the kinds of messages that are conveyed by women's bodies in motion, singing, laboring, and even sprinting. In "'The Kingdom in the Midst': Sounding Bodies, Aesthetic Labor, and the End Times," Casselberry studies liturgical performances in which women's bodies run, sing, pray, mourn, and labor. In doing so, Casselberry implies the limitations of the protocols of gendered liturgical space whereby men may claim authority at the pulpit while women rise and make their stand amid the community. In the scenes she reconstructs, Casselberry suggests the various stages and locations of women's liturgical and theological authority. Moreover, in a context in which Pentecostals are routinely portrayed as seeking and expecting salvation *now*, Casselberry highlights the eschatological tension, the "already and not yet" captured by their interpretive practices. In the community she studies—a church in the Church of Our Lord Jesus Christ of the Apostolic Faith denomination in Queens, New York—women make choices about how to read God's will regarding past events and events yet to be disclosed. In both instances, women express their faith and confidence in God's promise to fully heal and gather together all saints' bodies, despite the realities of paralysis and death. The women become exegetes of God's will and word and, in turn, offer their spiritual gifts (their work, their words) as supplemental texts. In a context of voiced doubt and confusion, these women's actions are *liturgy*—that is, "public service." They increase the repertoire of signs available for getting on in the world and for imagining, and even feeling, the promised redemption, albeit without directly altering configurations of power or dissolving the tension of present realities and anticipated futures.

How does spirit power compare with or interact with state models and institutions? This is the subject that unites part IV, "Modeling the State." In "A Critical Approach to Concepts of 'Power' and 'Agency' in Ghana's Charismatic (or Neo-Pentecostal) Churches," an account of Neo-Pentecostal churches in Accra, Ghana, Jane Soothill finds that these churches model themselves on state patronage relationships that reinforce the wealth and influence of elite men and women. In contrast, Laura Premack's chapter, "Bless Us with Children: Pregnancy, Prosperity, and Pragmatism in Nigeria's Christ Apostolic Church," finds that

Nigerian Pentecostal women's demand for varied and reliable maternal care drove both church and state resources toward the building of such institutions in the middle decades of the twentieth century

Soothill's chapter extends and problematizes the scholarly consensus that Pentecostal and charismatic Christianity in the global South empowers its female adherents. According to Soothill, this empowerment is evident in three key areas: the provision of leadership roles, the message of social change and the tools to change destructive male behavior, and the emphasis on individuation and self-development. Soothill digs deeper to examine the precise contours of this empowerment in the Ghanaian context. What she notices is that religious rhetoric and practice has tended to mirror political rhetoric and practice. The state has adopted the international gender development agenda and thus promotes women's equality. So, too, the Pentecostal and charismatic Christian churches promote spiritual equality and the democratization of charisma (while retaining an ideology of gender complementarity).[17] Yet women's political and religious leadership has been largely spectacular or iconic—cultivating a mass public of adulation, submission, and consumption. Political First Ladies are mirrored by pastors' wives. Consequently, power—political and spiritual—remains highly concentrated among an elite rather than democratically distributed. Soothill challenges scholars to avoid declarations of a generalized empowerment for women in Pentecostal practice by showing how elite women's tremendous power is coincident with the powerlessness of many.

Premack argues that central to the success of divine healing churches in Nigeria was and is their focus on *alafia*, a Yoruba term that means "peace" and encompasses health, success, and prosperity. Although the prosperity gospel of what is frequently referred to as Neo-Pentecostalism has prompted significant controversy with regard to both its claims to biblical support and its perpetuating or exacerbating disparities of wealth and power, Premack argues that, in the Nigerian context, prosperity is understood holistically to include material goods but is signified primarily in people and, especially, in the blessing that is children. Although much scholarship on the emergence and spread of divine healing churches in Nigeria has focused on male leadership, Premack seeks to offset that disparity by highlighting not only the fact that women provided the majority of membership and support for divine healing churches, but also that women's understandings and experiences of well-being or prosperity drove the popularity and institutionalization of such churches in Nigeria. Premack focuses on fertility and maternity centers sponsored by the Christ Apostolic Church (CAC) in the 1950s and 1960s. In opening these centers, the male leaders of the CAC sought to counter government criticism and interference; to invest in midwife training for women in order to compete with the colonialist-initiated health clinics; and to keep the church viable. Premack's analysis corrects the androcentric reading of Christianity in Nigeria, undercuts conventional readings of colonial regimes as instituting the separation of reproduction from governance, and highlights the pragmatic bent of Nigerian divine healing churches.

NOTES

1 Pentecostals have frequently envisioned themselves not as "worldly" but as "set apart" and their struggles as taking place against a sinful world. Nonetheless, some scholars of American Afro-Pentecostalism argue for an emerging trend toward increased engagement with the world. One key rationale for such a shift, they argue, is the emergence of a Black middle class since the civil rights era (see Yong and Alexander 2011: 6).
2 Here we find ourselves agreeing with Kevin Lewis O'Neill who prefers to speak in terms of an international or transnational rather than global Pentecostalism. He reasons that Pentecostals refer to nation and national citizenship and that the "actual movement of Christianity in the world is remarkably uneven." He adds: "Christians and discourses of Christianity flow across borders and between nations rather than saturate the world evenly" (see O'Neill 2009: 174, 176).
3 For a reading of the common feature of divine healing in Pentecostalism, see Gunther Brown 2011.
4 For analysis of the historical antecedents on intersectionality, see May 2015.
5 Clarence E. Hardy III, "Church Mothers and Pentecostals in the Modern Age," in Yong and Alexander 2011: 83, quoting the Arthur Huff Fauset Collection, Special Collections Department, Van Pelt Library, University of Pennsylvania, Philadelphia, box 5, folder 96, n.p.
6 For detailed critiques of the assumption that secularization entails the privacy of religion, see Casanova 1994; Pritchard 2014.
7 See http://www.pentecostrevival.nl. The Pentecost Revival Church in Amsterdam is part of the International Convention of Faith Ministries founded in 1979 with headquarters in Arlington, Texas. Early leaders included Kenneth Hagin, Jerry Savelle, Kenneth Copeland, and Fred Price, all of whom pledge their support for the Word of Faith movement.

8   Austin-Broos (1997: 235) continues: "And even in the small rural churches where patriarchy seems to prevail, women as the active members of a church can withhold their tithes, the pastor's wage." On the economic power of the overwhelming female majority in the Sanctified church, see also Gilkes 2001: 53. On the relative power of ordained and non-ordained, Butler writes, "There is the power of ordination, but there is greater power in controlling the ordained" (2007: 6).

9   Toulis (1997: 235) notes that this monopolization may also occur through speaking in tongues, prophesizing, or giving testimony. See also Toulis 1997: 239.

10 See "Kyeiwaa vs. Mercy Asiedu," video clip posted May 27, 2100, http://www.youtube.com/watch?v=CaRBanuq14w.

11 As Arjun Appadurai (2001: 5) remarks, "It has now become something of a truism that we are functioning in a world fundamentally characterized by objects in motion. These objects include ideas and ideologies, people and goods, images and messages, technologies and techniques. This is a world of flows."

12 Best is describing the desire for African Americans to participate in the Great Migration from the South to the North (1915–52).

13 Marla Fredericks (2012: 397–99) notes a shift in focus from race to class as Neo-Pentecostals seek to address a global public. She cites Bishop T. D. Jakes in particular.

14 Burdick's account suggests that Brazilian Black Gospel women singers perform a kind of exorcism of the sins of slavery and racism, similar to what Austin-Broos (1997) describes.

15 For an analysis of the ways in which bodiliness and eroticism stubbornly adhered to perceptions of African American women preachers, see Best 2005: 101–27.

16 Women's Bible Bands, started by the Baptist missionary Joanna P. Moore in 1884, were designed to teach literacy in general and biblical literacy in particular. They became key venues of African women's literacy, leadership, and networking from their founding through the first two decades of the twentieth century (Butler 2007: 16–25).

17 Martin (2001: 54) describes the democratic promise of Pentecostalism this way: "Whatever the organizational hierarchy may imply about the locus of religious authority, the sacred is not so easily reined in in the Pentecostal tradition. The Spirit 'goeth where it listeth' and lights indiscriminately upon women, the young, the poor, the unlettered, the marginalized of every kind." Nonetheless, the democratic promise of Pentecostalism is compromised by an enduring gender complementarity that entails asymmetrical status. "It establishes an *experience* of greater gender equality," she writes, without destroying what [Salvatore] Cucchiari (1990) has felicitously called 'gender integrity,' that is, the possibility of experiencing the gendered self as a 'good *woman*' or a 'good *man*.'"

PART I

Saving Race

VOICES OF GOD — 1

*Blackness and Gender in a Brazilian
Black Gospel Music Scene*

JOHN BURDICK

The struggle to alter dominant views about race in Brazil is a long, tortuous, uphill battle. Despite more than thirty years of sustained Black movement activism (Bailey 2009; Rodrigues and Prado 2013), views about race in Brazil today continue to be dominated by a cluster of deeply troubling ideas, such as that racial discrimination is not really a serious problem in Brazil; that slavery in Brazil was less oppressive than it was in the United States; and that political activism about race is both unnecessary and at odds with Brazil's mixed-race national identity (Alves 2012; Cicalo 2012; Reiter 2008; Reiter and Mitchell 2009; Soares 2012). Brazilian Pentecostals[1]—still, the fastest-growing religion in Brazil—tend to embrace these ideas (Burdick 1998, 2013). They regard the secular realm as irredeemably corrupt, reject Afro-Brazilian spirituality as the devil's playground, believe converted Christians already enjoy full equality before God, and see the individual soul as fundamentally more important than any this-worldly collective identity (Corten and Marshall-Fratani 2001; Freston 1998; Novaes 1985; Pedde 2002; Pierucci 2006; Prandi 2004; Selka 2005).

Given the pervasiveness of such views among Brazil's Pentecostals, it is worthy of note that in the past two decades a growing number of Brazilian Pentecostal musicians have begun to play, deliberately and self-consciously, what they call *música negra* (Black music), of which the most prominent subgenres are *música Black gospel*, *rap gospel*, and *samba gospel* (Pinheiro 1998, 2003, 2004, 2009). São Paulo, Brazil's largest city, is the epicenter of this trend and now includes more than twenty major Black gospel choirs, two hundred amateur and professional Christian rap groups, and dozens of samba gospel groups.[2] Thus, on almost any evening, in any neighborhood of São Paulo, one can hear a Black gospel choir, gospel rapper, or gospel sambista crooning the message of Christian salvation. During nine months of fieldwork between 2003 and 2005, I sought to understand how, and how much, these musicians might be pushing back against their religion's rejection of Black identity politics by configuring that identity in new ways. The relationship between Christian music and Black identity, though thoroughly explored in North American scholarship (see, e.g., Monson 2007; Radano and Bohlman 2000; Ramsey 2004; Reagon 2001), has not been much investigated in Brazil. In striving to grasp this relationship, I have paid special attention to the role of gender (cf. Selka 2007, 2009, 2010). This chapter details my finding that, while male and female Black Christian singers both articulate a positive Black identity, they do so in subtly different ways.

A note about methodology: on the Black gospel scene, I conducted in-depth interviews with twenty female and twenty male singers age eighteen to forty-five.[3] I interviewed only people who identified themselves as *negro*. Use of this term self-referentially in Brazil tends to affirm a sense of belonging to a group that historically has been stigmatized; in contrast, self-referential use of the terms *moreno* (brown) and *mestiço* (mixed) is less group-affirming, drawing attention only to the individual's skin color or mixed ancestry (see Silva and Reis 2011). In São Paulo, however, everyday use of the term "negro" has become so common that it is no longer markedly group-affirming. Its very commonness pushed me to dig deeper, to see the different underlying meanings it possessed.[4] Working with this group of forty interviewees, I asked: To what extent and in what ways did female Afro-Brazilian singers of Black gospel understand what they were doing in ethnoracial terms? How did these understandings differ from those of male Afro-Brazilian singers? In what ways did these understandings lead female and male Black gospel singers to push back against their churches' and Brazil's hegemonic stances toward racial politics?

My most striking finding was that almost all of the Black gospel singers I interviewed, male and female, thought of their music in intricately racial terms. In contrast to gospel rappers and gospel sambistas, Black gospel singers spoke spontaneously and extensively about the rootedness of their genre in the North American Black church (*a igreja negra*), its connection to the Black civil rights struggle in the United States, and the idea that their African descent conferred on them a predisposition to excel in this art form. But they went further and supported controversial (for Brazil) political projects, such as creating forums to discuss racism in church and teaching about the role of Africa in the Bible. I discuss these projects in more detail later; the point I wish to underline here is that, along with their strong consensus that *ser negro* (being Black) was directly linked to their art, male and female Black gospel singers conceptualized the linkage in different ways, which revealed gendered ideas about God, history, theology, and suffering. In this chapter, I draw attention to three of these differences. First, I suggest that the male and female Black gospel singers I got to know experienced and thought in different ways about the role of their voices in spiritual battles with the devil; second, they thought in different ways about the role of their voices, as Black voices, in God's plan for humanity; and third, they had in mind distinctive Black political projects.

WOMEN, MEN, AND THE SPIRITUAL BATTLE

I begin with Priscilla, a self-identified negra in her late twenties who was a soloist in her neighborhood's Pentecostal Church of God in Christ (COGIC). For her, singing was a constant inner spiritual battle. "The devil," she would say, "knows the power of gospel music to save souls. We singers are his worst enemies. His goal is to break our will." Indeed, when I listened to Priscilla sing, I could hear the sound of a soul engaged in life-or-death hand-to-hand combat. One afternoon, during one of my visits to her home, she glanced at the CD player on her dining room table, which was playing "Somethin' 'bout the Name of Jesus," by Kirk Franklin. "That song," she said, "is armor for me when I go into battle. Every morning I make coffee to that music. I don't know what the words mean,[5] but I could listen to this song all day long, because I need to do battle all day long. I hear in the singer's voice something that makes me ready to do battle."

"Can you say what that is?" I asked.

"Just listen."

So I listened. There it was, Dalon Collins's voice, belting the line "just like fire shut-up in my bones / The holy ghost is moving and just won't leave me alone." Listening, I thought I understood what Priscilla meant. Along with the ache and yearning in Collins's voice, I heard something else: ferocity, as if the singer were engaged in gladiatorial combat. "I think I hear it," I said. Priscilla pressed her lips together, closed her eyes, and nodded.

"I hear a force of power," she said, "a supernatural force, because that singer is engaged in a spiritual war. That is what I go through when I sing. It is a very deep war, John. When I sing, I am fighting. When I sing, I confront the devil. When I sing I'm in a battle. When I sing, I feel the devil is near. I can feel him."

A lengthy silence settled on us.

"How do you feel him?" I asked. "How do you know he is close?"

"I feel his hot breath on my cheeks," she replied. "And his voice. When I am about to sing, I hear a little voice trying to plant doubts in my mind about my right to sing before the multitudes. He speaks to me about my past, about the bad things I've done, and says, 'Priscilla, how come you think you can ascend the pulpit and minister to anybody, with all you have done in the past?' He reminds me of my past sins. He makes me think, Who am I? I can't be doing this. So the first minute, he makes me feel uncertain, because he is saying to me, 'Ha! They're making fun of you, Priscilla. They're looking at you, and they think you're drunk. They think you're crazy! Ha! Why do you think you can sing to them?' That's what I hear in the first minute. It is the devil, trying to plant an inferiority complex in my brain."

Priscilla proceeded to tell me some of the things she felt inferior about: she had been tempted in the past; she had slept with men she should not have; she had felt lust, greed, and jealousy; and she had not always walked in the ways of the Lord. She had felt moments of pride in her own voice: "There are times, yes, that as I was singing, I began to feel that pride in being listened to, replacing my pleasure in God with pleasure in myself."

"So," I asked, "then what happens?"

"Well, I can hear the devil's words. I can feel his hot breath. When I feel him near, I draw down God's power so I can battle him directly. I praise

God louder and stronger, so I am doing battle with the devil. That's when I need the Holy Spirit. Because all alone, I cannot face the devil. The only way I can survive is by drawing down the power of the Holy Spirit."

When I asked her what she did to draw down the Holy Spirit, she replied in brutally physical language: "To draw it down, to let it fill me, I must rip myself apart, to break my heart open." She placed two fingers on the V of her blouse, right below the collarbone. "I must rip myself in two," she said again, "right here, at the bone, digging down to a place deep inside my heart. When I do that, then the spirit enters. And when faced with the Spirit, the devil cannot remain. And so I feel a welling up of joy, as the devil slinks away, and I sing with even greater joy, because the Holy Spirit has won." She clenched her fists and started to spar against an invisible opponent. In fact, all this talk of bones, ripping, and digging made Priscilla sound like a prizefighter, down but not out, climbing back up, adrenaline rushing, preparing to deliver a knockout blow.

Suddenly she lowered her voice to a near-whisper. "I know," she said, "that demons can surround you, but when the power of the Lord arrives, I close my eyes and see angels, singing all around me. We put up such a ruckus the demons cannot remain. They have no choice. They must leave. They can't stand to be in the presence of such intimacy with God."

The experience of singing as spiritual battle is far from unique to Priscilla. Many other female Black gospel singers I got to know spoke at length about how, when they sang, the devil fought back by getting them to feel fearful, embarrassed, and ashamed, all emotions that impeded full-throated song. Deborah, a Black gospel singer in her forties, explained:

> What happens is that when the Holy Spirit arrives, I lose all my fear. I am up there singing, at first shy, at first timid. I hear my own voice and I wonder whether I have a right to be there. That is the devil at work. He is trying to tear me down; he does not want me to sing. He is afraid of that, so he whispers in my ear, "Deborah, ha! Deborah, you piece of filth, you nothing, you have no right, no right to stand before the multitudes. This is all a lie. You are sinning even now. You are doing my will; you are mine, all mine." But then I seek fervently the Lord. I break into a cold sweat. I seek the Lord; I invite the Lord to come and be with me. And then I lose all timidity. I open my mouth, and the power of the Lord, it is Him, not me, that sings. And from that comes

this power, this strength, I feel no fear. I shed those doubts, that feeling of inferiority.

I want to suggest that this interiorization of the spiritual battle is gendered, an effect of discourses that teach Brazilian women in general, and female Pentecostals in particular, to regard themselves as unworthy of standing before the multitudes. In the Pentecostal churches I spent time in, women performed roles as evangelists, prayer leaders, and Bible study teachers, but only men could become pastors and preachers. This was justified by the epistle to the Ephesians in which Paul states that God ordained men to lead women, and, in fact, many of the women I got to know held the view that God wanted men to be the leaders—both in church and at home. This reading of the Bible shapes how women think of themselves when they ascend the pulpit to testify or sing, making them feel they do not belong there. "When I stand before the church," says Marta, a singer in her twenties, "I am full of doubt. For a full minute, I hear the voice of the devil."

Yet these same women believe in the power of the Word and know that if they speak or sing with sincerity, God will move within them. Thus, for women in Pentecostal churches, the experience of standing before the congregation can be a deeply tense one, with tension arising between their religiously ingrained self-suspicion and their conviction that God is moving within them. They experience within their bodies a collision between these two forces. "It is a deep battle within me," Marta says. "At the start I don't believe I should stand there, a sinful, imperfect vessel. So I close my eyes when I'm up there. I'm so shy that I just can't stand to look at everybody looking at me. The devil wrings my heart. It is like a pain in my heart. But then the Spirit comes and gives me the victory."

The gendered nature of this experience of inner spiritual combat became clear to me when I asked men to describe their experiences of singing. Of my sample of twenty male singers, only two spoke of singing as causing collisions within their souls. More commonly they described spiritual battles as happening to *others* or as external assaults on the church, not as struggle within their own hearts and minds. This discursive pattern, it turns out, appears among male Pentecostals in other parts of the world. Shaunna Scott's analysis of a Pentecostal revival in Appalachia notes that male preachers spoke of the devil as a force external to themselves. Male testimonies revolved "around identifying signs of the supernatural struggle and aligning [one]self with God's side." Men's discourse was an externalizing one, in which the devil troubled other people, not them. "The devil is getting people's spirit today," Scott reported one preacher as saying. "I feel like Satan is here. . . . Do you know why [Satan is winning]? Because [people here] are wanting it. They're wanting it" (Scott 1994: 232). Another analysis of Pentecostals in New Zealand similarly points to men describing spiritual warfare as about battling the devil "out there" rather than within. "It is common," Andrew Monteith (2010: 55) writes, "in a deliverance session for demons to be directly rebuked or commanded away." In contrast, self-accounts of female Christian singers suggest an intimate, interior battle against the devil: they sing tentatively at first, until they "find" their voices. As Toni Morrison describes redemptive singing in *Beloved*, women's arrival at full-throated song is always an accomplishment, the outcome of a search, rarely all there right away. "The voices of women," she writes, "searched for the right combination, the key, the code, the sound that broke the back of words. Building voice upon voice until they found it, and when they did it was a wave of sound wide enough to sound deep water and knock the pods off chestnut trees" (Morrison 1987: 308).

Tentativeness and searching were decidedly not the pattern among my male informants. Most of the male Black gospel singers I interviewed spoke of a spiritual battle, but they did not speak of it as an interior one; theirs was, rather, an external battle between them as vessels of the Holy Spirit on the one side and the devil on the other. The image they painted was of themselves as fearless guardians of the church, standing up against an external force that penetrated the congregation from without and circulated in search of the church's weaker members. "When I stand before the church," explained Sérgio, "I feel the Holy Spirit speaking very clearly to me: 'Sérgio, now is the time to fight against the enemy. Look out across this church, the enemy is haunting this place, he has wandered in from the street, he is doing the rounds, striving to tempt the souls of these people.'" In this scenario, the devil is a stranger, a con man who has wandered in off the street. This is not an intimate whispering of threats into the anointed singer's ear. Nothing about the picture raises questions about the male singer's right to stand before the multitudes; nothing about it evokes an inner wrestling match with self-doubt. Here we are in the presence of a full-scale Brazilian ethos of masculine self-assurance. Male singers told me they arrived onstage strong in the spirit and launched right away into their singing. Mariano looked at me quizzically when I asked whether the devil ever bothered him when he began to sing. "No, not me," he said. "I am anointed by God, and the devil cannot touch me. But he is here. He comes to the church to trouble souls among the multitude. When I sing, that chases the devil away."

WOMEN, MEN, AND GOD'S PLAN FOR *A VOZ DO NEGRO*

I turn now from how gender shapes the intrapsychic experience of singing to how it shapes Black gospel singers' understandings of God's plan for *a voz do negro*. With consistency, fervor, and theological precision, both male and female Black gospel singers told me repeatedly that God had entrusted to negros the distinctive world-historical mission of using their vibrant, inimitable voices to bring humanity to salvation. All of my informants, male and female, insisted that the most powerful singing voices in the world—voices that had the power to penetrate into the marrow of the human soul, rip hearts in two, flush listeners clean, and cause them to cry out for Jesus—belong to Black people. "I'm not saying that White people [*brancos*] can't develop their voices," said Priscilla. "They can. But there are no two ways about it: for this kind of singing, negros have better timbre; they are capable of expressing more." Duglass, another Black gospel singer, said the same thing. "In a really good choir in church," he explained, "maybe you have a few Whites. But they are not the lead singers. You look around, and who are the artists who really stand out? Silvera, and Robson Nascimento, and Sergio Saas, and Daniel, and Ton Carfi. All negros!"

Of course, the association between Blackness and singing is enmeshed in Brazil's four hundred-year history of slavery and racism, as it is elsewhere. As Ronald Radano and Philip Bohlman (2000) and others have taught us, the attribution to Blacks of fine singing voices is the legacy of centuries of racist, essentializing ideas such as slave masters' effort to paint a picture of slaves contented with their lot. But it is also a result, as Paul Gilroy (1991) reminds us, of the African diaspora's deployment of voice as a source of survival, coping, resistance, and identity. Whatever the ultimate sources of this complex clustering of stereotype, fantasy, vision, racist belief, and source of racial pride, there is no denying that it is alive and well among Black gospel singers in Brazil. The question I wish to focus on is how female and male singers understand this cluster of ideas and practices in different ways.

Let us begin with female Black gospel singers. When they explained to me what they saw as the special power of Black voices, they did so through a narrative of collective suffering and overcoming. "Negros bring their suffering into every note they sing," said Priscilla. "Listen, really listen, and you can hear in the voice of the negro something unique. We sing with this emotion because we have suffered so much in the past, and we still suffer; we endured slavery, and we are still discriminated against today. So you hear all of that in the voz do negro. We have a sadness that White people will never know, but they can hear it in our voices." Priscilla continued,

> As I have learned about our people's history, I have concluded that God made us so that people can always hear weeping in our voices. I think that negros are the ones who have the sound of weeping in their voices. The sound of pain. The negro with this history, even today . . . we still suffer. So when we offer our voices to the Lord, it is a voice full of pain. A voice full of pain and ripped apart. It is a voice that expresses that. There's all of that history of pain in everything we sing.

Although Priscilla's references to the suffering of negros and its manifestation in their voices may strike a North American ear as something less than surprising, in Brazil they are a very serious departure from the hegemonic ideology that minimizes the reality of Afro-Brazilian suffering, both past and present. The departure is especially noteworthy when it comes from deeply committed Pentecostals, who in Brazil, tend to regard concern with racial history and identity as an expression of spiritual immaturity. Yet Priscilla, and other female Black gospel singers, expounded on the meaning of Blackness in world history. This counter-hegemony comes articulated with elaborate theological details. Here is Priscilla's commentary on the *Incidents in the Life of a Slave Girl*, the US slave narrative by Harriet Jacobs, which a friend had lent her:

> In that book, this woman says it so clearly: that singing was what they had, they could not cry out against their oppression in any other way,

but they could sing. And so I think that is what God had in mind for us: He needed us to sing, to express our pain in that way, because He knew that this would cut through to the very hearts of listeners. Not that God planned that we would be enslaved. That is the evil of man, that is sin. That is free will. Yet God is all-powerful. He sees and uses all to the benefit of all. He uses the benefit in everything. God needed the tears we shed. He needed the tears in our voices. He needed our brokenness. He needed the sadness in our voices. He needed this because this feeling of brokenness, when we sing, touches the hearts of man. So, you see, negros are part of will of God for humankind. Our voices are His instrument to reach humanity; it is through us that God will save the world. That is our anointing. That is our destiny.

This theological picture portrays Black suffering ultimately as part of the divine design. It is, in this view, enslavement and oppression that ensure that Blacks' singing voices have the power to touch the deepest parts of listeners' souls. I heard this point of view expressed by most of my female interviewees. Thus, as Deborah said, "God needs this praise so full of pain. This praise that expresses the broken heart. So when we enter truly in the act of the Lord, we offer our voices to the Lord, and it is a voice full of pain. It was all of that history of pain behind everything that we sing. I believe that the voice of the Black is a dream of God for the Black race in order to touch and reach other people."

Still, in a cognitive synthesis some readers may find paradoxical, this view of the theological utility of suffering goes hand in hand with celebrations of Black refusal, rebellion, and resistance. Thus, for example, the image of the militant, resistant, rebellious North American Black is central in these women's testimonies. Priscilla explained that the book she was reading about slaves in the United States

> brings us a very important lesson. In your country, negros wanted to change history. And they did it with this strength, this force, and it was this force that their throats put forward and made real. They really fought for themselves. The slaves in the United States refused to lower their heads. They refused to give up; they wanted to change their history. They wanted to figure out how are we going to change our history, and they did it through their voices. And song was a very strong expression for the slaves. It was like they were saying to their masters,

"OK, you can beat me, but I am going to sing. OK, you can do these things to me, I cannot say no, but I'm going to sing. You imprison me by ordering me, you imprison me by a beating me, punishing me. But I can confront you by saying that even imprisoned. I can sing."[6]

When we turn to the male gospel singers, we encounter a different set of discursive emphases. Male Black gospel singers accepted, in its basic outline, the narrative that Black voices derived their power to save souls, in part, from their history of this-worldly suffering. But these singers' hearts seemed to be elsewhere. When I asked them to talk about God's plan for Black voices, they spoke of Blacks' history of suffering tentatively and as an afterthought. What they really wanted to focus on were Old Testament prophecies that God planned to call on a strong, brave, powerful people from Ethiopia to offer their gifts to the world. I heard this idea for the first time from the Black gospel singer Sérgio Saas onstage in front of thousands of fans. As he ended a set, he opened his Bible. "My friends," he said, "the eighteenth chapter of Isaiah speaks of a people from a land beyond the rivers, from Ethiopia. Listen to the seventh verse: 'In that time shall a gift be brought unto the Lord of hosts by a people tall and of glossy skin, and from a people terrible from their beginning onward; a nation that is sturdy and treadeth down, whose land the rivers divide, to the place of the name of the lord of hosts.' Do you see? It is a prophecy. The Black race is fulfilling the prophecy. It began with the Americans, because they followed Jesus before we did. They filled their churches with praise before we did. But now we are doing it too. Now is our moment, now it is our turn, Brazilians! Through our song, our voices in song, we are delivering souls to the Lord." Isaque, another male Black gospel singer, iterated the same point in an interview:

> We are fulfilling the prophecy of Isaiah, and God is using our voices to speed the return to earth of Jesus in the Second Coming. Do not doubt that God has anointed the Black race as His preferred instrument to bring about the arrival of the kingdom of Heaven on Earth, because the more souls come to Jesus, the quicker Jesus will return. Do you see? He has endowed us with the most beautiful, powerful singing voices in the world to fulfil prophecy, so that we may convert the masses throughout the world. He is using us to prepare the round for the last Judgment.

Later, when I asked male Black gospel singers to explain what it was that God had done to endow their voices with such qualities, they spoke not about histories of suffering but about their voices' anatomical qualities and physical prowess. In fact, they articulated a full-fledged bio-racially determinist view of their own voices. "The Black has natural resistance or strength in his voice," Saas declared. "His throat muscles are stronger, more numerous, more resistant than any other race." There was no mistaking the pride he took in this declaration. "We have the strongest voices in the world. Others would love to have the strength of our voices, but they don't—they just don't have the equipment that we do. God gave us this [equipment] so that we could fulfil His prophecy."

At a deep level, Saas and these other male Black gospel singers are no doubt appropriating the racist bio-essentializiation of the voice, transforming it into a source of pride. When they say that God has bestowed on them a vocal apparatus that is strong, sinewy, and well suited to the strenuous demands of belting—a key singing skill of Black gospel—we may be forgiven for characterizing such statements as a kind of sociopolitical ju-jitsu. The racist narrative that depicts Blacks as enjoying a natural musical endowment has periodically served Blacks in paradoxical ways as a source of identity and pride. To classify music as God-given inscribes it as a possession "beyond the grasp of whites; accordingly it offers performers and insiders a powerful tool for inventing an exalted racialized space" (Radano 1993: 1–2, cited in Wong 2000: 72).

I cannot claim fully to understand why male Black gospel singers spoke to me more about the physical strength of their vocal cords than about the collective suffering of their people. It may be that ideas about "natural" vocal prowess are one more expression of Brazil's culture of patriarchal masculinity. After all, these clearly took pride in describing their vocal apparatuses, as they might other parts of their bodies, as impressive, muscular, large, resilient, and thick. And by downplaying the history of suffering, these men may have been distancing themselves from a narrative that focuses on what some could construe as underlining masculine weakness—their this-worldly disempowerment at the hands of slave owners and their vulnerability to God's inscrutable will. By emphasizing the natural physical endowment of the Black voice, these men seem to be thematizing their own strength, toughness, invulnerability, prowess, and God's will as altogether scrutable. Female Black gospel singers, meanwhile, seem more interested in a narrative of suffering and overcoming, perhaps mirroring more accurately their own experience of their place in and experience of the world.

RACIAL POLITICS IN PENTECOSTAL CHURCHES

In her introduction to this volume, Elizabeth Pritchard reminds us that the "emotional reformation" resulting from Pentecostalism's reconfiguring of dominant ideologies "is simultaneously a mobilization: a willingness to stand apart, to call out, to set out, to get ready. Whereas we distinguish *feeling* powerful or empowered from *having* power, we would not dismiss the significance of the former and we would insist on the need to be thoughtful as to the criteria we use to distinguish various kinds of power and their effects." Mindful of this point, I want briefly to consider how the contrasts between male and female Black gospel singers' worldviews eventuate in projects—plans about how to bring about real-world change.

I have suggested in this chapter that female Black gospel singers think of their singing more as an internal spiritual battle, while men think of it as more of an external one, thereby reproducing patriarchal ideologies both within Pentecostalism, in particular, and Brazilian culture, in general. I have also suggested that while both male and female Black gospel singers in Brazil see themselves as chosen by God to hasten the world's redemption, women thought of this power primarily in terms of a history of collective suffering, while men thought of it primarily as God's bestowal on them of natural equipment. Both men's and women's narratives challenge dominant ideologies of race, though mediated by dominant ideologies of patriarchy. I suggest that these ideological reconfigurations have as one of their effects the growth of commitment, energy and conviction that things in the world—at least, within the church—should not, and cannot, stay as they are.

These men and women are neither revolutionaries nor full-time activists. But the views they hold about race, nurtured by their understanding and experience of the Holy Spirit, have consequences for what they think ought to happen institutionally within their churches and in Brazilian society. All of them declared that it would be good for their churches to teach more about the role and presence of Africans in the Bible; that racism had not ended in the church; and that their churches ought to dedicate more time to discussing efforts to remedy the effects of racism. Such thinking is a first step toward pushing, in small ways, for this-worldly change. Black gospel singers have become increasingly visible participants in activities that have to do with the collective pro-Black movement. The Pão da Vida church, home of several Black gospel singing groups, regularly organizes educational forums on Blacks in the church and buying from Black-owned businesses. Black gospel groups have been directly involved in planning these events and take the stage during such discussions to set the tone. The Black gospel singer Sérgio Melo's Pentecostal church, COGIC-Azusa, is at the forefront of the *movimento negro evangélico* (Black evangelical movement) through the organization of interchurch meetings of pastors to talk about racism and the need for more proactive, pro-Black polices within churches. Other Pentecostal churches that feature Black gospel choirs have organized events that address issues facing Black people. One such church, Igreja Apostólica Renovação, has become the home of a major Black gospel choir that regularly performs at "Blackness and Faith" events. Coral Kadmiel, one the country's great Black gospel choirs, sings at events to promote the agenda of affirmative action and social inclusion, and in 2010 it established a special chapter as the choir of the University of Citizenship Zumbi dos Palmares. Clearly, Black gospel singers are not just thinking about the need to struggle against racism; they are increasingly directly involved in the struggle.

Here, again, I have found subtle, though significant, differences between male and female singers' approaches to change. The male singers spoke spontaneously about institutional changes they wanted to see in their churches—above all, the possibility of a church in which people of African descent held more positions of leadership. "What we need," said Saas, "is a church led by Black people." In fact, several male Black gospel singers had taken steps to survey land and buildings they might purchase to start new Black churches, a clearly institutional step to create a space in which Black male leadership might flourish. The female singers, in contrast, never suggested to me any interest in founding Black churches. What they suggested, rather, was that in addition to talking about Africans in the Bible, their churches ought to teach about slavery and about Blacks in secular history, in both the United States and Brazil. "A lot of people don't even know that Martin Luther King was an evangelical pastor," said Priscilla, in a comment that echoed the views of other female singers. "I think that would be very valuable for us, to have more teaching about the history of the civil rights movement in the United States." Then she added, "But we should also hear and learn more about slavery in our own country, something we don't learn that much about." I never heard such suggestions from the men.

I suggest that these contrasts between male and female singers' political views are rooted, in part, in the differently mediated relationships of men and women to the Black singing voice. As male Black gospel singers focus on their roles as guardians and protectors of the church from the devil, it is not surprising that they would be interested in furthering this role through building their own churches. It may also not be surprising that, encouraged by the Pauline theology of male leadership and buttressed by Brazilian patriarchal norms, Black male gospel singers conceptualize their mission as building an institution—a Black church—that they themselves lead. Female singers, in contrast, who understand their voices as rooted in a history of suffering, are more interested in spreading the word about how people of African descent around the world have raised their voices to articulate and resist that oppression.

CONCLUSION

The patterns of gendered and racializing thought that I have explored here underscore three key points. First, they should push us to complicate the assumption on the part of Brazil's Black movements that Pentecostals do not much care about race, racism, and Blackness. I suggest, in contrast, that as Pentecostalism continues to grow in Brazil, scholars and activists would be well advised to delve more deeply, as I have endeavored to do here, into the subterranean layers of consciousness about racial matters that exist among Brazilian Pentecostals. Second, the patterns underscore the difference that gender always makes, indicating at least some of the intersectional ways that gender shapes modes of thought and action about racial identity and struggles for racial justice. Finally, how male and female Black Pentecostal singers in Brazil think and act about race brings to the fore multiple scales of power. As Pritchard puts it in the introduction, "To study Pentecostals in general, and Black Pentecostal women in particular, requires, we suggest, sensitivity to the full range of power's frequencies: persuasive and coercive, material and spiritual, subtle and palpable, hidden and ostentatious, injurious and expansive, exploitative and accountable." The point is an important one, drawing our attention to the ongoing possibility, or likelihood, that small, hard-to-see, everyday triumphs of thought and feeling are allowing men and women to move—often slowly and quietly, but sometimes quickly and with their voices booming—toward collective struggles to change the world.

NOTES

1. I use the term "Pentecostal" to refer to churches and their members who embrace the mission of active, daily evangelization and approve as normal and desirable the experience of the gifts of the Holy Spirit (see Bastian 2006).
2. These figures are based on interviews with musicians, ministers, and music promoters between 2003 and 2005. One analyst of the Christian music industry estimated that total sales of Black music gospel CDs in 2004 amounted to about half a million units in São Paulo alone. "Black gospel" refers to Christian-themed music built around the human voice singing in a style referred to in Brazil as *canto Black* (Black singing). This includes belting, twang, melisma, and rapid timbral shifts (Jungr 2002; Williams-Jones 1975). "Gospel rap" refers to Christian-themed rap sung by baptized members of Protestant denominations. "Gospel samba" refers to Christian lyrics set to samba rhythms.
3. Of the three genres I focused on for the larger project—Black gospel, gospel rap, and gospel samba—the first enjoyed the most proportionately balanced participation of male and female singers. In the Black gospel singing groups I got to know, men only slightly outnumbered women. Gospel rap and gospel samba groups, in contrast, were constituted almost entirely of men. While the causes of these asymmetries are not the focus of this chapter, it is worth noting that women's underrepresentation in gospel rap and samba is likely the result of long-standing cultural identifications of these genres as domains of tough hypermasculinity (Pardue 2008).
4. The congregations I spent time in—groups of sixty to two hundred people—exhibited majorities of people of African descent (roughly 60 percent), and most of the people of African descent identified themselves as negro.
5. The song is sung in English.
6. There is no question that Hollywood and television images of African Americans, North American gospel music videos and DVDs, and the incorporation of US history into Brazilian school textbooks all contribute to and reinforce the image in Brazil of the assertive, tough, spiritually favored North American Black. But Brazil has its own, complex cultural sources of imagery around Blackness, such as general Brazilian nationalism; the image of Zumbi, the national runaway

slave community leader from the seventeenth century; Afro-Brazilian religions such as candomblé; expressive cultural traditions of dance, martial, and graphic arts; and a dense repertoire of musical and rhythmic genres. Thus, while this essay focuses on the symbolic and narrative effects of participation in Black gospel music, I in no way intend this discussion to imply that North American cultural forms are hegemonic in Brazil. Their influence is substantial, and the particular views of women and men who participate in the Black gospel scene certainly show that influence. I explore the other cultural traditions' influence on Black Protestants via music in my book *The Color of Sound* (Burdick 2013).

RACE, GENDER, AND CHRISTIAN DIASPORA — 2

New Pentecostal Intersectionalities and Haiti

ELIZABETH MCALISTER

Along with the other authors in this volume, I aim to better understand the intersection of diaspora, race, and gender as defining forces in the lives of Black Pentecostal women. My focus is on how Haiti fares conceptually in one rather extreme yet influential strand of Pentecostal thought: Third Wave evangelicalism. Also known as the Spiritual Warfare movement, Third Wave evangelicalism is a loose network of born-again believers who share in the dramatic revelation that they are "prayer warriors" specially chosen to fight as intercessors in the cosmic battle that Satan wages against Jesus.[1] These born-again evangelicals and Pentecostals share the sense that they are called by God to engage in spiritual mapping and spiritual warfare—practices that involve discerning the demonic activity of Satan and his legion of demons and doing battle with the demonic realm through fasting, prayer, and other rituals.

The movement is made up of a vocal minority; nevertheless, it wields a great deal of influence across the charismatic world, especially among large swathes of Pentecostals in the Caribbean and Africa. Third Wave theology is crafted by both (White) American and (Black) Haitian Pentecostals (and others), who reconfigure racial narratives, gendered images, and notions of citizenship in new ways. The role Haiti plays in this network is, dramatically enough, "the only nation dedicated to Satan," and this, therefore, bears unpacking and deconstructing by scholars.

Just after the earthquake in Haiti in 2010, the right-wing media mogul Pat Robertson said on his television show that the quake was a result of a "pact with Satan," a notion commonly held by evangelicals oriented toward spiritual warfare. I have researched religion in Haiti for years, and I wanted to better understand this extreme view. I made the acquaintance of Pastor John Flynn, a longtime missionary from the American Midwest.[2] He had traveled to Port-au-Prince in the days following the earthquake with Robertson's Christian Broadcast Network (CBN) film crew. Flynn led the crew to film various churches so that the CBN viewers would have an evangelical Christian perspective on the earthquake. He graciously allowed me to join his mission team in Haiti in July 2010, six months after the quake. Traveling with Flynn was surprisingly easy, considering that he is a missionary dedicated to ridding Haiti of its demons and I am a blue-state feminist with a spotty attendance record at a mainline Protestant church in New England. It turned out that we both held in high regard a female pastor, Pastor Yvette, who headed an independent Pentecostal church that ran a school, clinic, and mission team that traveled across Haiti to evangelize and heal. The church formed groups for youth, several choirs, intercessory prayer cells, and a circle of twelve prophets. Our mutual respect and admiration for Pastor Yvette became a strong bond.

TENT CAMP WEDDING

Pastor John took me to visit Pastor Yvette's Pentecostal congregation, whose many members' houses had collapsed in the earthquake. They were camped out on a soccer field in tents and under tarps or simple sheets, together about five hundred strong. They had sanctified a large space for worship services, and had set up what pews they could salvage from their own collapsed church. I had expected the hot Caribbean sun beating down on tents and the stench from the latrines and cooking fires, the flies, and the dust. But what surprised me was that enduring these conditions were not abject refugee quake victims, but rather an energetic community preparing a wedding. Several days later they celebrated the largest and most elaborate wedding I have ever attended, right there in the refugee camp. Undeterred by the catastrophe or their resulting displacement, they were following God's revelation that the wedding must come to pass.

Hundreds of people in their Sunday best dress sat in rows in the festive church tent, where standing plants formed a center aisle and crepe paper streamed from posts overhead. A hymn in French played over speakers, and as people craned their necks to look behind them, a set of twenty teenaged dancers, boys in one line and girls in another, danced a slow minuet down the aisle. They wore matching hand-made outfits of gold and white, the girls in long white gloves and the boys in gold ties. After them two more sets of youth danced forward together, this time in different but also matching outfits. Children ring-bearers and several bridesmaids followed. After almost an hour of procession the groom stepped out, all in white from head to toe including his tie. At long last the bride paraded down the aisle, resplendent in a full-length white wedding gown, long veil, white gloves, and rhinestone tiara. They sat in two enormous chairs at the front and were treated to performances by three different choirs, each in matching robes, a band with accordion and guitar, and several vocal soloists.

At some point someone whispered to me, "It was God who chose the bride and groom and put them together. He revealed the match to one of our prophets and gave them time to decide whether to accept. This way they can be strong and build the Kingdom of God." Pastor Yvette's church shares the general Haitian Pentecostal belief that marriage sanctifies and strengthens. The church had celebrated twenty-one weddings at the church the previous December, so new couples could begin the year together.

Apparently, the bride was living in the tent camp, but the groom was from Miami. He was "from the diaspora."

AFRICAN DIASPORA, CHRISTIAN DIASPORA

In fieldwork with Pentecostals in Haiti and the Haitian diaspora, I bumped up against a curiosity (McAlister 2011). Even though evangelical Protestantism is not a diaspora in the established sociological sense, many Caribbean Christians conceive of their "spiritual lineage," their past and their future, in ways that mirror a classic ethnic diasporic consciousness. Christians are not a diaspora by social science's definition, since they do not share an ethnic identity or a common homeland. But at certain moments, many fashion themselves as one people through the transcending of ethnicity in the universal possibility of Christian salvation. And do they not have a homeland for which they are nostalgic? The Christians' true homeland is not Jamaica, Trinidad, or another birthplace; it is the Jerusalem of the ancient Israelites, whose identities they have appropriated as God's new chosen people. And do they not actively long for an immanent "return," in the future ingathering in the New Jerusalem of the

Heavenly Kingdom? And will the Holy City not be prepared as a bride adorned for her husband?

Among evangelicals in the Caribbean, a common rhetorical stance is to proclaim that citizenship in God's kingdom trumps one's national identity. In Brooklyn I heard one pastor preach, "I don't need to go back to Haiti because I have Jesus." A young woman in the Virgin Islands said, with great rhetorical flair, to another researcher, "I am Christian. I am first and foremost a citizen of God the Father's kingdom, adopted into his family through Jesus Christ, whose ambassador I am to his honor and glory, in the power of the Holy Spirit" (Harkins-Pierre 2005: 33). How much more glorious it is to hold a passport to God's kingdom than a passport from Haiti, now declared a "failed state" and a ruined land.

My first point here is that evangelical Christianity (including Pentecostals) seems to function as a diaspora for many Caribbean peoples. Evangelical and Pentecostal discourse, prayers, images, and hymns produce a temporal and spatial past and future that mirror the kinds of diasporic sensibilities that ethnic groups cultivate. After all, brothers and sisters in the church, "the body of Christ," span the globe in a great, imagined kinship network. In adopting a saved and sanctified identity, born-again Christians also produce a new form of futurity and spatiality that, in turn, inflects national, racial/ethnic, and gendered identities. To be saved is to be oriented toward biblical geographies, past and future. We can see that, on a rhetorical level, some Caribbean evangelicals keep one foot in the African diaspora and another in the Christian diaspora (see Johnson 2007). For Haitians, the "African diaspora" becomes articulated with the second, Haitian diaspora. Haitians are more recently known in the Caribbean literature for being self-consciously diasporic; the term *yon djaspora* (a diaspora) in Haitian Creole designates a person who returns to Haiti from outside. Evangelicals, in turn, fit these various diasporic frames into their understandings of Christians as a diaspora.

My second point is that if we take into account what I term the "evangelical diasporic imaginary" in theorizing these overlapping diasporas, we can learn about the complex and contradictory ways people and groups produce space, experience time, and produce new raced and gendered collective identities. By reminding ourselves of the interplay of the notion of diaspora in social science and in Christian thought, we might better understand certain post-diasporic, extra-ethnic global identity formations (McAlister 2011). We will also gain insight into transnational flows, as evangelical Christian networks work out affinities and ideologies for Caribbean, African, and African American evangelicals, who may (or may not) have developed an Afro-diasporic consciousness, this extra-ethnic identity still must provide a way to account for race, for Blackness, and for African ancestral religiosity. What is more, we will be able to understand how the intersectionality of raced and gendered identities can be produced through evangelical theology.

"SONS OF THE SOIL": RACE AND BLACKNESS IN SPIRITUAL WARFARE

If Caribbean Pentecostals' longed-for return to homeland is the eternal Kingdom of God, then how do they understand their earthly national histories and racialized, gendered identities? The racialized aspects of Afro-Atlantic Pentecostal women's experience has been a focus of much fine work on US and Brazilian Pentecostals, and this essay adds the case of Haiti to the literature. Because of the different histories of racialization across the world, the ways that raced and gendered processes shape various African, North American, Brazilian, and Haitian Pentecostal lives reflects their national contexts. Cheryl Townsend Gilkes's scholarship on the US case makes the point that Black churchwomen are leaders in an autonomous sphere that constitutes its own base of power, prestige, and support (Gilkes 1985). John Burdick (1999) examines how Brazilian Pentecostal women are often accused of giving up racial consciousness and the project of Black liberation in favor of a Pentecostal identity. While both arguments can be said to hold true for Haitian women, their case is distinct from both of these cases in the sense that Haiti is a Black-majority country, and, in general terms, Haitian identity is already wrapped up in the idea that all Haitians are Black by definition (ever since the first Haitian constitution declared all citizens legally Black). Yet differently from African Pentecostals, who are also part of a Black majority, Haitian history unfolded in the American hemisphere. Even as these various national cases are distinct, they are also increasingly bound up in transnational flows of movement and in global conversations within evangelicalism, including the sense of being part of a Christian diaspora.

As Haitians participate in global circuits of thought and practice, they revise previous narratives of nationalism, race, and gender, and some co-create an alternative Christian one. This new conception of history, nationalism, race, and gender is part of the popular intellectual work of creating a new social formation with a new understanding of history, an alternative sense of political authority, and new ideas about nationalism and citizenship. There are both continuities and tensions between old, colonialist, Christian forms of racialization and new forms of racialization and racial identity in Haiti that are themselves complicated and contradictory.

The most extreme strand of Pentecostalism in the Haitian sphere overlaps with the Spiritual Warfare movement. That movement's best-known theologian is the American C. Peter Wagner, who taught for decades at Fuller Seminary in Pasadena, California. His thought has been taken up by conservative seminaries and Bible colleges across the Bible Belt. Sometimes embraced but often rejected, the theologies and practices of Spiritual Warfare have nevertheless inflected the vocabulary of global Pentecostalism, and both Haitian and American seminary students have brought his ideas to bear on Haiti. This revival movement stresses that all of human history consists of a cosmic battle between good and evil; between Christians and the demons ruled by Satan. The battle began, of course, in the Garden of Eden when the serpent tempted Eve to disobey God. However, in the contemporary moment, God has inaugurated a special new age in which He is calling prophets and apostles to break through and affect history, just as they did in biblical times. Those who answer God's call become intercessors and usher in the Kingdom of God through "warfare prayer." This group of divinely "anointed prayer warriors" understand that they are doing battle in the "spiritual realm" with Satan's high-ranking demons and take their understanding of this war from Ephesians 6:12: "We do not wrestle against flesh and blood, but against principalities and powers, against the rulers of the darkness of this age, against spiritual hosts of wickedness in the heavenly places." Spiritual warriors discern specific spaces to be demonic strongholds and declare certain cities, towns, or areas under attack from "the enemy" (see also chapter 5 in this volume).

This new evangelical thinking about Haiti retraces much of the well-trodden path of racialized thought that the Roman Catholic church laid out during the colonial era and beyond. Just as it was for the Catholic orthodoxy, for evangelicals the Afro-Haitian creole religion of the Black majority, known as Vodou, with its African sources, is "of the devil." The religious culture that originated in Africa is classed as paganism, which, in turn, is un-Christian because its engagements with ancestral spirits goes directly against God's commandment to "Have no other gods before me." For Third Wave evangelicalism, the spirits central to Afro-Creole religious practice are in reality numerous demons in the army of Satan. Afro-Haitian ancestral practices, Afro-Creole cosmology, and spirit work are equated with evil (McAlister 2012).

Insofar as "Africanness" and "Blackness" are often conflated in popular discourse throughout the hemisphere, it is important to interrogate whether racial Blackness is therefore closely associated with evil for these evangelicals. Third Wave thought teaches emphatically that racism is a sin against God. Yet, as we see later, it also teaches that indigenous spirits, including African deities, are essentially evil, and working with them spiritually is to commit the sin of idolatry (as written in the Ten Commandments). The evangelical movement in Haiti, with much of its funding coming from politically conservative US churches and seminaries and its centers of education in the US Bible Belt, opens itself to critique as a neo-imperial process in which mission groups of the North bring "salvation" and resources to the South and work to orient Haitian churches toward a Protestantism that is more central to US history and culture than the Roman Catholicism that prevails in Latin America. Since the earthquake of 2010, foreign Christians serving in short-term missions and Christian NGOs have become ubiquitous throughout the disaster zones.

The argument that evangelicalism in Haiti is neo-imperialist and racializes evil bears complicating to fully understand it, however. That diagnosis ignores some fascinating progressive countercurrents. I was surprised to discover that contemporary Pentecostal thinkers work to account for the postcolonial critiques of power. White American mission professors read critical theorists such as Michel Foucault and Homi Bhabha and make presentations at conferences about how to avoid reproducing unequal relations of power. The White American groups I interview who undertake missions in Haiti explicitly eschew relocating to the mission field and living in foreign countries. Rather, their slogan is, "Empower Local Pastors."[3] In their literature, they "emphasize the importance of *indigenous* leadership in the church around the world" (italics in original). One Haiti missionary writes, "I firmly believe that God's greatest and most effective leaders in any country are always the local 'sons of the soil'" (Williams 2008). In a fascinating implicit critique of colonialist missions typical of the past, the groups work explicitly to privilege the local, native missionary and pastor.

In their practicality, as well as in their decolonizing politics, these ideas eliminate the long-term foreign missionary and give agency to the local leader—as long as he is male. They are part of the contemporary current toward "empowering partnerships" written about by a coalition of evangelical and missionary organizations in the document called "Standards of Excellence in Short-Term Mission" (2003). The Third Wave missionaries assert emphatically that it is part of God's plan for national missionaries to lead the church and expand the kingdom, many of whom are "the spiritual children and grandchildren" of earlier pioneer missionaries (Williams 2008). This strategy creates the conditions of possibility for local leadership, local theological production, and local decision making, and it often brings investment for entrepreneurship. This trend nuances the neo-imperial, North-South framework.

These contradictory neo-imperial and decolonizing crosscurrents reflect theological dimensions. Local leaders in the evangelical movement in Haiti largely agree with the diagnosis that ancestral, "African" spirituality is demonic. Born-again Haitians themselves work to elaborate this theological point, and they fill in culturally specific details. I have traced the Spiritual Warfare movement in Haiti in detail elsewhere, and revealed the way that (White) American missionaries to Haiti, studying with Peter Wagner and Charles Kraft at Fuller Seminary in the early 1990s, formulated the logic that the entire nation of Haiti was "demonically entrenched" from its very founding (McAlister 2012). These American evangelicals worked out what they term the "spiritual mapping" of Haiti and produced a new *spiritual* interpretation of Haitian national origins. It began with a sin: the French enslavement of Africans in the colony. So, they say, it was natural and right that the African and Creole enslaved population would rise up to fight for their independence, which they did in 1791 in the world's only successful slave revolution.

Spiritual mappers stress a particular mythic event in Haitian history: standard accounts report that several weeks before the slave uprising in

1791 that led to Haiti's War for Independence, an enslaved leader named Boukman Dutty held a political and religious meeting on the outskirts of the northern capital in a place called Bois Caïman. Boukman and an African priestess named Cecile Fatiman sacrificed a wild boar to propitiate and strengthen their ancestral spirits. In the ritual logic of the Afro-Creole system, the life force contained in the animal's blood was given to spirits as a form of "feeding" in return for strength and protection in battle. In many versions of the account, the revolutionaries also embraced the African gods and rejected the Christian god (Hurbon 1993).

The story of this foundational political and religious gathering has been the subject of numerous tales, speeches, and writings by Haitian and foreign intellectuals. For spiritual warriors, the slaves of Saint-Domingue were the triple victims of sin and iniquity. Not having had the benefit of the Gospel, they were first unsaved sinners by birth; then, second, they fell victim to the French iniquity of racism and enslavement. Slavery was so terrible it created "welcome mats" for more sin and for demonic infestation. So, third, "in their desperation" and without the benefit of Christ's salvation, they had very little choice but to turn to whatever force would aid them: their demonic ancestral spirits. The sacrifice of the boar at Bois Caïman was nothing less than a "blood pact" with demons, legally sealing the fate of the new nation. Haitians freed themselves from French slavery only to sell themselves as slaves to Satan.[4]

When the earthquake hit Haiti in January 2010, evangelicals in churches and newspapers and on television, radio, and the Internet strained to discern what the quake might have to do with God's plan. Two days later, Pat Robertson stated on CBN: "They were under the heel of the French, you know, Napoleon the third and whatever . . . and they got together and swore a pact to the devil. They said, 'We will serve you if you get us free from the prince.' True story." A media storm surrounded Robertson's remarks, because it seemed so outrageous that he would be blaming a Haitian pact with the devil for the quake. Yet for many evangelical and Pentecostal viewers, the quake's devastation made theological sense. The principalities and powers of darkness that rule Haiti were causing their devilish mischief, and the people were engaged with them to such an extent that even God had lifted his protection.

In this evangelical nationalist narrative, as we can see, African deities are demonized as ontologically real embodiments of evil, and any distinctions that Christians would want to make between racial Blackness and African culture become elided in common popular thought. However, spiritual mappers *would* be quick to make this distinction; to emphasize that God created all "people groups" in His own image; and to say that no race or ethnicity is superior in His eyes. Further, each ethnic or racial group has a special destiny, and God has a plan for each group: "All members of the current population of Earth have an earthly indigenous identity that connects them through their ancestors to the geographical land of some nation or nations on the Earth. This we call national identity, and it is a key part of God's plan for man to exercise effective dominion in some spot of land in the Earth" (Chosa and Chosa 2004: 92). According to Jim Chosa, a Native Ojibwe and a spiritual warfare teacher at the Wagner Leadership Institute, the longer a person has had ancestors living in a particular place, the more spiritual authority the person has over that place. The evangelists called to work on missions or revival must "truly be agents of God to bring His deliverance into our assigned territories." In the United States, this means that Native peoples must be recognized as the original "hosts of the land" and must be invited as active participants in any Christian activities. If this principle is enacted, then racism will be impossible: "If you as a believer in Christ Jesus know who you are with respect to your heavenly and earthly indigenous identity, then honoring all indigenous people and recognizing them as host authorities in their spheres or territories makes racism a non-issue" (Chosa and Chosa 2004: 105).

Christians who are indigenous to a particular land have more spiritual authority over that land, such that entrenched ancestral demons will obey Christian local "sons of the soil" to a greater degree than they will foreigners. With the God-given (they might say "blood-covered") spiritual authority of a native Christian comes a greater ability to carry out the spiritual mapping and warfare necessary to break the strongholds of the devil, "bind the strongman," and usher revival into a territory, locality, or nation. This is not a political authority derived from the state system of governmentality but posits a truer, more real political authority that stems from God and is inherited through long-standing ancestral inhabiting of particular territory. If Christian prayer warriors truly understand the political authority vested in them by God, they will be successful intercessors who can hasten the coming of the Kingdom of God.

We can see that according to this theology, national citizenship is important mostly as a platform from which to act as a citizen of the kingdom. Any (diasporic) Christians have primary authority over their own ancestral, ethnic territory; a Jamaican British person has spiritual political authority in Jamaica (and, by extension, West Africa), just as an Anglo-American carries this privilege in the United States and then, further back, in any ancestral seats in the United Kingdom. Such Christians may receive revelations about particular customs, sins, or moments in their own ethnic histories that can be brought to bear on intercession and revival.

Thus, Haitians have been filling in the details of the Neo-Pentecostal interpretation of Afro-Haitian religion begun by White Americans in the 1990s. Pastor Yvette, who presided over the tent camp wedding, belongs to a group of churches under the leadership of Pastor Max. He, in turn, leads a confederation of churches with a branch in each of the *départments* of Haiti and often visits the United States to preach. He has a radio show and two (self-)published books. His knowledge of Haitian culture, together with revelations from God, allows him to analyze the cosmology of Vodou and discern exactly how and on what grounds Vodou is demonic. He asserts that Dambala, an important Afro-Creole spirit who is associated with snakes, waterfalls, and healing, is none other than the serpent who tempted Eve in Genesis 3. Both figures personify deception and ruse; "the serpent seems to manifest love and wealth for his servants.... He marries women that he desires, and enters into sexual relations with them while they sleep under the guise of a man. But this is how they will contract cysts, fibroids, and cancer" (Joseph n.d.: 67, author's translation).

Pastor Max speaks to Haitians in local religious idioms and works to read Vodou symbols through a biblical lens. For him, sin and iniquity are located not in Africa or in racial Blackness but, rather, in the deeds of Haitians (the serving of other gods, corruption, sexual iniquity, and so on) who have been under the influence of Satan since the moment of the "blood pact" of the Bois Caïman slave revolt before the founding of the nation.

For Haitian Pentecostals, the demonized condition of Haiti is not a conceptual product of the White American racism of spiritual mappers, as social scientists might argue. Rather, it is the effect and consequence of the sin of French colonial racism, which, in turn, led to the sin of slavery that created a "welcome mat" for demons in the form of the idolatry and covenant of the Vodou ceremony at Bois Caïman. The answer, rather than relying on help from American rescue missions, is for Haitians themselves to "break the blood pact" and accept Jesus Christ—and for Haitian Christians to lead the revival with the spiritual political authority they authentically hold as born-again "native sons of the soil." By looking at the revival movement from a historical perspective, and then from its own, inner logics, then, we can see two very different accounts of the racialization of Haiti and its relationship to Africa, to France, and to the (White-dominant) United States. What for some is a case of southern White American neo-imperialism that retraces and reactivates colonial routes of racialized demonization is, for others, a movement with a political imperative that native Haitian men become leaders both of the Christian revival and of the self-governing of the Haitian nation. In turn, Haiti is important only as a nation whose citizens will one day join the Kingdom of God. Haitian (and all other) Christians are part of the Christian diaspora that one day will gather and return. It is the task of every national citizen, standing in a Christian space of conceptual tension between nation and diaspora, to pray for the nation while ultimately working for the Kingdom of God.

DJAB RASYAL AND THE PROBLEM OF SEXUALITY

As the tent camp wedding demonstrated, one way born-again Haitians work to build the Kingdom of God is by marrying whom God choses for them and raising a Christian family. But even when converts live a Christian life, marry, and are faithful to their spouses, the Vodou spirits hunger to continue their relationships with their spiritual children, because people inherit ancestral spirits through family lines. Thus, any given person may be reclaimed (*reklame*) by a particular spirit, for whom she or he must periodically provide ritual food and prayer. New converts often are embroiled in personal dramas in which they feel they have been visited by Vodou spirits and called back into old relationships and obligations. Just as worldly marriage is an important step for Pentecostals to take, spiritual divorce from family spirits is often necessary. Christians graced with the gift of charismatic healing—in conversation with deliverance ministers internationally—are developing ritual methods to break ties with familial spirits who continue to hold people in spiritual relationships:

> One evening after church as the sun set and people lit small kerosene lamps or sat in the dark streets together talking, I made my way with a small group of women prophets from church across the muddy street to Pastor Yvette's house. Pastor Yvette changed from her dressy church clothes and hat while the prophets gathered around a married couple whose spiritual problems overwhelmed them. It seems that a sultry light-skinned woman with long flowing hair appeared regularly in the husband's dreams and made love to him, igniting sexual pleasure so intense it would wake him up. He was fighting the constant temptation to masturbate and to seek out prostitutes. In an earlier session of confession and repentance with Brother Miso, a young man with the gift of healing, the husband realized that he had inherited several ancestral spirits called djab rasyal (lit., "spirits of the race," but better translated as "family spirits"). This contested category of spirits is, for Vodouists, a type of family spirit that must be honored with certain foods, according to its requests. But for evangelicals, djab rasyal is often shorthand for the totality of Vodou spirits that Haitians are subject to inheriting. They are demons sowing discord, misery, and sickness in families and individuals.
>
> Brother Miso discerned that the husband had married Ezili Freda, the well-known spirit who flirts, rules the domain of romantic love, and is modeled historically after the colonial-era mixed-race mistresses of planters who were famous objects of sexual desire (and exploitation). It seemed clear to Brother Miso that Ezili was reclaiming her role as spirit wife in a marriage undertaken years ago for both luck and as a solution to some bouts of fever. Perhaps Ezili Freda was jealous now that the husband had both been born again and married an earthly bride, and the spirit wanted attention. This situation amounted to an iniquity whose cause was clear: the man had married the spirit, and she expected his prayers and occasional gifts of food. We were gathering to do a ritual called kraze alyans (lit., "break alliance" or "end relationship"), and the man would in effect divorce his spirit wife in the name of Jesus.
>
> Pastor Yvette's sisterhood of prophets formed a circle around the man and began to sing hymns. Standing in the fading evening light, they each wore simple skirts and blouses and head wraps or small white lace doilies pinned to their heads in symbolic covering, their beautiful brown complexions glistening with the last perspiration of the day. Some held their Bibles; one cradled a small boy in a suit and tie who had fallen asleep. Their hymn seamlessly gave way to prayer, and they became an intimate chorus, sensing one another's mood and the moving

of the Holy Spirit among them. Sister Rose began a slight tremor and began to speak in tongues, her holy syllables punctuating a stream of "Hallelujah!" and "Praise God!" The Lord was calling them together to heal this man of his spiritual persecution, and He demanded obedience; He demanded fidelity; and He was prepared to bless this couple if they would follow him strictly. The chorus of the sisterhood of prophets shouted and sang underneath this divorce ritual in a holy soundscape matching the gravitas of the man's salvation.

Brother Miso stepped forward as the sisters continued their soft stream of prayers and sighs punctuated by loud "amens." He asked the man to repeat after him a series of declarations and denunciations: "In the name of Jesus I tear up every covenant I accepted, every engagement I signed with any demon. I have signed a new covenant with Jesus of Nazareth. I break every covenant I made with any demon either in sleep or wide awake and I declare today that I am no longer a slave either in sleep or awake. My spirit is for God and my body is a temple for the Holy Spirit. In the name of Jesus, I divorce Ezili."

After a series of closing prayers, we all drank a cup of sweet hot cornmeal akasan and made our way through the muddy streets into the night. The sermon at church the next Sunday would be on the relationship between Haiti's national history and the Ezili spirit herself.

THE JEZEBEL SPIRIT: AS EVE CORRUPTS THE GARDEN, CECILE RUINS THE NATION OF HAITI

As theories of intersectionality demonstrate, racialization and nationalism are co-constituted through gender. Anne McClintock (1993: 69) has pointed out that all nationalisms are gendered and "the nation emerges as the progeny of male history through the motor of military might." The male-led slave revolt at Bois Caïman and the Haitian Revolution are a typical beginning in terms of masculine, if not Black, revolutionary success. After winning its independence from France in 1804, the new Haitian nation followed European gender norms, granting citizenship to men but not to women (although importantly, citizenship was extended to all men, including those formerly enslaved). As in France after its revolution, women in Haiti were ultimately incorporated into the nation through male members of the family: "The Code Napoleon was the first modern statute to decree that the wife's nationality should follow her husband's.... [A] woman's *political* relation to the nation was thus submerged as a social *relation* to a man through marriage" (McClintock 1993:

91; italics in original). Even today, Haiti's legal codes are largely drawn from their nineteenth-century beginnings. It was not until the 1950s that women gained a limited right to vote (with their husbands' permission), and they won full equal suffrage in 1957. A landmark decree in 1982 made women equal to men, particularly within marriage (Charles 1995: 147).

Haitian masculinity is still very much informed by the legacy of the Haitian Revolution. An iconic nod to the male Unknown Soldier of so many other nations, a statue of the "Unknown Maroon" graces the square outside the National Palace in Port-au-Prince: "As the Unknown Soldier could potentially be any man who has laid down his life for his nation, the nation is embodied within each man and each man comes to embody the nation.... Women are scripted into the national imaginary in a different manner. Women are not equal to the nation but symbolic of it.... In the national imaginary, women are mothers of the nation or vulnerable citizens to be protected" (Sharp 1996: 99). If Haiti has a mother (aside from the Virgin Mary), it would certainly be the woman who entered history through the story of Bois Caïman: Cecile Fatiman (sometimes narrated as an "African priestess").[5] While Boukman led the oath to fight for freedom, Fatiman performed the boar sacrifice under the spiritual auspices of African forces—which is to say, as a medium embodied by spirit. The spirit who "danced in her head" that night was an Ezili—but not Ezili Freda, whom we met in the divorce ritual narrated earlier, but Ezili Je Wouj (Ezili Red Eyes). It is said that Ezili Je Wouj's tongue was cut out by rebel slaves during the uprising to prevent her from giving away military secrets if she was captured. The spirit continues to appear after even two hundred years, and when she embodies an adherent, the person speaks in a guttural "ge ge ge" sound as if the front of the tongue is missing. In this story, the war for independence, a male military project, is powered by the supernatural strength of a female spirit possessing a female priest.

Fatiman and the better-known Ezili are icons of strong feminine power for the Haitian Black majority and in Haitian literature. Ezili's ongoing presence maintains the memories and experiences of enslaved Africans and a deep African past (Dayan 1994). There are a multitude of Ezili spirits, along with Ezili Freda and Ezili Je Wouj, such as Ezili Dantò, known as a poor, dark-complexioned lesbian and single mother who "turns" men and women homosexual, and numerous others. Spanning the color and class spectrum, the Ezilis enact a multiplicity of gendered ways of being and a range of sexualities. And in Haitian Vodou practice—contrary to both Roman Catholic and Protestant gender systems—possession can be multiply gendered, such that a male or androgynous spirit can possess a female, and vice versa. While the jewel-seeking mulatress Ezili Freda recalls the colonial concubines exploited by the French, the darker and poorer Ezili Dantò wears no gold but is pictured with a child on her lap—not the Christ child but a daughter known often as Anais. Dantò's mother is known as Gran Ezili. Together they form a kind of female trinity. Ezili Dantò with her mother and her daughter embody the highest value in Haitian womanhood: that of the mother. Their iconography also reveals a lesson in Vodou that the mother-child bond is stronger and more important than the bond of marriage. As one common prayer song sung for Ezili in Port-au-Prince says, "Ezili, if your mother dies, you will cry. / If your husband dies, you'll find another one." In a society that is oppressive to women in multiple ways, it is telling that the two worst insults that can be hurled at a woman are whore (*bouzen*) and lesbian (*madivin*). Yet two major spirits are divine embodiments of these stigmatized identities. Ezili Je Wouj, who fought in the Haitian Revolution, is a soldier and a hero, but her story is even less elaborated. I have encountered Ezili Je Wouj numerous times in Port-au-Prince and in New York City, when she blesses or admonishes members of congregations in spirit possession. Yet tellingly, the Ezili most associated with the Haitian nation is forever mutilated and silenced. Strong and central to Haiti's history, yet voiceless, Ezili Je Wouj "dramatizes a specific historiography of women's experience in Haiti and throughout the Caribbean" (Dayan 1994: 6; also cited in McAlister 2000).

The Spiritual Warfare movement tells a very different story here about Ezili, as we might imagine. Spiritual Warfare reveals that the spirit Ezili is an incarnation of "the Jezebel Spirit," who has become the most powerful feminized force in Spiritual Warfare demonology. The movement's thinkers draw from scriptural passages in Revelation 2:20 in which Jesus says, "Notwithstanding I have a few things against thee: because thou suffrest that woman Jezebel, which calleth herself a prophetess, to teach and to seduce my servants to commit fornication, and to eat things sacrificed to idols." A high-ranking demon in Satan's kingdom, Jezebel has been associated with the whore of Babylon, with feminism, and with prostitution and all sexual iniquities, as well as with idolatry and "the spirit of disobedience," especially manifested in women (Pierce 2007: 129–30).

Gregory Toussaint, a Haitian American pastor based in Miami, absorbed the American pastors' interpretation of Jezebel and applied it to the Haitian case. In his book *Jezebel Unveiled* (2009), he traces Jezebel to the slave revolution. Although he misnames the Ezili (replacing Je Wouj with the better-known Dantò), according to him, Cecile Fatiman, the woman who sacrificed the boar at the Bois Caïman slave revolt, "was possessed with Erzulie Dantò (i.e., Jezebel) when she was doing the ceremony.... Therefore, at the ceremony of Bois Caïman, it was Erzulie Dantò (i.e., Jezebel) who got the pioneer of the nation to drink the pig's blood. In short, on that night, Haiti made a blood covenant with that spirit" (Toussaint 2009: 83). In a weeklong revival campaign called Dezabiye Jezabel (Unveiling Jezebel), Shalom, the largest church in Haiti, focused on the terrible temptress and her wily ways, encouraging its thousands of congregants to search their worldly behaviors and spiritual ties for signs of demonic influence (*pesekusyon*).

For Pastor Yvette's colleague Pastor Max, "the Spirit of Jezebel" and "the Queen of Heaven" (the Virgin Mary) are both identified with Ezili, who often comes to possess her devotees in a sensual, coquettish persona. (Evangelicals point out that various Ezili spirits were creolized with appellations of the Blessed Mother in Roman Catholicism, and this is further argument that Catholicism is also a demonically infused institution.) Pastor Max finds Vodou's emphasis on the mother-child dyad improper and unbiblical and writes that "the Jezebel spirit incarnates the mother-child religion, which gives to women the place of the heavenly Father and the role of creation (and fertility)" (Joseph n.d.: n.p.). Ezili is a direct counter to the male God and his divine son; her spiritual power represents a profound threat to developing forms of evangelical masculinity. For Pastor Max, Toussaint, and others, the rule of the Jezebel spirit is the root cause of Haiti's downward political and economic spiral. Just as Eve succumbed to the wiles of the devil in the garden, it was Cecile Fatiman, more actively than Boukman Dutty himself, who opened the gate to the enduring female demonic at Bois Caïman. Here the divine feminine is literally demonized, and on the female demon is laid the blame for the myriad problems of Haitian national history.

Evangelicals would like to change how Haitians practice marriage, as well as how they create families. In fact, official marriage relationships were fairly rare historically for many reasons, including African social practices of polygamy and the dearth of Roman Catholic priests in the countryside. It was long common for men to have multiple "wives" and sets of children in systems of *plaçage* (common-law cohabitation). In the cities and among the wealthy, marriage was more common, but men were reported to keep mistresses and support second, "outside families" as a normal practice. Evangelicals (and other Christians) throughout the world understand adultery to be a sin, and for this reason they preach against polygamy, mistresses, and cheating, as well as against extramarital sex and non-heteronormative forms of sexuality. Third Wave evangelicals name "the demon of adultery" as a satanic force that is both inheritable and responsible for extramarital sex. Haitian converts often experience and depict the spirits of Vodou as active forces intent on ruining their marriages, steering them to illicit erotic encounters, rendering them impotent or infertile, or preventing them from having a peaceful family life. Haitian evangelicals preach a life of obedience to a Father God and his divine Son, a heterosexual marriage (without premarital sex), and male household leadership that is vulnerable to constant attack by inherited spirits/demons who must be fought using warfare prayer.

We can now see that evangelicals work to replace the extended family and its ancestral religious practices with a male-headed nuclear family solely worshipping Jesus Christ. In the process, they do away with the female spiritual power of the Ezili spirits (and others) and her multiple representations. The new evangelical nationalist script places blame for Haiti's problems on a female spirit's possessing of a female medium who committed an idolatrous sin and connects the fate of the nation to the fate of individual families. In turn, however, women are also potentially powerful agents of redemption for individuals and families—as long as they are working in the power of the Holy Spirit.

SISTER ROSE AND THE SURGICAL NEEDLE OF JESUS'S BLOOD

Women must be submissive to their husbands, as scripture instructs, and it is uncommon for a woman to take the role of pastor like Pastor Yvette. Still, male leadership in Pentecostal churches is often mitigated by the strong respect and authority women command, especially older women. For Pastor Yvette's church in Port-au-Prince, women are profound agents of holy healing. Sister Rose is a prophet with a powerful gift of intercessory prayer who considers herself "an employee of God." In a country where medical care is prohibitively expensive, it is common for Pentecostals to engage Jesus-as-physician and seek faith healing, one of the charismata, or gifts of the spirit. I end this chapter with a glimpse of a powerful woman whose accomplishments rival those of medical doctors in the narratives of her community:

> Amalie, a church sister, was married and had been pregnant numerous times but kept miscarrying at six months. As is often the case, the church sister had been to the doctor and received a medical diagnosis but had no means to pay for the recommended procedure—in this case, a cervical cerclage, or stitch to the uterus that would hold the fetus in place. At a deeper level of diagnosis, the family was convinced that a jealous neighbor was attacking Amalie's pregnancies through sorcery. Amalie was born-again, but her faith was not strong enough to withstand the demonic attacks. Amalie's mother saw in a dream that Sister Rose would save the baby. Together they shaped an understanding that, because Sister Rose was anointed with the gift of healing, through her the Holy Spirit was able to work to bring the baby to term. Sister Rose and her household (her husband and several cousins) acted radically in taking Amalie into their home for almost a year and acting as her caregivers. Amalie moved in with Sister Rose and they prayed together "morning, noon, and night."
>
> At the six-month mark Amalie started leaking amniotic fluid and began to cry and fret that she would miscarry once again. According to Sister Rose, "The Holy Spirit filled me and told me to do a cerclage. He said to take the blood of Christ as my needle and the amniotic water as my thread. He told me to sew up the womb. I declared in the name of Jesus that the baby would stay there until the ninth month." With this stunning ritual performance "in the spirit," Sister Rose assuaged the anxiety of the expectant mother. And indeed, Amalie carried the baby to term. Said Sister Rose, "On the day the baby was born God told me to prepare to receive a princess named Berakah, which means blessing. Truly they called me from hospital to say the baby was born." After staying for four more months with Sister Rose, Amalie returned to her own home.

Sister Rose shows us that, much like the "big-man-ism" of charismatic male leaders who develop high status through their own skills networks (McAlister 2002), Pentecostal woman in Haiti can become power brokers, often through manifesting direct relationships with the Holy Spirit through prophecy and other spiritual gifts. The focus, of course, is always on guiding converts in the principles of born-again life and in battling the demonic world. Women must still be submissive to their husbands, as scripture instructs.

FINAL THOUGHTS

In this portrait, we can see that race, gender, and Third Wave theology intersect to create an imagined diasporic Christianity in which men are heads of nuclear families; sons of the soil have the ultimate dominion and authority over the Christianizing and history-making of their own nations; and older schemes of racialized hierarchy festers in new logics. The essence of African ancestral traditions/spirituality is evil, and the feminine demonic is a particularly strong force of evil and enemy. Yet we can see that women themselves remain strong and empowered.

Pentecostals in Haiti and throughout the world are rewriting national histories that revise gendered nationalist ideals. The Christian male leader is the heroic and redemptive figure for both the nation and the family. And, of course, this has profound effects on the composition of households, the definition of the family, and gendered roles of everyday life for converts. The evangelical movement in Haiti follows global forms in arguing that the nuclear family, with the father at its head, is the most "biblical" form of kinship. In this sense, Haitian evangelicals align with political advocacy groups in the global Christian right that name a father, mother, and their biological children "the natural family," to distinguish it from family configurations they believe to be ungodly (Buss and Herman 2003: 2). While in the United States the natural family is positioned against the "gay family" and households headed by single mothers, in Haiti the natural family is the preferred replacement for the extended family networks in the rural traditional family compound called the *lakou*. Not only does the lakou contain multiple family dwellings, but it also generally features both a family cemetery and a family spirit house. The extended family, the recently dead, and the spirits—including the djab rasyal—that live in the land and are inherited through family lines all make up the totality of the family lakou. Families are compelled to divorce their ancestral spirits and base their authority on Jesus Christ, as his heirs. We can see intersections of identity constructed in quite different ways than they were in the past. In Haiti, as in other parts of the Americas, Pentecostals are rewriting the diasporic past and orienting themselves to the terms of a future Christian kingdom.

NOTES

1. The Third Wave has many names, including the Revival Movement and the New Apostolic Reformation; each carries nuances, but they overlap substantially. I use them interchangeably here.
2. The pastors' names are all pseudonyms.
3. The next lines of the slogan are "Encourage Local Women and Support Local Children," which encourages male leadership and female submission, as well as a paternal stance toward children.
4. In this narrative, the French, who began the chain of sin with racism and slavery, go unpunished, while the Africans, victims of French racism and slavery, are consigned to centuries of demonized misery (and then eternal damnation). Christians affirm this logic by saying that in biblical law, quite simply, idolatry breaks one of the Ten Commandments and constitutes a great sin, while slavery does not. This puzzle is a mysterious matter of the will of God.
5. Fatiman was a high-status mulatto woman married to Louis Pierrot, who served under the command of Jean-Jacques Dessalines and was a leader of the Battle of Vertières. Others say the manbo was not Fatiman but Manbo Marinette, who is now the spirit called Marinette.

PART II

Scrutinizing and Sanctifying the Body

WOMEN AND THE AFRO-BRAZILIAN PENTECOSTAL WAR IN MOZAMBIQUE — 3

LINDA VAN DE KAMP

"We are in war," Joana said to me on the way to a Brazilian Pentecostal church in Maputo, the capital of Mozambique, in August 2006. I had met Joana, age twenty-nine, at her office at the University Eduardo Mondlane before going to her church. She gave me a meaningful look as she said, "It is Friday." I remember the conversation I had with her the week before, when she explained the difficulties she experienced in relating to men. She told me about Friday and how it was "men's day," when men visited bars, drank, and chatted up women, or when they secretly visited their *amantes* (lovers). Joana had not accepted her former partners' "Friday sessions."

Friday evening is also the weekly time for liberating evil powers in Brazilian Pentecostal churches. Joana and I entered the church building, where about a thousand people, mostly upwardly mobile women like Joana, had already started praying under the guidance of the pastor who was screaming through huge speakers, "We are in war [*Estamos em guerra*]. Go awaaaaaaaaaaayyyyyyy, you demon, go, go, go, go...., burn, burn, burn [*queima, queima, queima*]." Everybody was furiously waving their hands to drive the evil out of their lives and screaming "go out" and, again, "go out [bad spirit], go out and never come back again." Sounds of distorted guitars and crashing cymbals played loudly. The pastor continued: "You, who follow these women everywhere, even into their beds, leave them, in the name of Jesus Christ." This was Joana's fourth liberation session in a series of eight. Over these eight weeks she was also fasting and preparing a financial offering of $2,000—she earned $100 a month[1]—that she would deliver during the final session. Her aim was to conquer all of the evil powers in her life and to open up a road to future success and happiness, including a faithful husband.

The spiritual war between God and the devil was central in every Brazilian Pentecostal church service I attended and in my conversations and experiences with pastors and converts.[2] The Brazilian Pentecostal churches that are featuring most prominently in Mozambique's urban centers belong to the new global brand of Neo-Pentecostal Christianity that stresses the importance of a direct personal experience with God through the embodiment of the Holy Spirit by followers of Jesus Christ (Anderson 2013; Asamoah-Gyadu 2013; Freston 1995).[3] These Pentecostals view the world as the site of a spiritual battle between God and the devil, and against this backdrop, in many African societies, they are concerned with the influence of ancestral spirits, which they consider demonic spirits that need to be combated by the Holy Spirit (Meyer 1998). Moreover, the Brazilian Pentecostal leaders in Mozambique concentrate on so-called Prosperity Theology, which underlines how a combative faith brings happiness, health, and prosperity in all aspects of life (Coleman 2000; Gifford 2004; Martin 2002).

While Pentecostals generally stress that the world is a place of spiritual warfare between God and Satan, for women frequenting Brazilian Pentecostal churches in Maputo, this spiritual war appears to have been appropriated in particular ways. Many women said that a certain spirit obstructed their intimate relationships, and I noted that the pastors were busy exorcizing a specific spirit or demon called the *marido da noite* (husband of the night) or *marido espiritual* (spiritual husband), who prevented women from marrying and conceiving and followed women everywhere—even, as the pastor quoted earlier said, "into their beds." When they are married, the relationship is tense; the husband is not interested in his wife but "views her as his sister"; sexual intercourse is problematic, or women do not conceive. These situations were important reasons for women to frequent Brazilian Pentecostal churches, where pastors fervently combated spiritual husbands and other "evil" spirits.

In their spiritual battle against such evil spirits, Brazilian pastors often referred to spirits that feature in Afro-Brazilian religions in Brazil, such as Candomblé and Umbanda. Since the transatlantic slave trade transported many African to Brazil, evil spirits from Africa, in the pastors' views, also crossed the Atlantic and came to figure in Afro-Brazilian possession cults, as Edir Macedo, bishop of the Universal Church, the most prominent Brazilian Pentecostal church in Mozambique, describes in his book *Orixás, caboclos and guias: Deuses ou demônios?* (2000). Brazilian Pentecostal pastors have created a cultural distance from "Africa" and are aiming to destroy elements of "African culture" on the basis of a historical cultural proximity in the South-South, or Brazilian-African, exchange (van de Kamp 2013). Brazilian missionaries are now recrossing the Atlantic to combat the roots of this evil. The examples of Afro-Brazilian spirits used by Brazilian pastors play an important role in how Mozambican Pentecostal women view occurrences with spirit husbands in their lives.

In this chapter, I examine the interaction between the Afro-Brazilian spiritual war and gender issues in Maputo. In line with the intersectional approach proposed in the introduction to this volume, which explores the interosculation of gender, race, class, religion and nation, I aim to shed new light on how Brazilian Pentecostals' gender constructions are entangled with postcolonial state formations in Maputo, a changing social and economic environment, and a rising middle class of women. Pentecostal women's bodily and intimate experiences—related to the family, spirits, marriage, and sexuality—are part and parcel of social transformations in Maputo (see also Cole 2010; Spronk 2012), a city that has been going through Portuguese colonialism (until 1974), a period of socialism after independence (circa 1974–89), a civil war (circa 1976–92), and the introduction of neoliberal socioeconomic and democratic structures (in the 1990s). Adopting and exploring the Afro-Brazilian Pentecostal approach to spirit power allows Pentecostal women to imagine and develop new forms of urban life, particularly when it comes to relationships, family, and sexuality, even though this can also imply increasing tensions in their relationships with non-Pentecostal kin.

With regard to the interplay of Pentecostalism, gender, and modernization, scholars have shown that Pentecostalism can enhance women's autonomy and stresses equality between men and women, despite their supposedly different qualities and roles.[4] The Pentecostal condemnation of drugs, alcohol, and polygamy—all of which are considered male domains—as well as the promotion of the household, positively affect the behavior of men who join their wives in church (Brusco 1995). These aspects of Pentecostalism may have special relevance in situations of social change. In Brazil, Pentecostal leaders have learned how to address the implications for family structures of intensifying industrialization and the growth of cities (Freston 1994: 539). This is also relevant in Mozambique's cities today. The majority of the converts are upwardly mobile women: they are educated and advancing in socioeconomic terms, working in the government and in companies as secretaries, officers and accountants.[5] They are teachers, nurses, or doctors and are setting up (informal) businesses, selling food or fashion. Their new social and economic positions go hand in hand with discussions about appropriate gender roles that are taken up by Brazilian Pentecostal pastors.

The question is, however, how Pentecostals' gender constructions relate to processes of social change (Martin 2001; Van Klinken 2013). While the observations on the connections between Pentecostalism and women's empowerment apply to the Mozambican Pentecostal field, I found that this very field is characterized above all by increased tension in households between men and women. I discovered that a lot of Pentecostal women were not finding a happy family life and consolation during and after conversion. On the contrary: the process of conversion often intensified tension in women's relationships, leading them to disconnect from partners and kin. This essay considers how conversion to Brazilian Pentecostalism in Mozambique has created such a tense environment, focusing on the interplay between the Afro-Brazilian spiritual war and gender issues in a post-civil war urban setting.

GENDERED CULTURAL POLICIES

Brazilian Pentecostalism in Mozambique is flourishing in (peri-)urban areas and among women. Based on fieldwork it is possible to affirm that nearly 75 percent of the visitors and converts at Brazilian Pentecostal churches in Maputo are women of varying age, and the churches are most visible and prominent in Maputo.[6] The majority of its inhabitants perceive Maputo as a city of both opportunities and uncertainties (Costa 2007; Paul Jenkins 2006; Lundin 2007). It is the place to be if one wants access to higher education or to obtain a good job. At the same time, however, it is a place where one has to compete with others and where life is expensive and demanding. Another set of challenges and uncertainties is related to questions about what Mozambican culture is. This has become an increasingly pertinent issue as a result of the country's turbulent history of social transformations and different colonial and postcolonial cultural policies.[7] Due to these histories with different cultural policies, conflicting practices and views exist on what society should be like (Macagno 2008; Sousa Santos and Trindade 2003). Notably, debates I accompanied with Pentecostal and non-Pentecostal Mozambicans on how their society should develop often focused on conflictive relationships, gender roles, money sharing, how to relate to kin, and how a marriage should work. More in particular, these issues were often articulated in gendered language and focused on the expected roles of women in society (see also Groes-Green 2011).

In her study on gender and nation, Nira Yuval-Davis (1997) demonstrated that the development of national identities involves particular views and attitudes specific to men and women. Gendered bodies have a central role as markers and reproducers of group identities, and this includes representations of a nation in terms of family and sexuality. Achille Mbembe (2001: 102–41) describes the semiotics of power in postcolonial societal formations in the form of an infinite erection, where political struggles are nearly always fought in the guise of verifying virility and femininity (see also Butler 2002). Such constructions and imaginations of the nation tend to position women as signifiers of the community's honor, making them subject to forms of control in the name of culture and tradition. At the same time, this position allows women to enter dialogue with other groups and to transcend and cross cultural boundaries (Grosz-Ngate and Kokole 1997; Yuval-Davis 1997). Aili Mari Tripp and her colleagues (2009: 25–28) describe how African women have used their position as mothers as a resource to demand changes in political culture, whereas motherhood can sometimes be seen as an obstacle to women's advancement. Social transformations in Mozambique have induced a certain loosening of the controls of traditional values and structures, and some cultural boundaries have become more permeable (Arnfred 2011; Loforte 2003). Pentecostal women are part of a growing group of upwardly mobile Mozambican women who have been able to embark on new socioeconomic and cultural roles and cross boundaries that touch on spheres of sociocultural reproduction such as the family and marriage.

After independence from the Portuguese colonial regime in 1975, the Frente de Libertação de Moçambique (Liberation Front of Mozambique; Frelimo) government introduced its so-called *abaixo* (down with) policy to reduce traditional sociocultural structures.[8] In its efforts to build one national culture based on Marxist-Leninist ideology, Frelimo was critical of all kinds of practices it labeled "traditional," such as chieftaincy, initiation rites, and ancestor veneration. In their attempt at modernization, Frelimo's leaders wanted to dismantle what they considered oppressive sociocultural structures by replacing lineage formations, banishing the suppression of women, and discouraging ethnic loyalties (see, e.g., Dinerman 2006; Newitt 1997: 546–50). However, it was far more difficult to implement the new structures than had been foreseen, and serious constraints prevented Frelimo from accomplishing this nation-state project. Its leaders underestimated the diversity of living conditions, power relations, and sociocultural roles in Mozambique (O'Laughlin 2000). For example, Frelimo did not recognize various local differences in women's roles and positions and the fact that, for some women, the existing structures could strengthen their position in society while Frelimo leaders said that many traditional rituals and social structures subjugated women (Casimiro 2004: 183–93; Sheldon 2002: 131–35). In some cases, the structures Frelimo implemented actually weakened women's positions (Arnfred 2011: 62–103).

These discrepancies were a contestation that was brought into play between Frelimo and the Resistência Nacional Moçambicana (Mozambican National Resistance; Renamo), and a combination of internal struggles, economic decline, and foreign intervention led to the devastating civil war between the two groups.[9] Renamo's tactics were to destroy everything related to the building of the nation-state to frustrate Frelimo's modernizing national project (Vines 1996: 87, 95; Wilson 1992). Renamo destroyed roads, bridges, hospitals, and schools; numerous stories are recounted of its soldiers making boys and young men kill their own family members as an initiation rite to become Renamo soldiers. Women were raped and forced to become the soldiers' partners.[10] The violent acts of killing and rape could be interpreted as part of a dispute on how life, including gender roles, should be reproduced (Owen 2007: 110–12; Vines 1996: 5; see also Wilson 1992: 564).

While Frelimo said it was committed to modernizing kinship, family, production, and sexuality, Renamo claimed it was in favor of reinstalling traditional lineage structures and rural chieftaincies. These different views of society also involved gender roles. Frelimo incorporated women into the production process but, according to Renamo, this happened at the expense of traditional cultural roles and activities. Correspondingly, Renamo called for the reinstitution of traditional gender roles. The conflicting views of the position of women became "shockingly literalized in the form of real physical attacks on women and girls, as well as in the physical and symbolic destruction of domestic home spaces" (Owen 2007: 110).

Even in such contrary circumstances, women became not only victims (Urdang 1989). In her stories about the war, the journalist Lina Magaia (1988) explores the role of women in the development of the nation at that time. Her stories center on women's reproduction of cultural life, such as work, cooking, dancing, praying, and participating in weddings and funerals, showing how women have restored society and transcended the gender boundaries that Renamo and Frelimo constructed. The war would also result in new roles for women. As their husbands died or were forced to leave home to fight, living conditions worsened, and many fled to the cities, where the number of households headed by women rose (Oppenheimer and Raposo 2002: 20–21). No longer able to rely on family ties, women were forced to become financially independent. Subsequently, this process was reinforced by the introduction of neoliberal economic structures in the postwar era, when many men lost their government-supported jobs and women intensified their activities in petty trade and the informal markets to generate income, particularly in the cities (Centre for African Studies et al. 2000). Although women had harder lives, as it became more difficult to buy food and to gain access to healthcare for their children, there were also women who benefited from the situation because of new possibilities for physical and social mobility that came with the reforms and with the emergence of nongovernmental organizations (NGOs) focusing on women's rights and emancipation (Casimiro 2004; Tripp et al. 2009). New ideas about men's and women's roles and the family were introduced. These developments have given women, especially those in the higher social classes, opportunities for new types of work, better education, and the chance to revise their thoughts about "traditional" and "modern" cultural practices.[11] More women have started to work in government positions and in companies, as well as in informal businesses. Increasingly, these upwardly mobile women are "invading" the city and doing so more prominently than ever before (Sheldon 2002: 235–39).[12]

Yet the subsequent mismatch between old and new gender roles is causing tension within families and generating conflicts (see, e.g., Sousa and Trindade 2003). For example, women are sometimes forced or encouraged to study and work but are blamed when they then cannot take care of the household. Along the same lines, the prevailing ideas about men show that they are expected to have a job and take care of the household financially, but in reality, many cannot live up to this ideal because they are unemployed and their wives are earning more money than they can. This becomes an obvious source of frustration that appears to influence increases in the occurrence of domestic violence (Centre for African Studies et al. 2000: 64–65).

The majority of the participants in my research said that they quarreled about money and gender roles with their partners. Most of the Pentecostal women I spoke to had professional careers and wanted to divide up the household tasks. Not all men were necessarily opposed to cooking and cleaning, but most felt uncomfortable dealing with these tasks (see also Cumbi 2009). Domestic roles in the home become a major source of tension when the in-laws confront young families with what they see as blurred gender roles. Mothers-in-law often find the behavior of their daughters-in-law unacceptable—a good woman should stay at home, cooking and cleaning for her husband—and they complain to their sons. Another source of friction is the extent to which a couple's salaries should be shared with their respective families, and the demands extended families are making on urban couples are further deepening conflicts within marriages to the point that the relatives are experienced as a burden. Frequently, distrust between relatives and couples about sharing is evident. People complain about the impossibility of setting up businesses and developing their lives because they have to take care of poor relatives, and as soon as they have some money, family members will show up asking for support.

The Frelimo government's changing cultural politics are adding a further dimension to these tensions and feelings of uncertainty about what it means to form an extended or nuclear family and to be a Mozambican man or woman in Maputo. With the end of its socialist policies, Frelimo abandoned the rules against traditional culture and started a strategy of rehabilitating pre-socialist cultural elements (Dinerman 2006; Sitoe 2003). Yet various Mozambicans, especially in the urban areas, had been exposed to and engaged in Frelimo's socialist modernizing ideals and in earlier attempts to banish "backward" cultural customs under the colonial regime. They have assumed new identities (Macamo 2005; Sumich 2008; see also Pitcher 2006: 102), become less dependent on their (ancestral) kin, stopped carrying out certain rituals, and now even question what the role of "tradition" should be.[13] I met some of them and their children at the Brazilian Pentecostal churches. To them, Frelimo's readoption of traditional culture is the reason for the failure of the postwar neoliberal and democratic projects to create more jobs and combat poverty and domestic violence. Others, both Pentecostal and non-Pentecostal, blame their parents for not having introduced them to Mozambican culture. Many parents, in line with the socialist project, did not allow their children to speak a local language while they were growing up, and now these people can hardly communicate with their grandparents, who do not speak the official language, Portuguese. This process, however, is currently changing as local languages are once again becoming important. There seems to be a "seemingly arbitrary circulation of the unknown" for many in African cities (Simone 2001: 17) in relation to what is being called "traditional culture." Are initiation rituals good or bad? What should the role of ancestral spirits be? What are appropriate gender positions?

Problematic access to money, distrust in (affective) relationships, and uncertainty about roles and the influence of spiritual beings all figured in rumors that were circulating when I was in Maputo. For example, stories were told about why there are so many beautiful, well-educated, and prosperous women who had remained unmarried. The explanation was that when they were children these women had been sacrificed to a spirit by their kin in order for the spirit to provide wealth. While the women were in possession of these powers, they were not allowed to marry and did not behave as an "African woman." This is a grave allegation not only because it points at involvement in witchcraft practices, but also because it illustrates how older structures of reproducing life, including the regulation of marriage and access to women and wealth, are under extreme pressure. As more and more people are becoming richer and others poorer, and as fewer "normal" households can be found, many people feel that the patterns of exchange and relating are no longer healthy and that Mozambique's future is unstable. It is in this reality that the Brazilian Pentecostal battle against evil powers has developed.

AVENGING SPIRITS

Indicative of the gendered characteristics of the changes that have been taking place in Mozambique are existing anxieties about so-called spirit spouses that frustrate women's sexual and marital relationships (van de Kamp 2011). I encountered various explanations for this phenomenon. According to *curandeiros* (traditional healers), the spirit spouse is a war spirit made up of the spirit of a murdered person who seeks revenge and attacks the murderer's family with illness and misfortune.[14] Compensation is needed to calm the spirit—for example, by letting the spirit marry a virgin girl from the murderer's family. This way the spirit becomes the girl's spouse, but the girl cannot later marry another man or special procedures have to be followed (see also Honwana 2002; Igreja et al. 2008).[15]

Another account explains how, in the current neoliberal economic order, parents and grandparents are selling children to spirits to become rich. The parents or grandparents consult a *feiticeiro* (sorcerer), who, in return, is given a girl (because the spirit is male) to "feed" the strong spiritual powers the sorcerer uses to produce luck and wealth (see also Cavallo 2013; Mahumane 2016). In the southern African region, this spirit spouse that "eats" human flesh refers to the spirit of people who have been appropriated or killed for the benefit of another person. This generally involves accumulating wealth at the cost of others, which points to witchcraft (see, e.g., Niehaus 1997; West 2005: 35–39). When telling such stories, people stressed how Mozambican society features unstable kin structures that affect women in particular ways, on the one hand, and, on the other hand, that people are often unfamiliar with the kinds of powers with which they have to deal. This is precisely the issue many of them feared: they did not know which powers were controlling and influencing their behavior.

In my conversations with Pentecostal converts, they emphasized the negative and oppressive atmosphere they had encountered in their homes.

Here, I present the cases of Paula, thirty-seven, and Julia, forty, whose experiences were typical of the educated upwardly mobile Pentecostal women of the same age who form a well-represented age cohort in Brazilian Pentecostal churches (van de Kamp 2012).[16] Paula said that when she started attending Brazilian Pentecostal church services, there was "no peace in our family. It is said that we carry the names of our ancestors and therefore our ancestral spirits. Spirits claim people. . . . It seems that my grandparents killed people during a war and that the spirits of those killed wanted some of us." That was the reason, she believed, that her family had a lot of trouble with marriages and that she and her sisters were unsuccessful in relationships. Only one of her five sisters was married.

Julia was afraid of marrying because her parents always quarreled. In her view, her father had brought misfortune to his children because he had refused to undergo a customary marriage (*lobolo*) when he started a family with her mother.[17] Julia's father had been educated at a Catholic seminary in the colonial period and had engaged with Frelimo's modernizing ideals after independence. Julia clarified that local customs, such as lobolo, were barbaric in the eyes of her father and that he "had been proud of having a car and civilization." For Julia, it was her father's arrogance that had made his family poor. Her father should have done lobolo because, without it, people do not belong to any family and lack protection from ancestral spirits. Julia visited a curandeiro to rebalance her relation with the family's spirits. However, when she felt that she and her relatives were only sending bad spirits to one another with the help of feiticeiros, she went to a Brazilian Pentecostal church to rid herself of spirits and the influence of kin. When I met her, she was afraid of the possibility of being involved in a spiritual marriage.

Worries about a new wave of spirits seeking vengeance have increased in the postwar era (Fry 2000: 80; Igreja et al. 2008; Schuetze 2010: 126–52). The destructive results of the latest civil war in Mozambique have been enormous. Curandeiros explained that the spirits of people killed in the civil war were expected to seek revenge in the coming years. As soldiers who underwent cleansing rituals (Granjo 2007) were getting old and dying, spirits that were temporarily calmed by these rituals were expected to become active again because they were still seeking revenge. According to both curandeiros and Pentecostal pastors, there are active avenging spirits in every (extended) family. Simultaneously, in the postwar neoliberal economy there has been a growing disparity between those who seem able to gain wealth and people who stay unemployed and poor. Suspicions arise about rich people's involvement with feiticeiros, particularly when they do not share their wealth, to which numerous stories circulating about the spirit spouse who "eats wealth" attest (see also Comaroff and Comaroff 1999).

Studies on spirit involvement and spirit spouses more specifically have been carried out in rural and peri-urban settings, in particular in relation to (traumatic) experiences in the latest civil war (Honwana 2002; Igreja et al. 2008). In line with an emphasis on religion's role in bringing certainty and security, these scholars have pointed to the crucial role of spirit spouses, and spirits in general, in the process of reconciliation and restoration in postwar Mozambican society (see Schuetze 2010: 412–39).[18] In the first place, the performance of war spirits in certain healing sessions offers a space for communicating about sexual violence and murder and plays a role in shaping memories of the war. In the second place, the marriage of the spirit to a woman contributes to restoring relations between spirits and the living, and thus to the renewal of communities and society. In this context, avenging spirits offer a way to deal with the traumas of war.

These forms of healing do not make any sense to Pentecostals and many other people in Maputo. The women I spoke to, including non-Pentecostals, questioned the idea that social life is kept in equilibrium by the combined existence of human beings and spirits. Some scholars have spoken about the "social schizophrenia" many Mozambicans are experiencing (Lundin 2007: 168–71), particularly in Maputo, where the number of people who engaged with Frelimo's modernizing ideals was the highest (Pitcher 2006: 102; Sumich 2010). To the outside world, people have to show that they are free of "backward beliefs" while they continue to be entangled with the past. Even though a national identity is being promoted in which "tradition," such as traditional healing, local music, and fashion, is being revived, the spiritual dimensions of "tradition" are still causing embarrassment and anxiety (Honwana 2003; see also West 2005). To the Pentecostal women, the growing influence of uncontrollable powers, including spirits, is disorganizing society. For them, Frelimo's return to "tradition" is the reason that the postwar neoliberal and democratic project is failing and that Maputo has become an inchoate city. Afro-Brazilian Pentecostalism, in contrast, is presented as a route to banishing the spirits and related cultural traditions forever and to reorganizing society.

THE AFRO-BRAZILIAN PENTECOSTAL BATTLE

When Brazilian Pentecostal pastors began holding church services in Maputo in the early 1990s, word quickly spread about how they were exorcizing spirits in spectacular ways—as described at the beginning of this chapter.[19] Mozambicans who attended these services stressed how, to their surprise, the Brazilian pastors were openly talking about spirits and witchcraft, which previously had been unheard of in an urban center dominated by a history of culture policies focused on abandoning "backward beliefs." Even though, today, Brazilian outspokenness about spirits is no longer newsworthy, converts are still fascinated by how Brazilians are able to discover the "devil's tricks" in Mozambique. Converts told me that there are numerous demons in Brazil, such as the spirit of *pombagira*, whose effects and actions were similar to what was occurring in Mozambique. In Afro-Brazilian imagery, pombagira is a female spirit that personifies the ambiguities of femininity and female sexuality (Hayes 2008) and is known as the Mistress of the Night or the Lady of the Cemetery. The spirit is attractive and dangerous and can be the spirit of a prostitute. Even though experiences of Mozambican women with the spirit spouse are not usually linked to prostitution, various women told me that a related problem is that women are not able to control their own bodies or marry because they are involved with "evil" spiritual forces.

After giving examples of women in Brazil who had been visited by spirits who interfered in their current relationships, a Brazilian pastor said, "This problem is the demon of pombagira. Here in Mozambique, you have the *marido da noite* (husband of the night), don't you?" It was March 2007, and the pastor had arrived in Mozambique the previous day. He had already prayed with several women, and spirits in their bodies had manifested themselves. According to the pastor, he immediately knew what kind of spirit he was dealing with because, as he said, "the spirits say who they are." The Brazilian pastors do not know the history of the spirit spouse, and Mozambicans are unfamiliar with the meaning and role of the spirit of pombagira in Brazil. To establish a connection between

Brazilian pastors and Mozambican converts, it is important that pastors show that they know the tricks of the devil, who uses local beliefs and relations to do his work. At the same time, it is necessary to have a distant position to "evil." The less one knows, the more "foreign" one can be(come) and one can thus break more easily with devilish ties (van de Kamp 2013).

Paula, who said that her family had no peace due to spirit spouses, emphasized that these spirits present themselves as ancestral spirits, "but it is the Devil who make us believe this. The devil knows that when your grandmother's spirit asks you to do things, you do it." She worked at a telecommunications company and was finishing her studies at Eduardo Mondlane University in Maputo. She had been attending a Brazilian Pentecostal church since 1994, when she had felt depressed and her family was facing problems. "I disliked tradition (*a tradição*)," she said, "but it was only after I entered the church that I had the power to protest. Before that, I participated in everything [such as family rituals dedicated to the ancestors]. What could I do? It was a struggle."[20] The vengeful spirit spouse or demon manifested itself through Paula at church services for two years. "I tore up various pastors' dress shirts," she said (this emphasized how strong and difficult to deal with the spirit was]. "Then I was finally free." Slowly, her life changed. Today, she said, "I can analyze difficult situations and react calmly." Compared with her depressive mood in the past, she feels more in control. At first, her family did not accept that she would not participate in any kind of family ritual, but now they no longer invite her. "I don't teach my children anything about tradition," Paula said. "More and more people are doing the same, so it will disappear." A few years after her conversion, Paula got married. Because of the violent relationship between her parents, she had decided not to marry, but the pastors convinced her that a different, happy life with a husband was possible. She had two children: a four-year-old and a baby. However, she recently started having problems with her husband "because of the young girls who run after married men who own a car." Paula told me that her husband wanted to be different from his father, who beat his wife and had *amantes* (lovers), but during his marriage to Paula he had become more like the father he so detested.

To deal with this situation Paula participated fervently in the daily church services at which converts learned to scrutinize their bodies in relation to the spiritual. At the start of the Pentecostal services, everyone must close their eyes, put their hands on their hearts, and start praying to allow the Holy Spirit to reveal the evil in their bodies. Under the guidance of the pastor, who is filled with the power of the Holy Spirit, the evil that is found in one's body is thrown out by going all over one's body with one's hands, by then pulling one's hands away from it and ordering the devil to leave one's body in the name of Jesus.

The Pentecostal rituals connect to and reinforce women's disengagement with local ways of living with spirits (van de Kamp 2011). Upwardly mobile women find it attractive to judge their situation privately, without depending on their kin. The important role of kin in finding out about the wishes of spirits, to find a way to live with them and, thus, to transmit a variety of messages (Lambek 2003), is unimportant and even destructive in the Brazilian Pentecostal realm. Converts are left to their own resources and self-consultations, primarily based on bodily revelations by the Holy Spirit and on what pastors say. The Pentecostal "art of living with spirits" (Lambek 2003) does not allow for a communication process with others, except for exchanges with pastors and God. Crucially, converts should not inform others, such as kin and partners, about the details of their spiritual battle, and only success stories were shared in public testimonies. Pentecostals have to learn to listen not to others but to the Holy Spirit, who will guide them in reading their bodies. The self-analysis and self-help that the Pentecostal setting allows for, and where only the Holy Spirit and the pastor are needed, is exactly the attraction of Brazilian Pentecostalism in Maputo. Upwardly mobile women are either disembodied from local spiritual communication structures or are happy to act independently of powers in the national and urban domains that, in their view, hinder their progress.

Julia, who was angry that her parents had neglected their ancestors because she and her unmarried sisters were now suffering as evil powers might attack them, felt that she could hardly trust the people around her, who were spreading rumors about why she had separated from the partner she had lived with for several years. The suspicions became louder when Julia, who worked at one of the government ministries and had a relatively good salary, bought a house with the help of a bank loan and therefore needed to save money from her monthly income. As a consequence, she could not always help her relatives, who frequently needed her financial assistance; they distrusted her and felt she would keep the money for herself. Julia, for her part, suspected that her relatives were "eating from her wealth" and were sending her evil. Julia saw her involvement in the Brazilian Pentecostal church as a way to protect herself from harm sent by others and to distance herself from the demanding relationship in which she felt herself entangled.

To live as born-again Christians, Paula, Julia and other converts are called by pastors to dress in the "spiritual armor" of God. Since the battles that converts face are spiritual in nature, they must fight with spiritual weapons that protect them and make it possible to act. Believers must put on the armor of God, such as "the belt of truth around the waist," "the breast plate of righteousness," and "the word of God as the sword which the Spirit gives," as described in chapter 6 of the book of Ephesians. Now and then, pastors distribute plastic swords and little wooden soldiers that stand for these spiritual moods of action. The spiritual armor not only symbolizes or imagines the spiritual battle but makes the battle happen (Meyer 2009: 6–11; see also Mahmood 2005: 161–67). By incorporating the Pentecostal arms, Paula was pushed and encouraged to find a better job and to improve her marriage. With spiritual weapons she would not be held back, and dressed in the spiritual armor she would be victorious. In fact, as a devout Pentecostal she had to be sure about her victory and needed only to collect the fruits of it. In her house, she stamped her feet on the floor to crush any demons that might be present. Paula decided not to talk to her husband about his nightly escapades and to speak about it only in prayer. Pastors normally advised not talking about demons with partners who were not Pentecostal because it would worsen the situation. Instead, born-again women take responsibility and use spiritual powers to convert their partners. As they pray and perform their warrior duties, they demonstrate how to be a winner, which, they believe, will then materialize in their partners, who often are not Pentecostal.[21] Moreover, Paula paid her tithes and other special financial offerings in church to demonstrate her dedication and to be able to collect the fruits of it by establishing a prosperous life.

At the same time, however, converts can become isolated. Her involvement in the spiritual war made Paula demonize her husband and silence the problems between them. The only things she could do, she said, were continue to go to church and fight for her marriage. Their relationship became very tense, and Paula became depressed. But leaving her husband was not an option, as this would mean she had failed as a (Pentecostal) woman, and her salary was not high enough to cover her daily living expenses. However, she made every effort not to become financially dependent on her husband. Similarly, the distrust between Julia and her relatives increased as she not only used her money to pay off the loan on her house but also gave tithes and additional offerings away in church.

Converts see the hardships they encounter as devilish attacks to prevent them from continuing their battle. Nevertheless, Paula became disillusioned with the pastors, who pressured her too much to become a successful *mulher batalhadora* (fighter woman), and changed to a newly arrived Brazilian Pentecostal church with similar doctrines but with a more relaxed atmosphere.[22] Julia stopped attending services regularly, because she was not sure they were really helping her. Instead, she prayed privately and merely followed the church's programs on television.[23] But some time later, she returned to the church because she felt she needed the Pentecostal push to become successful. Despite the challenges of the Pentecostal battle and increasing distrust, Paula and Julia, like other converts, stressed the conviction that increasing tensions and difficulties are part of the spiritual war and actually demonstrate that they are bringing about change. In other words, Pentecostal women are put to the test, and if they are able to continue the struggle, they can learn and demonstrate their capacities to open up a promising future in Maputo.

CONCLUSION

The Afro-Brazilian Pentecostal space of spiritual battling has become especially relevant to upwardly mobile women in Maputo who are seeking to direct and control their new socioeconomic positions in a changing, uncertain, and challenging urban environment. Uncertainties about new ways of living demand a critical cultural reflection, especially in the reproductive domain, such as in relationships with (ancestral) kin and men. By involving themselves in Afro-Brazilian Pentecostalism, women are exploring possibilities and anticipating a life trajectory to find and create alternative life options. As relative outsiders but with specific and powerful Afro-Brazilian spiritual knowledge, Brazilian pastors appear to be helping Mozambican women cross sensitive cultural and spiritual boundaries. In this respect, upwardly mobile women and Afro-Brazilian Pentecostalism find and reinforce each other in their capacities to challenge and move boundaries concerning gender roles and spiritual relationships.

Yet to bring about Pentecostal transformation, women enter a spiritual war that seems infinite. While the Pentecostal leaders claim that women can become free from bondage through the burning power of the Holy Spirit, their experiences reveal that they become part of a continuous struggle. The process of seeking to regain cultural and spiritual certainty does not always result in improved relations between husbands and wives, and it does not automatically bring harmony to household and family relationships. On the contrary, it often encourages further breaks and discontinuity that reinforce distrust and tension, as in the cases of Paula and Julia. The Pentecostal emphasis on breaking with kin fuels the relations of distrust in which women are entangled that results in an even greater need to participate in the spiritual battle. The Afro-Brazilian Pentecostal techniques of demonization and disconnecting from one's surroundings impede sensitivity to (religious) forms of dialogue and consensus, and converts who engage in these practices often lose touch with their partners' and relatives' reality and find themselves far removed from the happy marriage and life promised by Pentecostal pastors.

The spirits that belong to former wars and seek revenge in the current era become part of a new war. In the light of Mozambican history, the Brazilian Pentecostals' emphasis on destroying local culture could be seen as a continuation, first, of the Portuguese colonial regime, and then of Frelimo's struggle to banish tradition and create a "modern" nation. Even though Julia's father had broken with traditions, for example, she and her nuclear family continue to be entangled with their kin's history. For Julia, the break did not go far enough. This being the case, the most important preoccupation for Julia and other converts is who controls the powers of the past. Who is in control of ancestral spiritual powers and the course of national history? Precisely because the past continues to be present in their lives, especially through the activities of ancestral spirits, kin, and spirit spouses, and can hamper new ways to progress, the need for a rupture becomes more urgent every day. Therefore, converts actively engage in what Joel Robbins (2007) stresses is a Christian culture that claims radical change and expects it to occur. In their efforts to effectuate change, converts distance themselves from kin and quarrel with partners and in-laws. Yet converts' emphasis on evil spirits keeps the past alive in a Pentecostal way (Meyer 1998). Pentecostal ritual power is meant to destroy other powers, but at the same time, this act of aggression creates new forms of fighting. In Mozambique, the creation of the Afro-Brazilian Pentecostal battle appears to interact with a violent history, such as the post-independence civil war. Past wars have resulted in many spiritual marriages that subsequently have become part of the current Pentecostal war.

Like the former wars, the Afro-Brazilian Pentecostal war has gendered dimensions. The spiritual struggle involves a dispute about how life, including gender roles and wealth sharing, should be procreated. Part of the struggle Julia and Paula face involve the possibility of being financially independent as women and what it means to be part of an extended family and a partner in marriage, a battle that increases distrust between them and their relatives. Yet, Paula and Julia are also examples of how Pentecostal women do not necessarily feel that they are victims of hardship created by the spiritual war. They are attracted by the fact that the Brazilian pastors are not offering help but, rather, are pushing them to help themselves by not depending on their partners and kin, by not sacrificing money, and by learning and demonstrating their capacities to shape new life options and establish powerful positions, even as uncertainty prevails. Thus, battling and struggling become crucial in women's conversion process as they evoke and enhance the experiences of social alienation that are intrinsic to upward mobility.

In contrast with the views of scholars who regard conversion to Pentecostalism as a sort of coping strategy, upwardly mobile Pentecostal women in Maputo are showing that their conversion to Afro-Brazilian Pentecostalism is not primarily a response to social change but is a force of change in its own right. Brazilian Pentecostalism is pushing women to move existing spiritual, sociocultural, and economic frontiers, particularly in the domain of family and gender, and to establish new ones. As Pentecostals, these women need to conquer social domains by spiritual force. The Pentecostal women do not capitalize on the support that religious groups offer, but they take on challenges and private initiative as a way forward, a practice that Rijk van Dijk (2010) calls "social catapulting." This often implies increasing uncertainty and tension, which comes with the battling spirit that is shaped in the interaction between Afro-Brazilian

Pentecostalism and a gendered urban and national domain in Mozambique. I therefore argue in favor of understanding Afro-Brazilian Pentecostalism in Mozambique as a gendered practice of spiritual warfare in which the lack of trust, sociability, and support becomes something to nurture as it pushes upwardly mobile women not to rely on others and to stay aware of the evil powers that impinge on their lives.

NOTES

1. The Mozambican currency is the metical, but the US dollar is the leading currency in the business circles in which Pentecostals move and operate.
2. Research about Brazilian Pentecostalism in Mozambique took place from August 2005 to August 2007, funded by the Future of the Religious Past program of the Netherlands Organisation for Scientific Research and hosted by the Vrije Universiteit, Amsterdam, and the African Studies Centre, Leiden. Follow-up field trips took place in July–August 2008 and 2011. From 2011 to 2016, contact with several interlocutors was maintained through e-mail, Facebook, and the Whatsapp messaging platform. This chapter draws on data that I presented in earlier publications (van de Kamp 2011, 2015, 2016), but here it is used with the particular aim to show how the Brazilian Pentecostal gendered spiritual war in Maputo is part of different violent histories in Mozambique.
3. In Mozambique's 2007 census, evangelicals and Pentecostal churches were counted together for the first time as one separate category, which shows their growing importance. In Maputo city, where the Brazilian Pentecostal churches are most prominent (Cruz e Silva 2003; Freston 2005), their share corresponds to 21 percent of the population that assumed a religious membership (Instituto Nacional de Estatística 2009). The most prominent Brazilian Pentecostal churches in Maputo are the Igreja Universal do Reino de Deus (Universal Church of the Kingdom of God, known as Universal Church), Igreja Pentecostal Deus é Amor (Pentecostal Church God Is Love) and the Igreja Mundial do Poder de Deus (World Church of the Power of God). Pentecostalism is relatively new to Mozambique, where before independence from Portugal in 1975, the religious landscape was largely defined by traditional African religions, Islam, Catholicism, classic Protestantism, and African Independent Churches.
4. For an overview, see Robbins 2004: 132–34.
5. Normally the women had at least completed primary-school education and thus spoke Portuguese (the official language). Some of them were studying at the university and at institutes of higher education. In principle, they all earned their own salary, though the amounts could differ from the minimum wage (about $70 a month in 2011) to the wages paid for junior positions in the financial and NGO sector (about $170–$500 a month in 2011). Based on their education and

income, converts could be said to be part of an (emerging) middle class, even if many of them had irregular jobs or earned their money through informal economic activities.
6 This is similar to worldwide percentages (Martin 2001: 56).
7 For detailed accounts about the dynamics of the civil war, socialism, and neoliberalism in Mozambique, see, among others, Cabrita 2000; Dinerman 2006; Pitcher 2006.
8 Frelimo was founded in 1962 to fight for independence from Portugal. Since independence in 1975, Frelimo has ruled, first as a single party and then as the majority party in a multiparty parliament.
9 Renamo fought Frelimo in the civil war and since then has been one of the main opposition parties.
10 Attacks were also committed by "freelance armed bandits" who operated opportunistically in the general chaos in rural areas (Vines 1996: 97).
11 I put "tradition" and "modern" in quotation marks to indicate their constructed and contested meanings.
12 In the colonial period, the city was a man's world (see Penvenne 1995; Sheldon 2003).
13 Of course, there were also urban residents who did not share the official state discourse on banishing cultural traditions, although they claimed to have broken with traditional practices to avoid punishment (Lundin 2007: 105–8, 147–49). Still, the point is that many people learned to live in and adapt to different realities that continue to be felt today.
14 I spoke to several curandeiros/as (male and female) from different regions (urban and rural) in southern Mozambique in 2006 and 2007.
15 The avenging spirits are often male but can also be female and married to men. Cases of spirit wives were less known and less frequent.
16 For reasons of privacy, these are not their real names. I met Paula regularly in 2006 and 2007, and we met again in August 2008. I have been in contact with Julia since I first met her in 2005.
17 *Lobolo* is often translated as "bride price," but it means an exchange between the family of the bride and bridegroom, who enter into a relationship (Arnfred 2011: 71–77).
18 For a different interpretation, see Mahumane 2016.
19 This sections builds on van de Kamp 2011, 2015.
20 People often used the word "tradition" when referring to local customs, including beliefs and rituals related to ancestral spirits.
21 Men are not converting to Brazilian Pentecostalism easily, and pastors explicitly directed their missionary efforts at women, who would be more successful at bringing their men to church.
22 One of the Brazilian Pentecostal female teachers writes that God's women are fighters (Cardoso 2009), and this concept was regularly used in church services. According to Cardoso, many women are not successful in combining the various

tasks of going to work, taking care of the home, and investing high-quality time in their marriage. But God's women are fighters. They are able to take care of their home and of their work and still end the day with a perfect appearance. It is all about equilibrium, planning, and efficiency, says Cardoso. Women should organize their days and plan the hours in which they pray and read the Bible, clean the house, go to work, and spend time with their husbands and children. Women have to police themselves.

23 Most Brazilian Pentecostal churches use and own television and radio channels.

"DRESSED AS BECOMETH HOLINESS" — 4

*Gender, Race, and the Body in a
Storefront Sanctified Church*

DEIDRE HELEN CRUMBLEY

SAVED, SANCTIFIED, AND COVERED

It was the Sabbath, and we were on our way to "The Church"—this is how the saints, its members, referred to this Sanctified Sabbath-keeping storefront church located in the inner city of Philadelphia. As saved and sanctified saints of the Most High God, we "dressed as becometh holiness" (1 Timothy 2:9–10; 1 Peter 3:3). Women wore the white of a separate and "peculiar people" (Deuteronomy 15:2; 1 Peter 2:9)—the white of that "great multitude, which no man could number, of all nations, and kindreds, and people, and tongues" who will stand before the Lamb when time gives way to eternity (Revelation 7:9).

It was the late 1950s. The US Supreme Court decision in *Brown v. Board of Education* had effectively reversed *Plessy v. Ferguson*, making segregated public facilities illegal across the nation. The civil rights movement was at its apogee, and the 1960s would herald counterculture movements that contested mainstream America's social and cultural conventions. Although ours was a millenarian congregation, this first generation of saints were quite aware of these historical events and responded to them proactively. For example, after the *Brown* ruling, several saints enrolled their children in newly integrated schools, even though the Philadelphia school system provided no transportation; before going to work, parents drove their children from Black neighborhoods in which they lived to White areas where "better schools" were found. The saints valued education highly; still, academic excellence, along with all forms of success, paled to insignificance before Jesus Christ's impending return.

I, too, awaited the Parousia, struggled to purify my carnal mind "because the carnal mind is enmity against God" (Romans 8:7). I also did my best to keep the law, found not only in the New Testament teachings of Jesus and his apostles, but also in the Ten Commandments and selected Levitical injunctions of the Old Testament. Were we not followers of Jesus, and was not Jesus a Jew who kept Sabbath and "was daily in the temple" (Matthew 26:55)? Furthermore, while the indwelling Holy Ghost "kept" the saints in the "way of holiness" (Isaiah 35:8), "keeping the commandments" was integral to salvation because "faith without works is dead" (James 2:20).

So, "working out [our] own salvation with fear and trembling" (Philippians 2:12), female saints complied with such paranetical injunctions as:

> In like manner also, that women adorn themselves in modest apparel, with shamefacedness and sobriety; not with braided hair, or gold, or pearls, or costly array; But (which becometh women professing godliness) with good works. (1 Timothy 2:9–10)

> Whose adorning let it not be that outward adorning of plaiting the hair, and of wearing of gold, or of putting on of apparel.... For after this manner in the old time the holy women also, who trusted in God, adorned themselves. (1 Peter 3:3, 5)

Female saints did not wear slacks or anything that "pertaineth unto a man... for all that do so are abomination unto the LORD thy God" (Deuteronomy 22:5). Nor did female saints cut their hair, because long hair is a woman's glory (1 Corinthians 11:15). Thus, in elementary school my head was kept at least partially covered. I was allowed to wear gym suits, grudgingly, as they exposed arms and legs, and swimming lessons were rejected because so much of one's body was left uncovered by bathing suits.

Our distinctive and rigorous dress code distanced us from a sinful world that was about to be destroyed. Still, as I approached my teenage years, I became rather self-conscious and began to harbor dangerous thoughts. On the first point, I had taken to folding my long white mantle and stowing it away in my pocketbook before we drove to The Church; I did not want to stand out, even in the eyes of the hell-bound "sinners" who surrounded and gazed at us. On the second point, I wondered, to myself, why my daddy's and brothers' Sabbath clothes were not especially distinctive from those of men in the world. Their black suits, white shirts, and bow ties made them look "dressed up" and a bit like the Muslims brothers selling bean pies and *Muhammad Speaks* on the street corners. So why were their suits not white, like our dresses? Why did "dressing as becometh holiness" make female saints look so different from women in the world?

QUESTIONS, APPROACHES, AND CONCEPTS

Why did female saints cover their bodies so distinctively? Why did Mother Brown, who so thoroughly rejected male-dominated church structures, enforce strict dress codes on herself and other women? What might "dressing as becometh holiness" tell us about what it means to be female, Black, and Pentecostal? This chapter explores these questions by examining practices related to the covering of girls' and women's bodies in a Sanctified storefront church established in Philadelphia during the Great Migration. I argue that first-generation female saints' covering practices were neither thoughtless nor ungrounded. On the contrary, covering in The Church can be understood in terms of a long tradition of Platonized Christian dualism that pits the spirituality of male bodies against the sinful flesh of female bodies; millenarian enthusiasm; a desire for protection from "thingafying" stereotypes; a symbolic pursuit of respite from collective legacies of structural violence; personal yearnings for purity and power; and the possibility of simultaneously accessing social capital, spiritual power, and institutional mobility.

My approach is informed by multidisciplinary and multi-area training; I hold a master's degree in theological studies from a divinity school and a terminal degree in sociocultural anthropology. This chapter is also composed within the interstices of insider-outsider ethnographic writing in that its findings are shaped by the observant participation of a trained anthropologist who was raised in the Sanctified storefront church, which is the essay's ethnographic focus (Crumbley 2012: 8–11).

After providing working definitions of key concepts central to this investigation, then, the chapter describes the beliefs, practices, and institutional processes of the case study church, with special attention paid to gendered power relations. Those relations are then situated within tensions between the Christian dualism of mind versus body and African worship practices that integrate body and spirit; this section also explores Holiness-Pentecostal paradoxes that liberate the body in worship while constraining its sexuality. The chapter then addresses ways in which Black women's bodies have been the object of desire, exploitation, stereotyping, and religious surveillance, with special attention given to the response of Black churches to these representations. It concludes with a discussion designed to tease from these findings a multifaceted understanding of "dressing as becometh holiness" as it is experienced and expressed by the saints.

Central to this investigation is how the terms "Sanctified church," "body," and "dress" are conceptualized. While I have explored its historical and sociocultural sources elsewhere (Crumbley 2012: 22–25, 134–38), in this chapter the Sanctified church is presented as a spirit-privileging tradition, which has institutionalized selected mutually reinforcing features of African spirituality and Euro-Christian revivalism; this new formulation of Christianity is housed within formal arenas of Black-founded and self-determined religious organizations.[1] The case study stands in this religious tradition; it is referred to as a "storefront church" because of its humble housing, first above a horse stable and later in remodeled homes, rather than in a conventional church edifice.

My working conceptualization of the body is developed along a continuum of agency. At one extreme, the body actively produces, mediates, and communicates experiences that impinge on it. At the other, the body serves as psycho-physical terrain on which sociocultural practices, including power relationships, are mapped (Blacking 1997; K. Douglas 2004: 354; M. Douglas 1966; Foucault 1981: 81–83, 95–98, 101–3, 105, 2003:7; Norris 2001: 112). Relatedly, I approach dress as the selective cloaking of body parts through which an individual complies with, resists, or reformulates shared identities, meanings, and power relations (Anijar 1999: 184, 187, 190; Arthur 1999: 6; Butler 2007: 69, 80–81; Evenson and Trayte 1999: 112–13; Fischer 1999: 75, 87–92; O'Neal 1999: 125, 129–30).[2]

THE RISE OF A FEMALE-FOUNDED SANCTIFIED CHURCH IN GREAT MIGRATION PHILADELPHIA

Of all the female saints, Mother Brown, our pastor-founder, was most rigorous in her dress.[3] Her dress and mantles were the longest, and whether she was arrayed in Sabbath white or her dark-hued daily garments, her head was always fully covered. Born less than twenty years after the Emancipation Proclamation was issued in 1863, in Mecklenburg, Virginia, home of the first recorded Black Baptist congregation in America (1758), she arrived in Philadelphia in 1914, the year the Great War started. Mother Brown was part of the Great Migration, during which 6 million African Americans emigrated from the South over a period of six decades (Wilkerson 2010: 9–13).

"Baptist bred and Baptist born," Mother Brown experienced a call to preach the Word, but on reporting it to church leaders, she was informed that "God never called a woman to preach." Still, she answered that call, not in the South or in the Baptist church, but within the anonymity of the urban North, where she affiliated with a Seventh Day Holiness congregation. At that time, though not without its own forms of gendered inequity, the Holiness movement gave women more opportunities for ministerial leadership than established Black churches, for Holiness tended to privilege the divine call and demonstrated spiritual gifts over educational credentials (Best 1998: 153; Carpenter 1989–90: 12, 18).

Eventually, Mother Brown founded and led her own church, and before her death she put in place a Bible-based organizational structure that institutionalized women's leadership across church structures (Crumbley 2012: 7, 13–20, 157–59). Before starting her own congregation, however, she had "witnessed" as a street evangelist and was a member of one of the "big churches" in the Seventh Day Holiness movement. In time, however, she got tired of their "fornication and lies" and started her own Sabbath-keeping congregation; she was determined that hers would be a "clean church." It was meeting over a horse stable around the time World War II broke out and attended by a handful of mainly married couples, most of whom who had recently arrived from the South. Their numbers would grow to, and stabilize around, one hundred adults and children. The saints moved into larger accommodations in North Philadelphia, where they have continued to keep Sabbath and worship in the Holy Ghost into the early twenty-first century (Crumbley 2012: 140–42). Mother Brown remained the church's pastor-founder until she died in 1984, at more than one hundred years old.

While a unique and charismatic personality, Mother Brown was not alone in her quest for the promises of migration or her pursuit of institutional space within which to preach the Gospel. During the Great Migration, major northern cities such as New York, Chicago, and Philadelphia saw the rise of storefront churches led by African American women. As Wallace Best argues convincingly, these women found any number of ways to subvert the resistance of Black male preachers to the presence of female bodies preaching from the pulpit. The survival strategies employed by these women demonstrated both creativity and fierce determination to avoid the sexualizing gaze of both Black and White men and included intentional measures to desexualize their bodies through comportment and strict dress codes (Best 2006: 101–3).

From the Seventh Day Holiness tradition, Mother Brown introduced into The Church the valuing of both law and grace in its doctrine of salvation, demonstrated by keeping the commandments in tandem with being "filled with the Holy Ghost." Thus, the saints were "commandment keepers" who evoked the Holy Ghost by "pressing through"—that is, repeating the name of Jesus until it "becomes tongues." They "shouted" the holy dance of the saints, echoing ritual and religious dance, as well as spiritual possession found throughout the Atlantic African diaspora and over the African continent (Ballard 1984: 28–29; Carawan with Carawan 1995; Crumbley 2008b: 75; Dodson and Gilkes 1995: 528, 537; Franklin 1989:18; Harding 2006: 16; Hopkins 1978: 24; Nash 2006: 40–41; Stuckey 1987: 11, 22–25, 40, 58–59, 83, 89–91, 97, 364fn53).

Because of its emphasis on personal purity, biblical literalism, spirit privileging, and glossolalia, The Church can easily be subsumed under the rubric of Pentecostal Christianity; however, first-generation saints did not use this label to identify themselves. The Church was founded more than a half-century ago, before Pentecostalism would become the twenty-first century's "next Christendom," with more than 100 million believers in Africa and Latin America and featuring a strong element of evangelical engagement to save the world (Corten and Marshall-Fratani 2001: 1, 8–9, 82; Jenkins 2011; Kalu 2008: xi, 105–21; Marshall-Fratani 2001:

91–96). In contrast, The Church arose when Pentecostalism was practiced by localized sectarian groups of people from lower socioeconomic strata. Furthermore, among the founding generation of saints, there was little coordinated evangelical outreach; boundaries between The Church and the world were explicit and unyielding. Social interaction in the world was limited, as much as possible, to encounters at work or in school. In addition, joining social clubs, voting, and "worldly" recreation were prohibited; interaction with family who were not "saved" was constrained, lest one become "unequally yoked together with unbelievers: for what fellowship hath righteousness with unrighteousness? And what communion hath light with darkness?" (2 Corinthian 6:14).

From Seventh Day Holiness, Mother Brown introduced other beliefs and practices. They included a literal reading of the Bible and, germane to this chapter, teachings about the body that focused on its sinful nature, against which saints were exhorted to wage war to "make the kingdom." Theirs was the work of preparing for the imminent return of Christ, avoiding all earthly distractions in doing so. This focus on the millennium gave rise to a sentiment well expressed by the female leader of a storefront church in Chicago in 1939: people committed to the Lord's work simply "don't have time to think about sex and the things of the world" (quoted in Best 2006: 156).

Paradoxically, it is through these bodies that the Holy Ghost is both evoked and embodied when saints "press through" and "receive the Holy Ghost." Gender-related paradoxes also surface with literal reading of scripture, for Mother Brown taught that Eve caused her husband to sin, and her sermons did not skirt passages requiring women to be submissive to husbands; however, her exegesis of these passages were presented in tandem with scripture that exhorted men to love and honor their wives (Ephesians 5:25; Colossians 3:19; 1 Peter 3:7). Nor did Mother Brown sidestep the passage directing women not to speak in church (1 Corinthians. 14:33–36). However, her sermons referenced the unnamed but beloved "elect lady" of 2 John; Phoebe, "our sister . . . and servant of the church which is at Cenchrea" (Romans 16:1–2); Priscilla, on whom, along with her husband, Paul relied (Acts 18:2, 18, 26; Romans 16:3–4); and Judge Deborah, who led ancient Israel (Judges 45). Furthermore, although Mother Brown rigorously modeled "dressing as becometh holiness," she also modeled female leadership from the helm every Sabbath.

During her pastorate, Mother Brown had the last word on doctrinal matters, as well as church administration. The sexual division of labor was such that female saints were ritual leaders (e.g., Bible study leaders, interpreter of tongues) while male deacons handled the physical plant and money matters. Before she died, the pastor founder, drawing on Acts 6:1–6, put in place an organizational structure, without a pastorate, governed by a bicameral power structure of elders and deacons. Male and female elders, who were usually founding members and often married to each other, make church policy and provide spiritual direction; male deacons, like the deacons during Mother Brown's pastorate, manage the business affairs of The Church. The Church survived the founder's death in 1984, and the saints have continued to use this bicameral system to manage church affairs into the early twenty-first century. Regarding covering, women still do not wear slacks or cut their hair, and although some younger women wear colored clothing to church on the Sabbath, their attire is modest, and their bodies and heads are well covered during worship.

CHRISTIANIZING THE AFRICAN BODY: HISTORICAL PRECEDENTS AND PENTECOSTAL PARADOXES

Denigrating the human body did not begin with the Sanctified church. Kelly Brown Douglas (2004: 351) situates her exploration of sexuality in the Black church within "Platonized Christianity," which elevates the human body through the doctrine of incarnation but "demonize[s]" it as the antithesis of the spiritual sublime. In his writings, Paul, enthusiastically anticipating the Parousia, struggled against his sinful body while trying to reconcile his Hebrew legacy of body-faith-integration with Hellenistic pitting of flesh against spirit (Brown 2004: 53–54; Bultmann 2007: 202; Jacobs 1997: 71, 86; Moltmann-Wendel 1995: 41).

Moreover, this dualism was (and is) gendered. In Hellenistic and early Judeo-Christian discourse, the female body was anomalous to the normative male body. Eve is not only described as having been derived from Adam; she is assigned responsibility for ushering sin into a perfect world (Turner 1997: 20–22, 24–25). Women's bodies were regarded as unmanageable and frequently impure and were relegated to the peripheries of society. Although Jesus is reported to have interacted with and to have been touched by a woman, this precedent of breached boundaries was soon displaced by the institutionalization of the Jesus movement into a state religion in which women were eventually excluded from ordination (Torjensen 1993). Indeed, Augustine so closely identified sin with sexuality that, for both Catholics and Protestants, flesh became dangerous; pleasure became suspect; and female bodies, in particular, became an object of moral surveillance. Even female theologians of the Middle Ages associated flesh with women and spirit with men (Best 2006: 106; Douglas 2004: 352–53; Moltmann-Wendel 1995: xii, 2, 9, 35).

Despite the debate on the presence or absence of racism in classical Greco-Roman civilization,[4] it is clear that early Christianity also introduced color coding that associated sin with the color black, and dark skin became an occasion for apology (Drake 1987: 70, 151–69, 239–50, 259–91; Hood 1994: 73–90, 96–100, 115; Smith 2004: 75; Snowden 1970: viii, 1, 169–95, 198, 216–18; Thompson 1976–77: 33–35). Indeed, by the Middle Ages a church council had already declared Satan to be Black; an image had been made of Satan with a large penis; and black skin had been rendered only conditionally beautiful. Thus, Blackness was associated with the demonic, the hypersexual, and the aesthetically deficient (Hopkins 2004: 186).[5]

As part of a religious ideology that went hand in hand with expanding empire, Christian dualism and color coding would be employed to valorize racialized hierarchies that "civilized" out-of-control savages through national agendas of colonization and enslavement (Asad 1997: 43; Hood 1994: 115–32; Pandian 1985: 70–84; Rigby 1996: 9–10). Savage others with female bodies were further targeted because of the uses to which their bodies would be put in advancing empire building.

The souls of Africa were divided among various Christian denominations much as the continent had been divided by and among European nations at the Berlin Conference of 1884–85, which, according to original documents, convened "to ensure by arrangements suitable to modern requirements the application of the general principles of civilisation established by the Acts of Berlin and Brussels" (Crumbley 2008a: 126–27).[6] Mission churches, backed by the power and protection of colonial authorities and commercial interest, would displace traditional religious systems until indigenized formulations of Christianity emerged with the rise of African Initiated/Instituted Churches (AICs). The AICs selectively incorporated African religious traditions into localized expressions of

Christianity (Anderson 2001; Crumbley 2008b: 6–65; Jules-Rosette 1975; Opoku 1990; Oshun 1983: 105–14; Ositelu 2002; Peel 1968: 148; Sanneh 1990: 176–98; Sundkler 1971).

In diaspora, enslaved Africans were forcibly removed to the New World without the comfort of personal possessions and symbolic objects from their homeland. Nevertheless, their bodies served as matrixes of memories and as literal culture bearers (Austin-Broos 1997: 6–7, 13; Starke 1990: 76). Selected religious practices were kept alive during almost two hundred years that elapsed between the slaves' arrival in North America circa 1619 and the end of the second Great Awakening in 1815, when, for the first time, a concerted effort was made to Christianize Blacks (Raboteau 1978: 149).

The Great Awakening's privileging of embodied spirit reinforced selective African traditions of worship, including religious dance and spirit possession; however, the cultural affirmation of such ritual acts as shouting and Holy Ghost indwelling was accompanied by Platonized dualistic images of the body as dangerously erotic and in need of taming. Diane Austin-Broos notes this paradox in other parts of the African diaspora, observing that moralistic, eros-denying elements of Christianity are salient features of Jamaican Pentecostalism. The ecstasy of being filled with the Holy Ghost, she argues, has its source in West African non-dualistic affirmations of life and spirit. At first, this coexistence of affirmed and constrained bodies may seem irreconcilable; however, Austin-Broos observes that Pentecostal asceticism and morality lend the social capital of propriety to members of lower socioeconomic strata—especially to poor, dark-skinned women—enhancing their ability to negotiate inequitable social structures (Austin-Broos 1997: 6–7, 13, 34–35, 38, 116, 156, 195–204, 233–34).

THE BLACK FEMALE BODY: EXPLOITED AND CONSTRAINED

In North America, enslaved Black bodies became bare wares on auction blocks; after the trade in flesh officially ended, slave owners "used Black women as brood mares and Black men as studs" to produce the labor they could no longer import (Kirk-Duggan 2004: 12). Sexually abused "objects of exploitation" as well as "agents of exploitation," enslaved Black women controlled neither their own bodies nor what those bodies produced

(Cannon 2004: 18–20). Their bodies were commodified and raped by slave owners. Still, demonstrating unfathomable agency, enslaved Black women forged lives as mothers, wives, and members of community.

After slavery was outlawed, many Black women found that they were widows: more than thirty-eight thousand Black soldiers were killed during the Civil War, and five thousand more were killed during the ten years of racial backlash that followed the war, when White southerners succeeded in reclaiming political and economic control of the South (Cannon 2004: 21). Black women's labor would be exploited through the sharecropping system, which kept them and their families economically dependent on White landowners, until some, "voting with their feet"—like Mother Brown and most of the saints—left the South as part of the Great Migration. In the early 1900s, when the American Book and Bible House published *The Negro a Beast* (Carroll 1900) and President Woodrow Wilson screened *The Birth of a Nation* (1915) in the White House (Stokes 2007: 129–62, 154–55), Black people were arriving in Philadelphia at a rate of twenty thousand each year from 1922 to 1924 (Gregg 1993: 13; Hopper 2008: 29; Sernett 1997: 40).

Restricted to segregated neighborhoods and paying high rents, Black men met discrimination from employers and labor unions alike. They were forced to take less desirable, unstable, low-paying jobs while their wives, sisters, and mothers entered the workforce to make ends meet. Having been barred from clerical and sales positions, these women were forced into unskilled jobs such as domestic service, where they were paid less than White women (Clark-Lewis 1994: vii–viii; Collier-Thomas 2010: 281; Dill 1994: 142). Mother Brown, for example, "did day's work" cleaning houses for White families, as did my mother, and although their physical labor was welcomed, these Black women met fear-infused images of themselves in popular culture as illogical, hypersexual, and lacking moral integrity (Carby 1992: 730, 747, 751, 753). Furthermore, these women encountered such representations of themselves in well-meaning White-controlled "helping" agencies and among other African Americans dedicated to uplift. In 1905, for example, Sarah Willie Layten, one of the most powerful women in the National Baptist denomination (Collier-Thomas 2010: 127–28), worked closely with a White social worker, Frances Kellor, who founded a branch of the National League for the Protection of Colored Women in Philadelphia. The goal of the agency was to prevent the repeated "story of failure, of want, of crime, of poverty, of disease that might be avoided had the girl only been safeguarded" (quoted in Gregg 1993: 37–39).

Independent Black churches have served as institutionalized spaces of respite from White-dominated power structures and associated ideologies of White supremacy. Anthony Pinn speaks of the rise of Black churches as theistic responses to the "thingafication" of Black men, women, and children, in that these churches have been self-determining institutional arenas for reclaiming the complexity of their members' humanness (Pinn 2003: 77–78, 80–83). He adds, however, that conspicuously absent from this process are efforts to reclaim the Black body. Without bold and creative assessments of eros in African American Christianity, Pinn argues, any theology of liberation is incomplete at best (Pinn 2004a: 158–59, 161, 174, 2004b: 4).

In the Sanctified tradition of this case study church, the body serves as the crucible of divine union; however, sharp distinctions are drawn between rhythmic bodily movements of "shouting" in church versus dancing in the world. Similarly, "worldly" music stands in sharp opposition to church music. But are Black religious music and movement really so easily dichotomized? In her ethnographic observations on the "Sanctified Church," Zora Neale Hurston (1981: 79–80) explores "Negro spirituals" not as historically fixed or purely spiritual musical forms, but as containing dynamic musical variations around a great range of subjects, with "jagged harmonies" and dissonances that "neo-spirituals" have "ironed out" for concert performances.

Arthur Jones, in line with Hurston, argues that the neo-spirituals were "stripped" of all erotic elements, such as the sensual rocking hip motion that accompanies more traditional performances of "Move Daniel." Jones also rejects the commonly held genre distinction between blues and spirituals, asserting that they overlap in ways that express tensions and paradoxes found in the Black body at worship as African Americans negotiate Euro-American norms of sensuality and sexuality (Jones 2004: 238–39, 241–42). In a similar vein, Cheryl Kirk-Duggan identifies "blues notes" in the work of the "Queen of Gospel" Shirley Caesar, whose music and performance demonstrate "sensual embodiment" through participatory listening, kinesthetic testimony, and cosmological intimacy with Jesus as lover (Kirk-Duggan 2004: 228–29). The outcome is a conflation of secular and profane, eros and *agape*, as a way to address the tension between African and European legacies of the body—a tension explicated so eloquently by James Baldwin in an interview with Studs Terkel in 1961 in which Baldwin (1989: 9) stated, "It's a guilt about flesh. In this country, the Negro pays for that guilt, which white people have about the flesh."

SANCTIFYING THE BLACK FEMALE BODY

In his ethnography of a Church of God in Christ (COGIC) congregation, the anthropologist Melvin Williams comments on an "obsessive" concern with the "sexual potency of the body," especially the covering of tempting female bodies (Williams 1974: 124–33). To date, COGIC, and the Sanctified church, does not ordain women, although women have provided leadership and wielded power throughout its institutional history (Gilkes 1985, 1986, 1987, 1994, 2001). Anthea Butler suggests that sanctifying the Black female body through dress does more than merely affirm male dominance. On one level, sanctification can be seen to mollify open wounds of diminishment left by historical sins that reduced Black women to reproductive units and hypersexualized stereotypes. Sanctification of the Black female body, Butler agues, transforms denigrated flesh into divine vessel (Butler 2007: 20). On another level, Butler adds, when a saved woman dresses "as becometh holiness," she communicates her allegiance to the faith community's beliefs, practices, and organizational structures; this, in turn, opens doors of institutional opportunity that empower COGIC women to climb ladders of church leadership, culminating in the prestigious and powerful post of church mother (Butler 2007: 3–5, 69, 80–88, 90). Still, Butler is no Pollyanna; she states, flatly, that the Black female body in COGIC is "unbounded in worship yet bounded in behavior and appearance," and that, while the Black church experience may hold the potential for historical redemption and theological liberation, it "is also about pain and subjugation" (Butler 2007: 7).

If control over dress codes reflects control over the body, and if control over the body signals inequitable power relations, it follows that in male-dominated organizational structures, strict dress codes symbolically bolster patriarchy. How, then, is one to account for the enforcement of a strict dress code for women in a church that was founded and led by a woman?

First, Mother Brown might be accused of "false consciousness" following from uncritically internalized sexism from her exposure to Holiness, and its underlying and intensified legacy of Platonized Christianity, which pits mind against body, spirit against matter, and male against female. But why did Mother Brown internalize Holiness so selectively? For example, the Doctrinal Points, a biblically grounded catechetical document studied and recited by the saints, is explicitly opposed to glossolalia, or speaking in tongues.[7] Nevertheless, speaking in tongues is a central religious practice in The Church. Why, then, did the pastor not reject the strict Holiness dress code for women, as she did the anti-glossolalia teachings?

Using false consciousness alone to explain the strict dress code for female saints suffers from at least two weaknesses. First, it assumes a lack of mental rigor and personal agency on the part of the social actors. This could result in a research approach that downplays or completely ignores nuances of thought and behavior that could shed light on the social phenomenon under investigation. Second, false consciousness can overemphasize the role of human consciousness and diminish the contribution of society, history, personal biography, and religious dogma to the endeavor of understanding human motivations and actions.

Attention to the personal does not readily leap to mind when one thinks of anthropology. With the exception of ethnobiography and what Alisse Waterston and Barbara Rylko-Bauer (2006: 405) call "intimate ethnography," anthropological studies too often lose track of the personal lives within vortices of theory-driven analysis. But as difficult as personal biography is to access or interpret, the life of one individual can steer many lives and redirect whole futures. For this reason, it is worth giving our anthropological attention to the private and personal in our analysis of the communal and public.

As an example, Mother Brown yearned for a "clean church." Indeed, churches full of "fornication and lies" drove her to start her own church. If "clean" is understood as a metaphor for fornication-free, then desexualizing female saints' bodies by imposing a strict dress code may have been her way to make her dream of a clean church come true. In addition, Mother Brown was a southern-born Black woman, newly migrated to the North, for whom a modest dress code may have asserted a counterimage to popular stereotypes of hypersexualized Black bodies, which she, as an

African American woman, would have negotiated both north and south of the Mason-Dixon line.

The Church's strict dress code for women, then, can be understood as reflecting collective memories of commodified Black female bodies and structural and physical abuse, as well as Black women's experience of living in a world populated with stereotypes of themselves. Stained by rape and bruised by social depredation, Black women who cover their bodies in white symbolically contest social and historical sins committed against them—sins yet to be fully confessed or reconciled. Furthermore, the saints' habit of covering their bodies would seem to provide some relief from the acquisitive male gaze and its displacement of sexual provocation onto women's bodies.

Millenarian enthusiasm may have intensified body-mind dualism as the saints struggled to avoid any distraction, including uncovered flesh, that might prevent them from being saved and entering the kingdom. Still, millenarianism alone does not explain the stricter dress code for women than men. This is not to say that adherence to a religious dogma does not shape human behavior; in fact, religious beliefs can inspire human behavior in radical and dramatic ways—functionally and dysfunctionally. However, I believe that the role of religious dogma in exploring religious behavior is most elucidating when wed with careful attention to the social eventualities, historical legacies, and power structures that believers deal with in their everyday worlds.

As an example, by covering modestly, female saints send a coded nonverbal message of institutional commitment, which identifies the wearer as a believer who has accepted practices, values, and standards of being saved and sanctified. As pointed out by Butler and Austin-Broos, female saints who comply with prevailing practices of ascetic morality can earn social capital in the larger society and in their communities of faith. In this way, covering enhances the possibility of institutional mobility and leadership opportunities within church structures.

The Church in the twenty-first century is changing. The millennium, while still anxiously anticipated, has been absorbed into a distant mystery of unknowable time. The dress code has modified toward greater individual expression and lessening distance from dress style of the world (Crumbley 2012: 155–64). In contrast, for the first generation of female saints, divine eternity was fast approaching and human history was about to end. Through symbolic action of covering, we veiled our Black female bodies from the gaze of sinners, countered misrepresentations of ourselves in society, and mollified histories of structural violence. This compliance also opened gateways to unlimited spiritual power, to deliverance from death and meaningless suffering, and to the respect and embrace of fellow saints awaiting the Lord's soon return, dressed as becometh holiness.

NOTES

1 "Sanctified church" refers to an institutionalized expression of a spirit-privileging tradition with cultural roots in West African spirituality. This legacy was kept alive within African American slave religion for almost one hundred years before it was selectively reinforced and reformulated through cultural contact with Euro-American spirit-privileging practices of American revivalism during the first and second Great Awakenings (1720–70s and 1795–1815, respectively). Euro-Christian spirit privileging harks back to Welsh revivalism and even earlier, to medieval mystics such as Hildegard of Bingen, who spoke in a "lingua ignota." European and African spirit-privileging spiritualities occurred within interracial worship practices of early Holiness in America and, later, in the Azusa Street Pentecostal movement, institutionalized in 1897 with the founding of the Church of God in Christ (COGIC). Thus, COGIC's founder, Bishop Charles Harrison Mason, ordained "scores" of White Pentecostal ministers, but by 1914 Jim Crow had undermined the interracial quality of the movement. Whites left COGIC and started White Pentecostal churches as a racially segregated religious phenomenon until public reconciliation was initiated by the Memphis Miracle of 1994 (Hurston 1981: 103–7; Lincoln and Mamiya 1990: 78–81; Llewellyn 1997: 1–5; MacRobert 1997: 295–309; Rosenior 2009; Sanders 1996: 4, 19–20, 29–32; Tinney 1971: 4).

2 In addition to Butler's (2007: 69, 80–81) exploration of sanctified dress as social capital, the reader may want to examine innovative uses of dress by Jewish immigrants for whom American fashion became a text for assimilation (Anijar 1999: 184, 187, 190); "switching back and forth" dressing practices of Christianized Dakota Native Americans as they negotiated nuanced and sometimes dangerous identities (Evenson and Trayte 1999: 112–13); and the "dress rebellion" against the Mormon leader James Strang after he attempted to control dissident male members through a dress code he imposed on their wives (Fischer 1999: 75, 87–92).

3 "Mother Brown" is a pseudonym.

4 In this debate, the classicist Frank Snowden and the anthropologist St. Clair Drake argue that structural racism as we know it today did not exists in classical

civilizations; however, the historian Alvin Thompson argues that ideational seeds of racism and color prejudice preceded the transatlantic slave trade. Thompson cites Hanno's fantastically derogatory observation of West Africans in the fifth century BCE and the writings of the Roman Pliny, who described these Africans as "human monstrosities," lacking language, and consuming dog's milk (quoted in Thompson 1976–77: 34–35). In contrast, in *Blacks in Antiquity* Snowden (1970: 132–34, 144) documents the presence of Africans across Greek and Roman society and culture, from wooly haired Eurybates in Homer's *Odyssey* to Roman diplomatic interacting with the "Ethiopian queen" or Kantake/Candace. Drake, doing battle with the "modern Manichaeism" position that denigration of blackness is "natural," argues that modern racism is a product of malleable social, economic, and historical conditions. To support this argument, he explores race relations in the ancient Nile Valley in volume 1 and in Early Muslim and Medieval European history in volume 2 of his magnum opus *Black Folk Here and There* (Drake 1987).

5   In his Latin Vulgate translation of Songs of Solomon 1:5 from Hebrew scripture, Jerome translates the Hebrew word *waw* (and) as *sed* (but). Thus, instead of "I am Black and beautiful," his translation reads, "I am Black but beautiful." Jerome would also link blackness to lust by describing the devil as black like the night and possessing "inordinate sexual powers" (Hood 1994: 83). On the association of blackness with sin and carnality in early church history, Hood also notes that the eighth-century Council of Toledo "declared the devil a monster with cloven hooves, horns, and the ears of a donkey, fiery eyes, an awful smell of sulpher, and enormous penis. In an Eighth Century manuscript, the devil is portrayed as Black and naked" (Hood 1994: 89).

6   "Convention Revising the General Act of Berlin, February 26, 1885, and the General Act and Declaration of Brussels, July 2, 1890, signed at Saint-Germain-en-Laye, September 10, 1919," accessed December 7, 2012, http://archive.org/stream/conventionrevisi00greaiala#page/no/mode/2up.

7   *Doctrinal Points of the Church of God (7th Day Apostolic) Re-organized 1933* (Church of God 1951: 19 consisted of "the original 40 points of doctrine ... herein incorporated, having been established in the year 1933, and were accepted by the ministerial council assembled at Salem, West Virginia, March 5, 1950, and reaffirmed by the Apostolic Council, July 7, 1951.

PART III

Sonic Power

WEST AFRICAN AND CARIBBEAN WOMEN EVANGELISTS

The Wailing Women Worldwide Intercessors

PAULA AYMER

In 2004, three West African missionary women arrived at the Pentecostal house church on the Caribbean island of Grenada, where I was residing and engaged in research as a participant observer. The West African missionaries were seeking devout, spirit-filled women who met regularly in evangelical churches and prayer and Bible study groups who would respond positively to a prophetic message the visitors had received. The foreign visitors recounted how, in a vision, the Lord had specifically asked that godly women from across the world be raised up, first, from across Nigeria's thirty-six states, then from the countries of the world, to intercede for the entire world that was under threat of God's fierce anger. The visitors shared that they had received clear instructions that Christian women must engage in specific forms of prayer that included visible and vocal signs of sorrow, as declared in the book of the prophet Jeremiah.

These Nigerian women were members of the Wailing Women Worldwide (WWW) missionary organization. The phrase "Wailing Women" comes from a short directive from the prophet Jeremiah. In it, the prophet calls for professional wailing women to stand at a public gate in the city and wail for the sins of the people of Israel: "Thus saith the Lord of hosts, consider ye and call for the mourning women, that they may come; and send for cunning women; that they may take up a wailing for us that our eyes may run down with tears, and our eyelids gush with waters" (Jeremiah 9:17). This organization, begun in Nigeria in 1998, by 2004 had sent out missionaries bearing the vision's mandate to Britain, North America, and the Caribbean.

I noted that the visitors' vision was a selective rallying call. It had singled out Nigeria as a special case within a wider troubled world, and the invitation to urgent prayer was addressed only to women—specifically those women across the world whose lives were influenced by the indwelling of the Holy Spirit. The leader of the house church and the visiting women testified that the Holy Spirit had miraculously connected them and made their coming together possible. Very deliberately, the Nigerian missionaries were engaging in a cross-cultural, international project with the goal of establishing a network of bases. From such bases across the world, saved and sanctified women would participate in incessant intercessory prayer. The international prayer project seemed to be an unusual and ambitious undertaking, especially since Pentecostal missionary organizations in North America such as the Assemblies of God tend to commission and support husband-and-wife missionary teams or single male missionaries to evangelize in foreign countries. In this phase of the missionary project, three Nigerian women had become God's emissaries sent to mobilize a global army, composed of women, to save a lost world.

The West African missionaries were intentionally seeking out evangelical (mostly Pentecostal) women's groups to present them with the millennial vision that called women to become intercessors with them on behalf of a sinful and hell-bent world. The WWW is a para-church organization that has carved out a unique theological and missionary niche that allows spirit-filled women to assume secondary forms of leadership and solidarity without threatening the traditionally male-led authority in evangelical communities. The WWW missionaries present their intercessory prayer vision as a collaborative effort that subsumes and replaces any cultural differences, long-established organizational arrangements, and national boundaries that they might encounter. Pentecostalism as a global evangelical movement has exposed converts across the world to elements of Pentecostal theology and practice, especially in its inclusion of noise, sound, and emotionality, which believers view as evidence of the presence and power of the Holy Spirit. However, although the West African missionaries and the Caribbean house church members were certainly united in obedience to scripture and some Pentecostal practices, they are inheritors of starkly different cultural and political histories. Such differences are reflected in their worship styles, representations of God, gender practices, and family arrangements.

This case study reveals that, although diasporic and global Pentecostalism is able to subsume some cultural differences in shared and intensive worship performances, historical and cultural factors matter and are deeply embedded within religious expressions and experiences. Wailing Women Worldwide will have to negotiate significant cultural and theological differences in building its global army of women.

In what follows, I first sketch historical and political differences that inform Pentecostal sensibilities and practices in Nigeria and the Caribbean. I then provide background as to the formation and organization of the WWW. In the third section, I describe the changes and challenges that attended the WWW members' efforts to secure the participation and ongoing commitment of a spirit-filled group of Caribbean Pentecostal women on the island of Grenada.

PENTECOSTALISM IN THE CARIBBEAN AND NIGERIA

Large numbers of poor women from countries in the Caribbean and across the world have positioned themselves at the center of the evangelical movement identified as Pentecostalism, a religious awakening that is now global in its reach and influence (Corten and Marshall-Fratani 2001; Cucchiari 1990; Gilkes 1998; Griffith 1997; Soares 2012). Pentecostalism as a religious movement emerged in the United States with gusto during the first decade of the twentieth century and became branded with recognizable characteristics. Influenced by an evangelical awakening—the Holiness movement—Pentecostalism spread, then seemed to wane, only to return more revived and expansive in its evangelization programs in the decades after the 1950s (Brown 2011; Poloma 1989; Womack 1968). Without a central ecclesiastical body that organizes Pentecostalism within a bureaucratic administrative structure, myriad independent Pentecostal congregations, as well as evangelical and missionary organizations, have proliferated across the world. They take different forms, such as megachurches, house churches, storefront churches, and para-Pentecostal organizations such as the Missionary Church International and the Assemblies of God. Evangelical and Pentecostal women display their spiritual zeal, too, in organizations such as the WWW, with its base in Nigeria, and the Women's Aglow Fellowship International, which was established in the United States in the 1960s (Griffith 1997).

The research suggests that glossolalia, or speaking in tongues, and wailing by worshipers in poor Black religious sects would have been unacceptable and punishable in British Caribbean societies before the post-1950s decades. Exuberant forms of Black Afro-Christian worship were regarded by the established colonial churches and other major institutions as deviant behavior (Cox 1994; Vessey 1952: 65). Thus, for decades in the British West Indies, Afro-Christian sects that engaged in intense emotion, physicality, trance, or the making of loud sounds during worship were declared illegal and driven underground (Bravo et al. 2001: 21; Cox 1994; Edmonds and Gonzalez 2010; Murrell 2010). During this period, the Anglican church had the most economic and political clout in the British colonies. However, on some islands, including Grenada, which had been a French colony before it was ceded to Britain in the late eighteenth century, Roman Catholicism was predominant. Once slavery ended in the British colonies, Caribbean Blacks—the descendants of enslaved Africans—were given at least three religious alternatives. People could choose not to practice any communal form of religion, and many—perhaps a majority—chose to do just that. Membership in the established, confessional, colonial denominations became more accessible to the poor. However, the requirements of full membership in the colonial established denominations were beyond the means of most. In the third alternative, some members of the majority-Black population embraced religious expressions created from the melding of bits and pieces of Christian theology and practices with African religious rituals and beliefs that had been passed down during the centuries of enslavement endured by their ancestors. Yet to do so was to risk being labeled deviant. In the Caribbean (and in the United States), this censure, imposed by mainline religious and other dominant institutions, created long-lasting class- and race-based divisions within Christianity (Gilkes 1998b; Sernett 1999).

By the 1950s, the established clergy in the Caribbean were facing serious competition from new and powerful, North American, Pentecostal rivals. Political changes in the Caribbean region in the second half of the twentieth century, and the strength of the global Pentecostal movement propelled by various forms of media and evangelical outreach, proved too strong for the colonial churches that, until then, had been bastions of religious and political power and privilege. Husband-and-wife missionary teams from the Assemblies of God, North America, began arriving in the eastern Caribbean in the 1950s and working among the poor and unchurched in rural communities. Although Caribbean women responded more readily than men did to the Pentecostal missionaries, the Assemblies of God began a campaign of indigenization and church planting, and the organization's mandate during this period sought to promote local men to leadership positions wherever new churches were planted (Hodges 1986: 85). At each Pentecostal mission site in the Caribbean, converted local men were trained for leadership, then ordained to take over from the US-based missionaries. Therefore, by the end of the twentieth century, nearly all Caribbean Pentecostal congregations that had been influenced by Assemblies of God missionaries and other US evangelical missionary outfits, were led by Caribbean-born pastors. Pentecostalism, with its flexible worship formats and ability to tolerate cultural diversity, seemed a good fit and provided a welcoming religious environment for many who felt marginalized by the mainline, colonial denominations in the Caribbean. Still, in the twenty-first century Afro-Christian sects continue to operate throughout the former British colonies but remain small in numbers and membership, while evangelical—and particularly Pentecostal—churches have outgrown the established colonial churches in influence and membership (Austin-Broos 2001).

The visiting West African women and the Caribbean women of African descent share histories of colonial exploitation and exposure to European colonial religions. The theological historian Ogbu Kalu (2003: 8) notes that "colonialism was actually a very short-lived phenomenon in Africa—it lasted only the span of a single human lifetime." In comparison, European colonization and enslavement of African people and their descendants in the Caribbean lasted nearly three hundred years. Although often clandestinely, enslaved and, later, free people formed Afro-Caribbean Christian religions that "show strong African connections and harbor African cultural memory" (Murrell 2010: 1). However, most people in the Anglophone Caribbean have no widespread and continuous socialization into religious systems that have mythical sources in traditional religions in the ways that people on the African continent do. Again, Kalu (2003: 9) writes about African Christianity, "The Africans read the Bible through their own traditionally 'charismatic' worldview. They know there are spirits in the sky, the water, the land and the ancestral world." However, like West Africans, the masses of Caribbean people cannot boast of a history of full inclusion in the established colonial, Christian denominations that were established in both regions. In the post-1950s decades, many in the Caribbean have helped to create and now claim what can be called Caribbean Pentecostalism.

Citizens of West African countries have been introduced to the Pentecostal religious drama and life-changing promises and realities of conversion into evangelical Christianity preached by indigenous and foreign evangelists and missionaries. However, it seems that Pentecostalism's emphasis on the presence and power of the Holy Spirit has served to strengthen pervasive cultural beliefs held by sub-Saharan African people in the power of spirits and the activities of the spirit world ruled by Satan (Marshall-Fratani 2001: 9). In response to real or perceived attacks by Satan and evil spirits, Pentecostal congregations in Africa organize deliverance services to rid members of traditional forms of religion and the supposedly Satan-led spiritual powers that inhabit them. On this theme, the WWW *Training Manual* (2004: 2, 6, 7, 8) warns its members to guard against spirit possession and especially evil spirits that disrupt families and insert themselves into the lives of wives and mothers. In particular, the manual presents Satan as a pervasive, evil, spiritual presence in the world. The urgent need for Christian women to thwart Satanic power is a recurring directive throughout the *Training Manual*.

However, US and Caribbean Pentecostals have shown some ambivalence toward the topic of demon oppression and possession and its theological emphasis (Poloma 1989: 237). Vague myths and even beliefs in spirits have been retained by the people of the Anglophone Caribbean, but no consistent or organized forms of socialization in the workings of the spirit world and their patterns of malfeasance are passed down through the generations. Nor is the pervasive presence of spirits from a cunning hoard of evil spirits encouraged in Caribbean Pentecostal theology. However, Caribbean Pentecostalism does teach that the wiles of Satan are to be avoided and his power thwarted by the power and presence of the Holy Spirit. It is fair to say, however, that African Pentecostalism's theological emphasis on the reality and pervasiveness of possession by evil spirits has been one of its most important contributions to global Pentecostalism.

Caribbean and Nigerian Pentecostalism share strong theological connections to the Assemblies of God, North America. The Assemblies of God, the largest and one of the oldest Pentecostal denominations in the United States, has a strong presence in Nigeria. In the case of its African influence, in the post-1960s decades, the Assemblies of God claimed sub-Saharan Africa as an important mission field (Corten and Marshall-Fratani 2001: 316). Rhema Ministries, an offshoot of Assemblies of God, USA, established a major theological center in South Africa to which many West African pastors go for training. Both the Reverend Mosy Madugba, director of Rhema Ministries in Nigeria, and his wife, Chinyere Gloria Madugba, have served as international coordinators of the WWW. Reverend Madugba wrote the foreword for the *Training Manual* (Wailing Women Worldwide 2004, 2008).

WAILING WOMEN WORLDWIDE AND THE GRENADA HOUSE CHURCH

During those first meetings in 2004, Pentecostal women from two distinct cultures agreed that their religious commitment and theological beliefs created the beginnings of an important and sufficient bond for future collaboration. The majority of Caribbean women who worship weekly at the house church are members of several different Pentecostal congregations, yet they are able to be united by their evangelical beliefs and experiences. The weekly house church meetings had grown steadily over a four-year period and on some days consisted of as many as fifteen evangelical and charismatic women. The meetings were led by a woman who had a tertiary level education and had lived abroad for many years before returning to retire on the island. Her assistant and co-leader, a younger woman, had barely finished grade school but had educated herself using the Scriptures. This woman often testified about the power of the Holy Spirit in her life; she was respected by the group and seen as a powerful prayer warrior and evangelist. In 2004, the Caribbean women's group met three times a week. The meetings began at 3 PM and lasted for about three hours. Each meeting usually began fairly quietly with a long session of Bible study, during which the women participated in exegesis and commentary, "as the Spirit led them." After about two hours of Bible study, the meeting would move to extempore prayer that began with one leading voice that was raised in praise of God. Slowly and steadily the woman's voice would be joined by others in prayer. As the women praised God, they inevitably interjected intercessory pleas on behalf of various personal or family needs.

For more than an hour at each meeting, the mumbling sounds of women's voices raised in emotional exhortation would rise eventually into a crescendo that resonated among the group, spread throughout the house, and echoed into the nearby streets. Two phrases punctuated the prayers. During the fairly calm, initial period of prayer, words of praise began or ended with the phrase, "Father God." As vocal intensity and emotion rose, the women's praise mixed in with supplication. Then the co-leader and prayer warrior, using her vocal strength and its resonance, would often take the group to the highest point of prayer emotion. Unlike the often whispered and reverent prayers heard in established colonial churches, the prayer warrior at the house church, in a clear, loud voice, called, demanded, and commanded the Holy Spirit to come near to hear and answer the fervent prayers of each supplicant. Now at the pinnacle of emotion, the repetitive phrase the women uttered at the beginning and end of their prayer sentences of intercession was always, "In the name of Jesus," with great emphasis placed on the last word of the phrase: "Jesus."

As individual prayers and supplications joined and rose in a cacophonic chorus, the separate but enjoined prayers being uttered by the women were often pierced by the prayer warrior's full-throated glossolalia, which seemed to emanate from the depths of her soul. Some women knelt while others sat, but all had both arms raised above their heads as they prayed. Occasionally, women cried quietly or wept as they prayed and testified about small miracles or temptations they had been able to overcome. Mostly, their supplications focused on their personal health, grief, losses, and material needs and those of their family members and friends. After an extended period of prayer, often, one of the women would break into singing a gospel chorus. This usually eased the heavy emotional tension and moved the prayer activity first into whispered prayer, and then into tired quietness. As the women gathered their handbags and Bibles, they whispered, "Thank you Jesus, Thank you Jesus."

MILLENARIAN EXPECTATIONS, TRANSFORMED WORSHIP

That first evening, and every evening of their short stay, the African missionaries introduced the Caribbean women to a very different form and focus for their study of Scripture and prayer meetings. Their accustomed prayer pattern, as well as the theological themes and focus of their Bible study, would change drastically under the influence of the WWW. The prophetic directive proclaimed by the Nigerian missionaries contains millenarian, apocalyptic Christian themes (Hunt 2001) that were also subliminally political:

> In January 2003, the Lord said these words to us: "I am raising a confrontational army to confront and counter the effects of the powers of darkness. An army that will fight and recover the lost grounds; an army that will take over territories, lives, and people. An army I will use as My workforce. An army I will depend on. An army I will use to demonstrate my power to the kingdom of darkness. An army that will march against the sophisticated weapons of the world." (Wailing Women Worldwide 2004: viii)

The prophecies of WWW missionaries' prayers and writings follow a language pattern that Andre Corten (2001: 115) calls "chains of utterance," a term that represents language that is not only used forcefully and incessantly by preachers during worship before their congregations or beamed by radio or television but also for private personal and public emotional effect. The following are popular utterances in the WWW's communication repertoire: "powers of darkness," "spiritual warfare," "salvaging the world from crisis," "unprecedented violence," "the deplorable state of the church," "an increase in satanic activities," "a wave of terror sweeping over the world," and "sin and abomination." In the organization's *Training Manual*, the women write about a complete breakdown in civil society in Nigeria and throughout the world caused by personal and collective spiritual weaknesses that have allowed evil demons and spirits to gain access to, and significant power over, the world. The women attested that, according to the vision they had received, this structural and personal failure among all the people of the world accounts for God's wrath.

Pentecostal theologians often seek to define and delineate theological positions and organizational arrangements that exist in the contemporary Pentecostal movement. Some see the spread of Pentecostalism as having become "an amalgam of diverse, and often theologically ill-defined groups, institutions, and traditions" (Mohler 1996: 32). R. Albert Mohler argues that the evangelical movement is at an impasse, with two strongly different theological interpretations of Christianity: the "Doctrine Party," which bases its teachings on core doctrinal essentials and an insistence that the Bible is the final authoritative source of all doctrines, in contrast with the "Experience Party," which "would establish a rather amorphous notion of religious experience as the evangelical essential" (Mohler 1996: 32). I see the WWW organization as attending to doctrine, as well as experience.

Wailing, in the form of groveling or remaining prostrate on the floor while uttering horrific sounds of intense sorrow as displayed and demanded by the missionaries, is not a standard prayer format or act of piety used by Pentecostals generally, or by the women of the house church. However, wailing, as an act of piety, was performed in response to the women's vision and was supported by Scripture. During the initial visit, the Nigerians not only explained their mission, but performed the requisite style of prayer. The house church members were taught to assume prostrate prayer positions and were given vocal demonstrations of how to pray effectively as women in travail. They were directed to avoid "a pretentious, dry, and passionless cry," but rather to express howling and screaming "like a woman who has lost an only son, and with incontrollable weeping in a way that touches even the most hardened hearts" (Wailing Women Worldwide 2004: 3). They directed that only the women's wailing in prayer would provide God's deliverance:

> Wailing is a very high form of intercession. Wailing and lamentation are called for when impossible cases need to be handled. The Holy Spirit helps us to pray with such intense groaning and wailing that can produce results (Romans 8:26). Interceding with deep lamentations in the Holy Spirit often helps us to secure results that ordinary prayers cannot produce. Deep wailing, which emanates from our innermost being like a big tidal flood, goes with passion. It comes from a broken and a contrite heart. Genuine repentance with tears always produces results. (Wailing Women Worldwide 2004: 3)

In addition, the missionaries introduced a strict meeting format outlined in a teaching manual. Each meeting had to focus on some aspect of global need or human failures, and attached scriptural texts were provided in the manual for each prayer theme. The women were told to steer away from devoting prayer time to personal and family needs and to focus instead on the global reach of the enemy.

Deliverance from evil forces, spirit spouses, and satanic powers are dealt with in much detail in the manual. The missionaries seemed to be inscribing this evil spirit pantheon into a global Pentecostal theology of the supernatural in which Satan's power is enhanced by a host of evil spirits, which strictly women's prayers can help obliterate. The women at the Caribbean house church were being socialized and acculturated into new forms of worship made possible by the flexibility that Pentecostalism allows and new worship themes strongly influenced by news of conflicts broadcast daily through globalized media outlets. The women's own knowledge and experiences of the terrors of Nigerian political culture were also included in their intercessions. Interestingly, the women's intercessory wailing is aimed at affecting male traits of sinful intransigence, as well as placating a male and angry God. Sicilian Pentecostal women revere an androgynous deity, since they worship Jesus who is God presented as a gentle and comforting mother who invites and pulls each convert (child) to his bosom or heart, much as Roman Catholics envision the Virgin Mary did in her special motherly relationship with her son, Jesus. In addition, during public prayer, Sicilian Pentecostal women use language that describes God as having the characteristics of a gentle lover. But Sicilian Pentecostals also include sterner representations of God that resemble the harsh, even violent, characteristics celebrated in Sicilian manhood (Cucchiari 1990).

The Nigerian and Caribbean Pentecostal women insisted that God is just and caring. But together they shared, proclaimed, and worshipped an awesome, strongly dominant, and fiercely vengeful God who, for the Caribbean women, had to be loudly placated and whose attention had to be demanded. In the West African women's prayers, God was leading a powerful army because the world has become disobedient and sinful. Therefore, God's plan is intent on uprooting and tearing down the structures of evil in the world. In response to the vision, the WWW missionaries have been directed to form a global army of wailing women "networking in prayer. It is through networking that watchmen from all over the world come together ... at the global or continental altar" (Wailing Women Worldwide 2004: 53).

At annual conventions, in their introductory talks to groups of women, and in their writings, the West African leaders of the organization describe, in metaphorical images that alternate between traditional notions of femininity and masculinity, the tasks that women must undertake. Women are to be handmaidens and helpmeets to men such as their mates, male religious leaders, and, ultimately, God. At the same time, their peculiarly feminine wailing is a sophisticated "weapon" that remains the only hope of God's ultimate triumph over evil. Thus, each committed woman is asked to transform herself into a disciplined soldier and even a ruthless warrior. At meetings, women are told to become instruments of war: "To root out wickedness, pull down strongholds of darkness; throw down altars of darkness, and serve as a disciplined squad in God's end-time, recovery army" (Wailing Women Worldwide 2004: 6).

Women are directed to serve as God's battle-axes and weapons of warfare for their faith as they evangelize the world. Moreover, as soldiers in God's army, they have to be prepared to fight to the end. In addition to offering women opportunities to don typically male and lauded characteristics, the WWW was providing them with a ritual to supersede their local relationships and daily routines. Ordinary prayers, even including glossolalia, seemed insufficient as a spiritual hook to tie the global army together. Wailing, if the missionaries were successful, seemed destined to surpass chanting, speaking in tongues, and feet washing—all of which are central to many Pentecostal congregations worldwide. Wailing during prayer was being presented as a new and unique ritual bond to unite and hold disparate global networks of women together.

CULTURAL AND CLASS DIFFERENCES

Caribbean Pentecostal women were being invited by Nigerian Pentecostal women to join a global evangelical prayer initiative. Committed women did not have to know one another or belong to the same congregation, community, culture, or nation. Instead, a "new type of negotiation between local and global" Pentecostal communities was being established (Marshall-Fratani 2001: 83). Significant cultural differences among women within the global army were thus downplayed or ignored and encapsulated in their common practice of intercessory prayer made effective through intense wailing. However, cultural differences infiltrate and influence Pentecostal communities. For example, the Nigerian missionaries brought with them cultural and religious tropes about the godly family. A chapter in the WWW's *Training Manual* is titled "The Wailing Woman and Her Home." The first of its ten directives is based on Psalm 127:1 and reads, "Every Wailing Woman should be properly married before witnesses and she must uphold the marriage vows as a covenant" (2004: 13). In addition, her duty as a Christian wife/mother demands that she stand beside her husband at all times and assume a quietly supportive role as his helpmeet. In Pentecostal communities, husbands lead their families in a patriarchal system as directed by Scripture (see Brouwer et al. 1996: 245).

The West African missionaries would take the marriage, family norms, and cultural expectations of religious Nigerians to the social-class complexities of the Caribbean family institution. All three female Nigerian missionaries in the WWW who visited the Caribbean in 2004 seemed to be in their late thirties or early forties. They were all residents of Port Harcourt, Nigeria. The leading missionary, Olaide Okafor, who is described as the head coordinator of women intercessors for the church and nations, is a medical doctor. The second missionary, Chinyere Gloria Madugba, is an educational administrator and author of several books. The third, Nne Gloriy Ebele, was a banker and is now a full-time missionary. The WWW's *Training Manual* reports that each of the visiting Nigerian women was a university-educated wife and mother. In the wider Nigerian society, family norms encourage the majority of women to have expectations of motherhood within marriage, often early marriage, and, for non-Christian women, even becoming second wives.

This emphasis on marriage, although well known in the Caribbean, is not widely practiced (Barrow 2011; Clarke 1966; Smith 1962). In the Anglophone Caribbean, many couples have children outside marriage and without the couples ever having engaged in residential cohabitation (Aymer 1997). Marriage is a religious rite in most mainline denominations, a sacrament in Roman Catholicism, and one of the marks of respectability in established churches in the Caribbean. Besides, marriage, if undertaken at all by couples from the region's poor and working class, usually occurs after individuals have had children, sometimes with more than one partner. Extended family and female-headed families are more prevalent than are nuclear, conjugal family arrangements. Motherhood, not marriage, is the female status celebrated by poor and working-class Caribbean women. The twelve to fifteen middle-age Caribbean women who gathered weekly at the house church were nearly all middle-age grandmothers. The majority had attained only grade-school educations, and a few were married.

Mating patterns among the poor may have roots in the centuries of slavery, during which time marriage among the enslaved was discouraged. For much of the Caribbean's colonial history, the established colonial denominations castigated the poor for their patterns of premarital sex, mating, and child bearing, and poor, unmarried mothers felt marginalized in mainline congregations. Caribbean evangelical Pentecostalism has employed evangelical theology and organizational systems to downplay, though not ignore, Caribbean mating patterns to pull in poor people. Single mothers are welcomed into and "saved" in Caribbean Pentecostal congregations. The women feel the tension of marginality born of poverty and the stigma of unwed pregnancies fade. Any charge against converts of having lived sinful lives before conversion would be almost forgotten, their sins washed away by their salvation experience and acceptance into the fold of the church. Personal religious conviction and conversion make for inclusion in the saved community, no matter the believers' previous mating histories. The grown children (mostly daughters) and grandchildren of unmarried mothers now constitute the majority of the membership of large and small Pentecostal congregations on Caribbean islands such as Grenada. Women, who once were mostly invisible in the organized mainline religions into which they were baptized as infants, have entered the Pentecostal churches in droves. In sum, the very existence and growth of Pentecostal missions and evangelism in the Anglophone Caribbean depend heavily on a large, energized female membership composed mainly of single women, many of whom are never-married mothers (Glazier 1980: 21).

Culture, class, and race matter in all encounters between missionaries and their potential converts. For example, a well-planned regional annual meeting held by the WWW organization in the Caribbean a few years ago consisted of all-day sessions and presentations over a two-day period. Women from the house church group that I studied arrived only for the last session of each of the two days of the meetings. This surprised and annoyed the visiting conference planners from the WWW. When the women were questioned, they calmly replied that their daily family chores prevented them from spending all day at the meetings. Besides, they argued, they found it unreasonable to ask or expect them to do so since they had family responsibilities and gained little from the sessions. In addition, to attend other annual meetings held in North America or the Caribbean islands, a few of the women had to organize cooking and baking sales to raise funds to attend. Because of this, only two or three relatively well-off women from the group were able to travel abroad to attend any of the WWW annual regional conferences.

Several women complained, too, that they missed the close-knit prayer group and Bible study, which tended to be more extemporaneous and personal. Thus, as the prayers against evil spirits and the emphasis on global deliverance increased, the group lost some of its members. Personal needs, and those of family members and friends, were very real and present to the women living in the small Caribbean island-state—more so than the imagery of worldwide warfare taught to them by the WWW missionaries.

CONCLUSION

The researcher Waldo Cesar (2001: 26), writing about women in Caribbean Pentecostal church membership, states that conversion and membership are drastic, life-changing events for converts not only because it is "a break away from a previous religion and 'the world,' but also [because it] means consecrating the majority of their non-working lives to participation in church-services and activities." In Caribbean Pentecostal congregations, women are often chief participants in their churches' youth, music, and service ministries. In other words, even within the predominantly female congregations, women assume on their own volition or are assigned to lower-level and crucially important gender-specific evangelization and leadership roles in public worship and in various forms of Christian service.

Women also bring energy and emotionality to the Caribbean Pentecostal worship experience. In the Anglophone Caribbean, gender informs public shows of emotion, and female worshippers, rather than men, are expected to display great emotion and physical movement during Pentecostal worship. Norms of masculinity practiced in evangelical churches often discourage intense and public displays of religious emotion from male worshippers; especially when women are present. However, the "magical charisma" (Poloma 1989: 94) of the Pentecostal preacher, a major attraction that pulled people into not only intense, emotional experiences but also deep commitment to faith in US Pentecostalism in the early twentieth century, continues to be popular in Caribbean and African congregations. Christianity, and Pentecostalism in particular, offer liminal worship spaces where, in theory, gender, racial, ethnic, national, regional, and social-class boundaries may be crossed and, perhaps, temporarily eliminated. After such outbursts, men leave the liminal space and return to the expected patriarchal order as if the boundaries had not been breached. Extremes of visible emotion, whether caused by joy or sorrow, are still typically gendered female in most congregations. Thus, in highlighting the *power* of women's peculiar intensities of emotion, the missionaries of the WWW have carved a theological niche in which they can engage and lead women to create particular female roles in religious practice and ritual that is dominated by men. However, these female gendered roles must not encroach on the male pastoral leadership of Pentecostal congregations in Africa or the Caribbean.

The women of the WWW have designed a missionary program that takes them to foreign countries to propagate their vision's message. This message is conveyed through workshops and conferences and various media outlets, including a publishing company with the interesting name *Man-Child Printing Press*. Although women can be missionaries, they are prevented from becoming pastors. In a chapter titled "Dealing with the Spirit of Jezebel," the WWW *Training Manual* warns against women in congregations who are "fiercely independent and intensely ambitious.... [Such women] lurk around the corridors of power to manipulate those in authority to use their positions to accomplish wickedness" (Wailing Women Worldwide 2004: 101). In addition, the manual states that such women carry around "a spirit of resentment and bitterness towards men" (Wailing Women Worldwide 2004: 102). Evangelical women invited to join the global army of the saved must be submissive and obedient warriors, servant leaders who work tirelessly behind the scenes and serve unobtrusively (Wailing Women Worldwide 2008: 3). Many West African societies have ancient traditions in which women are celebrated as spiritualist mediums, midwives, and priestesses in traditional religions. The WWW rejects outright all forms of African traditional religious practice and would therefore eschew women's power being displayed through formal leadership of religious communities. Thus, educated, spirit-filled, urban women from strictly conservative Pentecostal backgrounds have designed leadership niches that do not threaten traditional patriarchal power relations in their religious communities.

The theologian Katherine Henderson (2006: 80) interrogates patterns of female leadership in religious congregations and asks whether women with obvious leadership skills "choose to lead from behind, within, and beneath, because of a conviction that this is more effective, or do they do it out of fear of what leading from the front may entail?" Some of the strongest evidence of Pentecostal women's leadership talent is showcased in women's para-church organizations such as the WWW. Another example is the Women's Aglow Fellowship International that was created in 1967 as "the fulfillment of a vision divinely imparted by God to a small coterie of women" (Griffith 1997). The evangelical organization welcomes single, divorced, and married women of various ages, all of whom are saved or are seekers on the path to salvation. Aglow finally added women to its Advisory Board in 1993, although male advisers were retained in the organization's state chapters. In contrast, the WWW retains male leadership and direction. Indeed, one of the WWW's five directors and advisers, the Reverend Abu Bako, was the main presenter each day of the three-day national conference at the Sheraton Hilton Hotel in Fort Lauderdale in July 2008.

The missionaries of WWW see their project as international but not ecumenical. To seem inclusive and welcoming, they refuse to describe their organization as Pentecostal. This is undoubtedly attributable to their desire to broaden their missionary outreach. I suspect that their disavowal of being strictly Pentecostal is also a political strategy directed at the women's home congregations in West Africa. The members of the WWW were at pains to avoid the appearance of being a group of ambitious women disguised as missionaries who were really seeking to be Pentecostal pastors. Any claim of leadership, especially at the international level, would conflict with evangelical theological emphases and compete with and threaten the support that the women have received so far from their pastors and home churches.

The vision of the leaders of the WWW reflects the political and religious cleavages in Nigeria, a vast nation-state composed of various tribes who often see themselves as separate, competing nations that have experienced decades of political turmoil and terror from dictatorial military rule. Although rich in human and natural resources, Nigeria has been unable to provide for and protect its millions of disparate groups of people. Tribal and religious internecine warfare, civil unrest and violence have been prevalent (Lewis et al. 1998; Marshall-Fratani 2001). In particular, Pentecostal Christians fear deeply that both Islamic and traditional religious beliefs and customs might contaminate and threaten evangelical Christianity's beliefs and practices.

Pentecostals take seriously their Christian mandate to expose, if not win, the entire world to the Christian Gospel. Members of these two powerful Abrahamic religions proselytize within the same national territory and thus arouse mutual feelings of threat and dread of religious subjugation in each group. In addition, the prestige of the Federation of Muslim Women's Associations of Nigeria, a well-known and powerful socioreligious women's organization that has been in operation for several decades (Lewis et al. 1998), may have prompted the activities of WWW. It is possible that the WWW organization feels an urgent need to confront this non-Christian organization by rallying Christian—and particularly, Pentecostal—women within Nigeria and globally in a competitive and defensive stance to safeguard Christianity from non-Christian faiths.

The WWW missionaries' invitation to evangelical women to engage in concerted worldwide intercessory prayer expressed through wailing has remained selective in that it is extended only to women of evangelical or Pentecostal, and sometimes charismatic, groups, large and small. Therefore, Christian women who are members of the established mainline denominations but have not had a conversion experience are not solicited. In addition, racial and cultural considerations have continued to limit the missionary outreach activities and composition of the global army of women who become members of branches of the WWW. Increasingly, the WWW missionaries have been invited to or have identified churches and groups in which evangelical women are immigrants from the African diaspora. Therefore, some of the strongest WWW groups have been formed in cities in the global North, such as London, New York, Miami, and Toronto—cities in which large numbers of African and Caribbean immigrants have settled. Thus, the army of wailing intercessors engaged in prayer is composed mostly of women of color from countries of the global South. Some groups also have been formed among women dispersed throughout Latin America and the Caribbean, and a committed WWW branch project composed mostly of West African immigrant women has been established in Barbados, in the Caribbean.

Ruth Marshall-Fratani (2001: 92) states, "Part of Pentecostalism's success in Nigeria is related to the community's ability, not only to give regular people access to global repertoires, but also to use this in its self-representations to an outside which has not yet been saved, an outside which comprises a potential threat, but also a challenge." In the case of the WWW, a band of professional women from a developing country in Africa have placed themselves at the vanguard of efforts to universalize the proselytizing aspirations of spirit-filled evangelical women. Thus, at the house church I studied, women were being invited to become members of a network in which women, including women of the African diaspora, were being united with other women globally in an intercessory prayer effort to save the world. According to the WWW, a worldwide army of saved women from different cultural and political backgrounds would be able to intercede on behalf of a world that otherwise is destined to be destroyed. Together, the prayers of the WWW could soften God's heart and deflect the terrible wrath to be unleashed on the world. The ultimate goal of the WWW seems to be the creation of a world body of Pentecostals and evangelicals who, as a global community of saved women, replace the kingdoms of the world with a virtual kingdom of the saved and sanctified who are ruled by God. It seems to follow, then, that sinful men throughout the world will eventually turn from their evil ways. The African women of the WWW see themselves as having been raised up by God for a worldwide mission. In other words, they regard themselves as having been bestowed with significant leadership positions in global Pentecostalism.

"THE KINGDOM IN THE MIDST" — 6

Sounding Bodies, Aesthetic Labor,
and the End Times

JUDITH CASSELBERRY

If you live right
Heaven belongs to you, if you pray right
Heaven belongs to you, if you sing right
Heaven belongs to you
Oh, Heaven belongs to you

—AFRICAN AMERICAN GOSPEL SONG

The body provokes theology. The body contests
its hypotheses, resists its conclusions, escapes its
textual margins.

—M. SHAWN COPELAND, ENFLESHING FREEDOM

Sunday morning worship services at True Deliverance Church of the Apostolic Faith Inc. (TDC) begin at 11:30 AM and end around 2:30 PM, depending on "the move of Spirit." For many, however, the day begins with Sunday school at 9:30 AM, so the relaxing dinner hour between 3 and 4 PM, in the downstairs social hall, is much appreciated. An hour of kneeling corporate prayer starts at 4 PM and is followed by 5:30 evening service. On one February evening, guest singers came from a sister church in Brooklyn to fellowship with the Queens, New York, TDC congregation.[1] Both churches, along with more than five hundred national and international congregations, belong to a Harlem-based denomination, the Church of Our Lord Jesus Christ of the Apostolic Faith Inc. (COOLJC).[2]

Oftentimes, when a soloist, choir, or minister visits a sister church, members of their congregation go along. Also, when guest singers or speakers are known to be adept at setting the church alight, members will invite friends and family, saved and unsaved, to come and have "a good time in the Lord." So the transition from corporate prayer into worship service, on this evening, saw people moving not only throughout the church, but also coming from outside. During the buzz of folks hanging up coats and greeting one another in the anteroom, the Praise and Worship Team worked in the sanctuary to "usher in the Spirit" through song.

While the congregation was settling, two visiting musicians positioned themselves at the organ and drums, which were tucked in the front right corner of the sanctuary below the elevated choir pews. Both "highly anointed" and highly skilled, the musicians' interplay with the TDC Praise Team and the growing congregation moved praise and worship to "higher heights."[3] Sunday evening services (and weeknight services) also incorporate testimonials into praise and worship, allowing anyone to offer a word or song about "God's wonder working power." It was not until the young drummer came out from behind the drum kit and hobbled to the front of the sanctuary to testify that it became clear: he did not have use of his left side. "I wasn't going to testify tonight," he said, "but I have to talk about the goodness of Jesus." A serious car accident had left him in critical condition and in need of major surgery. He had survived the surgery, only to suffer a paralyzing stroke during recovery. A husband and father of a toddler, he described the anxiety of coping with the impact on his young family and the emotional devastation of ending his musical career. Once out of the hospital, he threw himself back into church and "playing to the Glory of God." Throughout his testimony, the saints praised God, calling out, "Hallelujah!" "Thank you, Jesus!"[4]

"God gave me back my drumming," the young man declared. "God has been faithful. The only thing I can't do is run. I still can't run. I need three people to run around this church for me!" Immediately, a woman jumped up and began to run counterclockwise around the sanctuary. Before she had gotten halfway up the outer aisle, a second woman, then a third, and then a young boy, about ten years old, joined them. As they whipped around the sanctuary, two of the women were crying, and all were calling out to God. Congregants began to stand, shout, clap, praise God, and speak in tongues, as the anointing fell on many. The organist joined in, underscoring the sound of bodies with percussive chord hits. Physical acts of running, crying, and shouting praises brought the Spirit down instantly. The runners physically and sonically incorporated themselves into the testimony of the young drummer, reiterating the church's confidence in divine healing and miracles. Proxy runners made God's promise of future healing for the drummer a present reality. Harnessing spiritual power and (en)circling the congregation, the women carried the entire church into the restorative present-future while actualizing the drummer as one member of a whole healthy body in Christ. Merging material, spatial, and temporal realms, women's religious sounding bodies signaled an "already and not yet" eschatology, which has been foundational to Christian theology.[5]

The paradoxical proclamation of Jesus that the Kingdom is both present and forthcoming ("already and not yet") permeates material and spiritual behavior and practices of COOLJC members.[6] Through close readings of two religious episodes, this chapter charts the ways in which aesthetic labor of churchwomen demonstrates a live relation to power that reveals supplemental texts; disrupts conventional notions of hierarchy; and resists linear time and space. The opening running testimony provides the first example. In this instance, I suggest that unrestrained and restrained bodily practices of women address gendered ideologies of respectability and power operating within the church. With these actions, women bring power and respectability together as a final state of being, which democratizes the "already and not yet" while leaving the male-headed church polity intact. The second close reading centers on an episode outside of church in which spontaneous singing by a church "mother," in the home of a recently deceased saint, mediates doubt arising from the paradox of divine healing and death, and the paradox of the power of prayer and predestination.[7] With her singing, she throws open a space that allows committed members to be uncertain and remain in the fold. Women, in both instances, show that aesthetic labor is a vital mechanism for replicating and reshaping religious understandings of "the end times" and "the Kingdom in the midst."

Seeming contradictions within COOLJC doctrine, rhetoric, and religious practices demonstrate both the paradoxes and ambiguities within a particular "already and not yet" eschatology. What do particular religious embodied strategies of Apostolic women tell us about the meanings of "the end times," beyond doctrine and rhetoric? In what ways does aesthetic labor (including self-presentation) of women reveal a projection of the end times? Ultimately, I argue the practices of COOLJC women reproduce and reconfigure church theology, doctrine, rhetoric, and aesthetics, creating a passageway that expands both the parameters of and also access to the past-present-future "already and not yet."

In addition to church teachings, which I describe later, aesthetic labor provides a particularly effective lens for examining the ways in which these women (re)produce and reveal "some sense of value and appropriateness" in expressive liturgical forms, as well as in self-representation and social relations (Herzfeld 2001: 289). Building on Anthony Pinn's approach to analysis of African diasporic religions, this study examines "the construction, presentation, and placement of Black [women's] bodies as a matter of aesthetics" *and aesthetic labor* to illuminate "the nature of religion and religious experience" (Pinn 2009: 2). The runners in church perform aesthetic labor by making community sensibilities audible and visible by the manner in which they present and place sounding bodies within the sanctuary. Birgit Meyer's work on Ghanaian Pentecostal filmmaking and images in the public sphere can be applied, as well. Instead of dividing the material and immaterial, she moves away from thinking about representation as an imaginary field. Meyer argues, "The relevance of aesthetics, and the concomitant importance of style," are key in "grasp[ing] the material dimensions of religious modes of forming subjects and communities" (Meyer 2009: 10; see also Meyer 2008). Aesthetic sensibilities embedded in practice and in conversation with an eschatological perspective reveal particular COOLJC paradoxes and ambiguities of doctrine and rhetoric negotiated in action. Central values reflected in aesthetic labor of Apostolic women, as we will see, hold tensions linking theology, religious practice, and raced and gendered histories.

GENEALOGY, THEOLOGY, AND DOCTRINE

The Church of Our Lord Jesus Christ of the Apostolic Faith Inc. is a classical Oneness, and the third largest historically Black American Pentecostal, denomination (Alexander 2011; Jacobsen 2003).[8] Robert C. and

Carrie F. Lawson founded the organization in 1919, after migrating to Harlem from Indianapolis, where they had been under Bishop Garfield T. Haywood of the Apostolic Faith Assembly Church (which would later merge to become Pentecostal Assemblies of the World [PAW]). Haywood came to Pentecostalism in 1908, after two believers, Glen Cook and Henry Prentiss, arrived in Indianapolis spreading a new message from the Azusa Street Pentecostal Revival in Los Angeles of baptism in the Holy Spirit, evidenced by speaking in tongues. In 1915, Cook returned to Haywood's church, now the most influential in Indianapolis Pentecostalism, with the "New Issue" of Oneness—the "Jesus Only" doctrine. The controversial teachings disputed long-held theology of Trinitarians, arguing for a unified godhead and that water baptism should be done not in the name of the Father, Son, and Holy Ghost but in the name of Jesus only. Haywood adopted the new theology and rebaptized the entire congregation, including Lawson, whom he also ordained (Alexander 2011; Clark 2001; French 2011; Jacobsen 2006).

Lawson and Haywood would soon part ways over doctrinal disputes; Haywood approved of women's ordination and believed that a pre-salvation marriage could be dissolved. Lawson disagreed. Oneness theology therefore set him apart from the majority of Pentecostals, while doctrinal schisms set him apart from Haywood and PAW. Lawson also stands unique as an early twentieth-century Pentecostal theologian who established an Afro-biblical exegesis that situated Black women at the center of the atonement through "Negro" women in the lineage of Mary and, thus, in the blood of Jesus (Lawson [1925] 1969).[9]

On the one hand, Lawson advanced gender-normative ideology regarding the role of women in the New Testament church by rejecting ordination; promoting Victorian ideals of genteel characteristics; and adopting stringent tenets of submission, obedience, comportment, and dress. On the other hand, through publications and preaching, he advanced a remarkable theology that placed the blood of Black women in the Christ and flowing at the crucifixion (Casselberry 2013, 2017; Lawson [1925] 1969).[10] Lawson's theology is of particular significance because, like the vast majority of Holiness Pentecostal organizations, COOLJC maintains majority female membership.[11] Given women's majority status and the egalitarian nature of spirit-infilling, religious sounding bodies of women most often actualize the "anointing"; in every Apostolic service, congregants work to bring down the Holy Ghost. In this way, members demonstrate the paradoxical proclamation of Jesus that the Kingdom is "already and not yet."

Church teachings that address final events in the end of the world can be traced back to late nineteenth- and early twentieth-century dispensationalist pre-millennialism (Clark 2001).[12] The church anticipates the Rapture in "the end times," when the saints will be "caught up in the air" and saved from the ensuing apocalypse.[13] In spiritual and mundane activities alike, COOLJC members operate under the overarching frame of the imminent Second Coming of Jesus Christ, "like a thief in the night" (1 Thessalonians 5:2). The return of Jesus has been at the heart of COOLJC doctrine since its inception. According to Bishop James I. Clark, the church's focus on the Parousia points to an "already" and "not yet" that privileges the "not yet" because institutional priorities, since the 1960s, have placed salvation above working toward social change for communities of color (Clark 2001: 68). Yet Clark's important focus on the political concerns of COOLJC overlooks the ways in which women negotiate gender politics within the church through embodied theological praxis.

A closer examination of women's practices positions "already and not yet" in a shifting equivalence and tension. The proxy runners kept the present on balance with the future, infusing both individual women and the community with realized power of the yet to come. At the same time, "already and not yet" holds that those who are not yet present—future generations and unsaved family members, and particularly children (such as the drummer's toddler daughter)—bind the paradox of hope to present reality. "Already and not yet" also embraces the past, allowing those who have "gone home to the Kingdom" to remain present while occupying the "not yet." Women's practices of materiality in COOLJC—the sounding body—therefore address religious, material, and social relations alike.

Here, the work of Catherine Bell on "ritualized actions" is useful. Ritualized actions are practical activities carried out in strategic ways in particular social circumstances, and this type of action should be analyzed "in terms of its vision of redemptive hegemony" (Bell 1992: 67, 85)—that is, by asking, "What are the ways in which actions reproduce or reconfigure relations of power in order to be socially and personally redemptive?" Specific to this discussion, what are the ways in which aesthetic labor of

COOLJC women uncover a particular "end of times" within socioreligious circumstances? In what ways does women's aesthetic labor shape the reproduction or reconfiguration of COOLJC eschatological ambiguities and paradoxes? As I show, unrestrained and restrained actions of women take place within a twentieth- and twenty-first-century Apostolic aesthetic milieu (that they make and remake) in which their sounding bodies remain contested terrain.

RUNNING FOR JESUS, RUNNING FOR A HEALING

Each runner at that February service dressed "according to the standard." Church teachings require women to conceal their bodies; tenets forbid sleeveless tops, hemlines at or above the knee, slit skirts that expose knees, open-toe shoes, bare legs (without stockings or tights), and uncovered heads.[14] The first runner, a small-framed woman who appeared to be in her mid-thirties, wore an A-line shirtwaist dress, falling to mid-calf. The cardigan sweater she wore over it could have been indicative of a sleeveless garment or an extra layer to move the shape of her outfit outward. Her inch-and-a-half-heeled pumps produced soft and insistent thumping on the church's red carpet, while the lace doily-style head covering strained against the bobby pin that kept it attached to the crown of her head. The other two women were adorned in straight-lined, mid-calf-length skirt suits with appliqué-lapelled jackets falling below the hips, a style commonly seen on Sundays. Both wore modest hats—one, a wide-brimmed cloche; and the other, a beret.

Ongoing attention to the presentation of Black women's bodies within COOLJC comes out of the American religious, cultural, and political landscape of the late nineteenth century and early twentieth century that gave rise to the wider Holiness Pentecostal movement. The sociohistorical and religious render the bodies of Black women "triply damned" through the stigma of enslavement, stereotypes of hypersexuality, and Eve's centrality to the "fall of man." At the same time, within COOLJC women's bodies become doubly "revered," showing both power, through spirit-infilling of the unbounded Holy Ghost, and respectability, through modest dress and comportment. With emergent Pentecostalism, notions of Black holy women's self-presentation were inextricably tied to a political and social history rooted in enslavement, a "sexual economy" in which each Black woman's body became the point of production (Davis 2002). The ensuing post-emancipation shift from Reconstruction to Jim Crow–era America found the majority of Black people precariously situated between the "politics of respectability" and Black "folk" cultural ways of knowing (Higginbotham 1993).[15]

Holiness Pentecostals adhered to certain markers of "respectability," such as strict codes regarding leisure activity and sexual behavior, whereas music, preaching and teaching styles, and other elements of worship remained firmly rooted in African American/Black Atlantic aesthetics (Levine 1977; Maultsby 1990; Williams-Jones 1975). Holiness Pentecostal theology of spirit baptism embraced ecstatic worship, which flew in the face of Black mainstream politics of representation. At the same time, members demonstrated restraint in dress and comportment, rooted in both a politics of representation and the Bible (Butler 2007; Crumbley 2012; see chapter 4 Crumbley). Holy Ghost infilling and the imminent return of Jesus for a church without a "spot or wrinkle, . . . holy and without blemish," required each individual to maintain a pure vessel, signified by outward appearance (Ephesians 5:27).[16] Pentecostal dress and demeanor also countered hypersexualized stereotypes projected onto Black people—stereotypes that always carried the real threat of violence when acted on by the barbaric. This history and its legacy helped shape COOLJC doctrine as wider sociopolitical concerns and Christian values internal to the church converged in formulating gendered aesthetics of holiness (Casselberry 2013, 2017).

Exploring the production of COOLJC women's attire broadens the work sites open to examination by scholars of on-the-job aesthetic labor, who consider "embodied capacities and attributes" that employees bring to a potential job and that employers further exploit for organizational gain (Warhurst et al. 2000: 4; see also Boris and Parreñas 2010: 98–99). (For example, a boutique owner may look for prospective employees who have a particular cosmopolitan demeanor in clothing style, speech, or carriage, which the employer will further tailor to appeal to her specific clientele.) Like workers in public contact service work who are "constantly on display," churchwomen, by their outer appearance and demeanor, reflect the institution (Warhurst et al. 2000: 5). Yet there is a key distinction between COOLJC women and service sector workers who bring (and further develop) embodied qualities and style to the job in that the bulk of aesthetic labor of presentation for a saint begins after she commits to a Jesus-led life. In fact, the community values a more radical transformation in dress and comportment after salvation as a marker of the new self. The work of presentation by COOLJC women shows the ways in which dress, as a religious aesthetic, is seen as an embodiment of holiness.

Operating within the COOLJC aesthetic-religious environment, the three women runners—the first responders—unleashed their spiritual power to bind the congregation, "believe God for a healing," and democratize "already and not yet." Their ability to push material boundaries sits in stark contrast to doctrinal regulation, most rigorously codified on women's bodies. Running and crying out to Jesus demonstrated active amalgamation of materiality and spirituality and revealed an "already and not yet" eschatology bound up in particular raced and gendered meanings. Actions of this sort reproduce and reconfigure the paradox of women's spontaneous and regulated sounding bodies. Worship places women's bodies at the heart of religious life, as "the body mediates that 'more' and makes visible [and audible] what cannot be seen" (Copeland 2010: 7). Holy Ghost anointing, prayer, singing, shouting, crying, speaking in tongues, and running collaborate, making women's bodies and the sounds they create definitive markers of community aesthetics, that which is deemed correct and valuable. The church relies on women's spiritual power, exhibited in particular agreed-on ways, to set the church alight.

When women catalyze congregational anointing, however, the actions sit in relief to male-headed hierarchical structure as the women pull "the true power of the living God" into the space from their position below the dais. The Episcopalian organizational structure of the church, which excludes women from ordination and other lifelong titled positions, can also be seen within gendered geographies of spaces (Massey 1994). Entering the sanctuary, one sees the backs of women's covered heads and the faces of ranking men on the dais, which buttresses the notion of concealing women's bodies and politically elevating men.

The ideology underlying COOLJC's gendered geographies becomes clearer when analyzed within the context of preaching and teaching. Men preach from the pulpit; women teach from the floor.[17] Regardless of a woman's scriptural knowledge, rhetorical excellence, and spiritual power, when she rises to "give a word" to the congregation at a weeknight or special service, she is teaching, not preaching. Protocol emphasizes the distinction: when women speak from the floor, gendered geography creates visual obstructions for the congregation and speaker. Not every attendee can see the speaker (thus, she is partially concealed); nor can she see each congregant. By submitting to the protocols of gendered space, however, she shows her own adherence to church doctrine, which strengthens both her individual religious grounding and the corporate identity as a holy body.

Sprinting counterclockwise around the whole of the sanctuary, each woman (called attention to and) displaced top-down hierarchy. She produced the "already and not yet" of "neither male nor female" in Jesus Christ, just as her enslaved pre-Pentecostal forebears, moving counterclockwise in ring shouts, activated "neither bond nor free" (Galatians 3:28). She reiterated the materiality-physicality of self and community making while operating in a spiritual register. Cleaving the tension between boundless spirit and gendered delineations of respectability, she yanked the democratized "not yet" of the Kingdom into "the already" of the earthly church. Running and crying out to heal the drummer also acted to realize healing of the "Kingdom in the midst" and restore it to the fullness of "already and not yet." This aesthetic labor of holy women addresses conflicting messages about the nature of belonging in the church: who belongs, and in what capacity? When situations outside the sanctuary call for women to navigate paradoxes of church teachings, as I show, they again bring a distinctive COOLJC aesthetic approach to bear on grappling with and transmitting eschatological meanings.

SINGING FOR JESUS, SINGING FOR A HEALING

Armed with ammonia and bleach, Mother Reeves left the pristine bathroom and came into the kitchen to begin the process of cleaning every utensil, dish, and surface. She and four other women from TDC had gathered at the home of Sister Louise Franklin to prepare to receive grief-stricken family and loved ones. Louise had passed away that morning. Forty-six years young and the mother of two teenagers, Louise had succumbed to a cancerous brain tumor just before surgery. Smells of Clorox,

Pledge, Ajax, and dust mingled in the air as the saints worked to ready the two-story, four-bedroom house in Brooklyn. Tending to the family and home of a saint who has "gone to sleep" is women's work,[18] so each oversaw an area: Sister Charles, the dining room; Sister Farmer, the living room. I took to sweeping the hall and stairway carpeting, and Mother Morris tackled an upstairs bedroom.[19]

Amid the sounds of cleaning and thick silence of grief, from the kitchen, in a rich, resonant alto/tenor register, Mother Reeves began to sing a slow plaintive hymn:

Thank you, Lord.
Thank you, Lord.
Thank you, Lord.
I just want to thank you, Lord.

Having spent most of her sixty-two years in church, Baptist into young adulthood and Apostolic for the past thirty-plus years, Mother Reeves had been singing "to the glory of the Lord" for a long time. She began singing softly, internally, and with each repetition the song swelled in volume and intensity. Pulling, squeezing each syllable—"thaaaa-kuuuu-Laurrrrd"—her resonant overtones cradled each syllable; her gospel vibrato carried sadness; her vocal mastery relayed conviction. Intoning "Thank You, Lord" just hours after a death reinforced church teaching "to be grateful in all things" as it more generally fixed the moment to a longer historical arc of ironic existence.

For African American women, gender and race have operated as "tool[s] for both oppression and liberation," and these mutually informing contradictions affect Black Apostolic women's religious lives (Higginbotham 1992: 252). On the one hand, because of systemic sexism and racism, they have been subjected to socially and politically oppressive forces that have circumscribed their authority within church and in society at large (Collier-Thomas 2010; Davis 1981; Roberts 1997). On the other hand, gender and race identification galvanized women in religious and civic spheres, as they created, defined, and implemented alternative systems of power (Collier-Thomas 1998; Gilkes 2001; Kelley 1993; Ransby 2001). Well aware of incongruities between the national image of a Christian democracy and realities of race, gender, and class oppression, Black Apostolic women have lived the American paradox.

Inconsistent and unpredictable circumstances have permeated various registers of life, and Black people have (re)produced an "aesthetic sense of paradox" in expressive culture. An early twentieth-century classic blues singer used blues irony to assert acquiescence "to male desire and, at the same time, affirm [both lyrically and sonically] autonomous desire and a refusal to allow her mistreating lover to drive her to psychic despair" (Davis 1998: xv). Prior to blues women, this philosophical approach rang out in nineteenth-century spirituals, in which "despair was usually intertwined with confidence and joy" (Cone 1972: 57–58). "Sometimes I feel like a motherless child" ends with "Glory Hallelujah!" as does "Nobody knows the trouble I seen. Nobody knows my sorrow."

The paradox of grief and gratitude in Mother Reeves's version of "Thank You, Lord" echoes the "despair" and "joy" in Negro spirituals, carrying a Black American aesthetic sensibility (Cone 1972: 57–58). Yet Mother Reeves operated within the specificity of Apostolic Pentecostalism. In keeping with the narrative structure of the religion, she sang to minister to those present. Saints engage music as deeply as prayer, scripture, and sermons; it is a core method for conveying the theological underpinnings of faith (Cox 1995; Ward 1997). "Music [is] not just an embellishment," Harvey Cox (1995: 15, 121) explains, "[but] the wavelength on which the message is carried." In addition to the work of the song text ("Thank you, Lord"), gospel music's "innumerable variations of vocal color . . . and nuances in vocal contour, which may be meaningful only to those who are sensitive enough to cultural practices to understand such subtleties," bind Apostolic bodies to generations of sacred sonic praxis (Boyer 1979; Levine 1977; Williams-Jones 1975: 381). Singing literally moves conviction through the body, which epitomizes the intimate embodied nature of applied Apostolic theology. The transformative power of music alters not only the body, but also psychic and spiritual space, linking members to the supernatural (Floyd 1995). Mother Reeves's unction to sing, therefore, threw open a space to hold the immediate eschatological paradox of divine healing and death, and the paradox of the power of prayer and predestination, in ways that are distinctly different from doctrine and rhetoric.

Louise's death flew in the face of the doctrinal and scriptural assurances of divine healing and answered prayer. Sermons, testimonials, and corporate and individual prayer geared toward her healing had been the focus of the church since she had taken ill four months earlier. One Sunday sermon came from Matthew 9:27–30, which tells of Jesus restoring sight for two blind men. Minister Lee's topic was "I Know He's Able." He read verses 28 and 29, "And Jesus saith unto them, Believe ye that I am able to do this? They said unto him, Yea, Lord. Then touched he their eyes, saying, According to your faith be it unto you." "This is about faith and praise," Minister Lee told the congregation. "I know that I know that I know, He is able. Not think, but know." Bishop Cook, the octogenarian founder and pastor of TDC, reinforced the message in closing remarks. "God is able to do anything but fail," he declared. "We're so glad to see Sister Louise. God is able. Louise made her way to church on Friday and today. She's to have a biopsy on Wednesday. Walk by faith and not by sight."

Over the months between her diagnosis and passing, neither Louise's medical treatment nor her scheduled surgery undermined communal certainty of divine healing. Healing can be instantaneous, or, in the case of a slower process, the earthly physician comes under the province of God. Jesus uses the physician to reveal the source of illness, guides the doctor's accurate and effective treatment, and strengthens the body in recovery.[20] "We believe in divine healing," Bishop Cook told the congregation. "But we don't tell you not to go to the doctor.... Go to the doctor and get verification of your healing." Members, too, use medical diagnoses to direct prayer. Deacon Charles testified quite often about his healing from lung cancer. "I had blood clots on my right lung and then that lung collapsed," he recalled. "Then they discovered blood clots on my left lung. Bishop was so precise with his prayers, 'take the blood clots,' and he asked the body to create no more." Charles was cancer-free and testified to the doctors' bafflement. After each of Louise's medical appointments, with each new bit of information, saints would come together to "touch and agree," to target prayers, to effect her healing.

Of even greater significance was Louise's confession to the church. "I'm nonchalant about how sick I am," she told the congregation, "because I got on the prayer line, and God told me I was healed." So her death one month later sent shock waves through the church community. "Divine healing [was] what she said she wanted for herself," Sister Holmes explained. "And the church was believing for her to be better. So her dying was the last thing that anybody ever thought would happen.... It wasn't even a consideration. When she passed, it was just like somebody pulled the rug from underneath [everyone]."

In the days and weeks that followed, others sang, spoke, and testified about "Jesus, the burden bearer." Saints encouraged one another to "Hold on to Jesus, to His hand," reminding themselves, "He's too wise to make a mistake, too good to do wrong." In the Friday night service, the evening after Louise's passing, Bishop Cook voiced the long-established position: "We don't mourn like others with no hope. We lift Him up. Don't feel sad. Be glad she died in the Lord." In both formal and casual settings, after Louise passed away, saints talked about salvation for comfort. Louise was saved and had gone "home." Mother Reeves later explained, "As long as you're sleeping [in Christ], that's the consolation. So it don't grieve you as much because you know that she's with Christ. She's saved. . . . It will be all right. That's what gives you peace." As it turned out, the peace Mother Reeves spoke of was not a complete peace for everyone—not even for her. "How do you accept that?" she asked eight months later. "It's HARD! *It's hard.* You're still baffling with yourself. *She's gone? What? What?* [It's] hard to accept because you're human; you're in the flesh. It's hard for you to accept it, to just let it go."

Time-honored teachings were insufficient. Questions remained. The confident declaration of Minister Lee—"I know that I know that I know"—eluded Sister Clark. "I don't know. I really don't," she stated painfully. Eight months after her good friend was gone, she acknowledged, "I'm struggling, . . . trying to understand . . . why my prayer wasn't answered. . . . Is this God's will? *Is it* God's will? I don't even understand. It's just hard." Sister Clark wrestled with the paradox of divine healing and death, of the power of prayer and predestination, and she was not alone. For months after the tragic event, in casual conversations, most saints voiced the understanding that the passing of Louise was most certainly the will of God while their faces and body language revealed a deep sadness that ran counter to Bishop Cook's directive to "be glad she died in the Lord."

Mother Reeves's singing on the morning Louise passed away, before many of these issues were articulated, can be viewed as an "exercise in the strategy of choice" in which she "exercise[d] her sense of economy of signification" (Smith 1980: 116–17). Her "choice" modeled "already and not yet"—that is, she was thankful for a state of gratitude, which she anticipated. "Not yet" is realized only insofar as "already" stimulates effective actions. Her singing in the "already and not yet" proleptically kept "already" viable, thereby sustaining the "not yet." Envisioning Louise with Jesus offered a long "peace," while singing supplied an immediate balm, in Mother Reeves' body and throughout the space. The good women gathered at Louise's house had taken primary responsibility for preparing the home and church for protocols of "home going." In those initial hours before the family and wider church community gathered, it was important to bolster one another, because some would later be responsible for conveying, in word and deed, confidence in the wisdom of God's plan for everyone.

At the same time, any death in the church family puts everyone on notice. "The Lord is trying to tell us something," Bishop Cook warned. "We need to ready ourselves.... Can't say how long you're gonna live.... [It would] do you right to get your house in order.... Those who live right have a hope in Christ." Grappling with the meanings of death, judgment, and the future state, saints anticipate and (work to) manifest a "new heaven and a new earth" (Revelations 21:1). At the same time, they know that "the fearful, and unbelieving, ... shall have their part in the lake which burneth with fire and brimstone: which is the second death" (Revelations 21:8).

What does it mean to be awash in the paradox of divine healing and death, and in the paradox of the power of prayer and predestination?

Mother Reeves, through spontaneous song, stood "in the gap" for uncertain, committed saints (Ezekiel 22:30). The prayers for divine healing of Louise's cancer did not have the anticipated result. Now they needed another healing. Mother Reeves performed a restorative act by sounding the conviction she might not quite have felt in her heart. In the midst of trials and tribulations, a key indication of a saint's religious confidence is her ability to thank and praise the Lord. Acquiring and maintaining steadfast faith is a process that has its ebb and flow. During times of trouble, if a saint feels spiritually weak, praising God and giving thanks becomes a strategy that shores her up: "I'm gonna praise my way out"; "The victory is in the praise." Consequently, the reservoir of techniques used to demonstrate faith is the same one used to instill faith—tools used to show what you have or to get what you need. With "Thank You, Lord,"

Mother Reeves sounded conviction and uncertainty, and she knew from experience, it would move her to a spiritually stronger place.

Ambiguity about the degree of faith being demonstrated levels the spiritual playing field, throwing open an interpretive and democratized space that allows anyone to enter, regardless of her spiritual grounding at a given moment. Carrying out aesthetic labor, Mother Reeves concocted a sonic salve to rub into the open wounds and, at the same time, created a passageway for "her sisters in the Lord" to access "the new heaven and new earth." Concocting the salve required pulling and mixing healing tones valued by the community. Simple, direct, and repetitive lyrics ("Thank You, Lord / I just want to thank you, Lord") allowed each woman to access what she needed personally from the song. Chanting created a sacred space for worship and fellowship in the midst of the scrubbing, sweeping, and polishing, bringing all closer to God and giving comfort.

So whether Mother Reeves was in fact grateful to God at the time she sang the song or was singing as a reminder to *be* grateful, contemplating gratitude while grieving kept everyone in the "already and not yet" and close to their spiritual sister who had "gone home." Mother Reeves later explained, "Our life and ... Hallelujah! [*She shuddered at the touch of the Holy Ghost.*] ... however it's to go has already been preset. You know, it's just that you got to fall in place." In the moments that saints are falling—some in place, and some out of place—acts such as those of Mother Reeves mediate doubt in a sacred sonic register. Her aesthetic labor pointed to eschatological meanings that may not be apparent in paradoxical rhetoric or doctrine. She democratized the space, allowing uncertain, committed saints to remain securely in "the Kingdom in the midst" while they regained their moorings.

CONCLUSION

Black American Apostolic women operate in a sacred milieu of "already and not yet." They experience Jesus's proclamations of the present and forthcoming Kingdom within the context of particular raced and gendered social, political, and cultural histories. The sounding bodies and aesthetic labor of COOLJC women can reflect much larger concerns about eschatological paradoxes. Who is included in the collapsed time and space of the "already and not yet," and in what capacity? In what ways does a saint's current state address her future state? To what extent must the future be realized in the present? In what ways is the future state proleptically reflected in her current state? In the end, to bridge gaps among theology, doctrine, and experience, women use sounding bodies as the conduit for aligning a democratized "new heaven" with hierarchies of "the Kingdom in the midst."

NOTES

Epigraphs: Traditional African American gospel song; Copeland 2010: 7.

1. Ethnographic data in this essay are drawn from fieldwork I conducted in January 2004–December 2005, May–August 2007, and June–September 2012. My methodologies included participant observation, in-depth open-ended interviews, and informal conversations, in social and religious settings, within the church community.
2. In addition to churches in the United States, the organization boasts congregations in England; Germany; Ghana; Grenada; Guyana; India; Ivory Coast; the Leeward Islands; Liberia; Manitoba, Canada; Mexico, Sierra Leone; Trinidad and Tobago; and Venezuela. It is, however, difficult to ascertain the size of international congregations, accessed January 15, 2013, http://www.cooljc.org.
3. Church members refer to those who exhibit spiritual maturity or highly developed spiritual gifts as "highly anointed." In this particular instance, a church mother leaned over to me during praise and worship (and my note taking) to inform me that the musicians were "highly anointed."
4. Converted members throughout Holiness Pentecostalism refer to themselves and one another as "saints." See Ephesians 4:12: "For the perfecting of the saints, for the work of the ministry, for the edifying of the body of Christ." *The Life Application Study Bible (King James Version)*, which is used in COOLJC, defines saints as, "'holy ones' who consecrate themselves for God's Service" (Barton 1989: 2427).
5. For analysis of "already" and "not yet" centered on the COOLJC, the focus of this essay, see Clark 2001. Clark applies an "already" and "not yet" analysis to the Sermon on the Mount and its lesson for the church today ("Blessed *are* the poor in spirit: for theirs is the kingdom of heaven" [Matthew 5:3]). He posits that the present tense indicates "a reality that can be experienced in the here and now.... This present reality is a form of realized eschatology in the sense that there is a future to the benefits it affords the believer" (Clark 2001: 125). The call to occupy a conflicted time-space realm is directed to a community already committed to Christ (and the Christian project)—"those ... having already accepted 'salvation' and understanding 'the requirements of eschatological revelation'" (Clark 2001: 127). He further argues that the COOLJC, in the eschatological tension of

"already" and "not yet," has abdicated its responsibilities to social justice, alluded to in Matthew, in favor of focusing on the heavenly kingdom. Clark thus analytically separates "already" and "not yet" while holding them in tension. My argument, however, keeps "already and not yet" as a unified conceptual model within women's practices.

Paul Ricoeur (1984) examines "already" and "not yet" through the transition of the Gospels from oral (preached) to written (scripture). Drawing on Jesus's proclamation "The Kingdom of God is within you" (Luke 17:21), Ricoeur (1984: 505) maintains, "The proximity of the Kingdom lies entirely in the anticipating capacity linked to Jesus' proclamation and in the crisis it opens." He sees "already" and "not yet" as dialectical, in that Jesus's preaching of the future Kingdom is "the sign of the already aspect of this expectation" (Ricoeur 1984: 507). For argument against dialectic analysis through Pauline text, see Chang 2007. The author contends that, in the book of Romans, Paul does not exhibit tension of "already" and "not yet"; Paul privileges "already" in chapters 6 and 8, which frame chapter 7.

For a study that takes this eschatological tension into the civic realm, see Carbine 2006. Carbine engages "already" and "not yet" as a means to construct an ideal political vision—a feminist public theology. Building on Schüssler Fiorenza's *ekklesia* of wo/men, Carbine proposes "ekklesia" in the context of Christian eschatology but operating within a human/political reality that recognizes the inability to actualize the ideal. By this reading, the "not yet" is unattainable, which undermines the proleptic and paradoxical characteristic of "already and not yet."

6 The present kingdom is referenced in Luke 17:20–21: "And when he was demanded of the Pharisees, when the kingdom of God should come, he answered them and said, . . . behold, the kingdom of God is within you." The forthcoming Kingdom is seen in Luke 21:28–31: "And when these things begin to come to pass, then look up, and lift up your heads; for your redemption draweth nigh . . . , know ye that the kingdom of God is nigh at hand."

7 "Church mother" is an official title granted to older churchwomen who have exhibited years of consistent spiritual and organizational leadership. According to C. Eric Lincoln and Lawrence H. Mamiya (1990: 275), "The phenomenon of the 'church mother' has no parallel in white churches; it is derived from the kinship network found within black churches and black communities." Gilkes (2001: 103–4) provides detailed analysis of the role of church mother across Black denominations—particularly, Black Holiness, Pentecostal, and Apostolic churches.

8 For the doctrinal distinctions among Charismatics, Classical and Neo-Pentecostals, Holiness Pentecostals, and Apostolics, see Synan 1997.

9 In 1925, Lawson published *The Anthropology of Jesus Our Kinsman (Dedicated to the Glory of God and to the Help of Solving the Race Problem)*, which espoused an Afro-biblical analysis linking early African civilization, biblical history, and

theology. He maintained that God deliberately created Jesus's mixed Hamitic, Semitic, and Japhetic bloodline; therefore, the atonement was for all. Tracing the Hamitic genealogy of Jesus in biblical scripture, he argued that Mary, the progeny of David and the tribe of Judah, descended in part from "two Negro [Canaanite] women," Shuar and Tamar, "two mothers of the tribe of Judah." He also identified Rahab, a "harlot" and great-great-grandmother of King David, and Bathsheba, mother of Solomon, as important contributors to the Hamitic lineage of Jesus (Lawson [1925] 1969: 24–26, 30).

10 In addition to its original publication in 1925, excerpts from *The Anthropology of Jesus* were republished, in 1949 and 2000, in the COOLJC organizational journal *Contender for the Faith*.

11 Majority status of women across American Christianity is well documented (see Pew Forum on Religion and Public Life 2008). Pew reports that women dominate in nearly every Christian group. Specifically, "Members of Protestant churches are eight percentage points more likely to be women than men (54 percent to 46 percent); a similar gap is seen among Catholics. Among historically black Protestant churches and Jehovah's Witnesses, however, women constitute a somewhat higher percentage (60 percent)" (Pew Forum on Religion and Public Life 2008: 63). Regarding the 60 percent participation of Black women, a 2009 report of African American religious affiliation notes, "No group of men or women from any other racial or ethnic background exhibits comparably high levels of religious observance" (see Pew Research Center Forum on Religion and Public Life 2009). Joel Robbins's study of Pentecostal and Charismatic Christianity notes women make up 75 percent of churches worldwide (Robbins 2004: 132). While no organization-wide survey has been conducted within the Church of Our Lord Jesus Christ of the Apostolic Faith, Inc., my data from New York churches are consistent with Robbins's global data, with women constituting closer to 80 percent of active membership.

12 The Church of Our Lord Jesus Christ of the Apostolic Faith Inc. traces its theological roots from late nineteenth-century Bible Conferences of John Nelson Darby and Keswick Movement revivalists Dwight L. Moody and Cyrus I. Scofield. The Scofield Reference Bible, published in 1909, significantly shaped African American Apostolic Pentecostal theology. Clark (2001: 85) argues, "It was the Bible of choice. The *Scofield Reference Bible* [King James Version] was the only Bible for my tradition and most, if not all, African-American Apostolic Pentecostalists from 1919 to the last decade of the 1950s." During the late twentieth century, alternate versions, most often the *Thompson Chain Reference Bible*, came into use. Clark (2001: 85) notes, however, that alternative versions that displace the centrality of dispensationalist pre-millennialism have been rare and controversial.

13 See 1 Thessalonians 4:16–17: "For the Lord himself shall descend from heaven with a shout, with the voice of the archangel, and with the trump of God: and the dead in Christ shall rise first: Then we which are alive and remain shall be caught

up together with them in the clouds, to meet the Lord in the air: and so shall we ever be with the Lord."

14 Dress regulations strictly apply within the sanctuary, but the vast majority of women carry them into daily life. Doctrine prohibits wearing pants, make-up, and earrings at any time.

15 For analysis of the "politics of respectability" as it relates to the Black Baptist women's movement in the late nineteenth and early twentieth century, see Higginbotham 1993. Higginbotham identifies the ideology and practices as politically resistant yet socially and culturally assimilationist. Black Baptists believed that adhering to dominant societal norms of decorum and aesthetics would lead to inclusion in the body politic, countering segregation. From the beginning, Holiness-Pentecostalism's relation to Black mainline denominations was conflicted, being at odds over cultural and organizational models. Ecstatic practices of embodiment in Holiness-Pentecostal worship were at the heart of cultural conflicts, which carried religious, social, and political implications. African Methodist Episcopal, African Methodist Episcopal Zion, and Baptist churches, working to develop religious and social profiles based, in large part, on a "politics of respectability" renounced Black folk culture, fueling the religious schism with Holiness-Pentecostals (see also Collier-Thomas 2010: 116–19; Hunter 1997: 137–44, 177–79). Many Holiness-Pentecostals rejected the large centralized organizational framework of mainline denominations, opting for locally controlled congregations (Best 2005; Taylor 1994).

16 Notable affinities exist with nineteenth-century Afro-Catholic women in New Orleans donning habits and twentieth-century African American Muslim women donning hijab (see Fessenden 2000 and Rouse 2004). Twenty-first-century COOLJC women, too, "use dress as a marker of the true soul beneath the fabric" (Klassen 2004: 41).

17 For details of teaching and preaching activities of the women of the Church of God in Christ, see Butler 2007. Also, Gilkes 2001 discusses power dynamics in sanctified women's teaching sites and practices.

18 Apostolics use the term "sleep" in the biblical sense—meaning death. In John 11:11–14, Jesus speaks of sleep when talking about Lazarus's death. See also 1 Thessalonians 4:13–14: "But I would not have you to be ignorant, brethren, concerning them which are asleep, that ye sorrow not, even as others which have no hope. For if we believe that Jesus died and rose again, even so them also which sleep in Jesus will God bring with him."

19 I was neither saved nor a church member, but I received a call from Sister Holmes on the morning of Louise's death; she asked me to meet her at Louise's house. When I arrived, Mother Morris greeted me at the door, with broom in hand. Within a few minutes, she handed it off to me to finish sweeping the hall carpeting. Sister Holmes had gone to the funeral parlor to make arrangements.

20 COOLJC attitudes toward medical science resonate with other evangelical organizations. In *God's Daughters*, a study of the Women's Aglow Fellowship,

a predominantly White American evangelical prayer organization, R. Marie Griffith (1997: 91) observes, "Doctors, hospitals, and the techniques of modern scientific medicine ... are more often readily accepted as complementary instruments in the total healing process. Miracles are believed not to be limited to instantaneous and inexplicable events but to encompass a whole range of more gradual movements toward health as well."

PART IV

Modeling the State

A CRITICAL APPROACH TO CONCEPTS OF "POWER" AND "AGENCY" IN GHANA'S CHARISMATIC (OR NEO-PENTECOSTAL) CHURCHES

JANE SOOTHILL

Charismatic Christianity is the most recent and fastest-growing expression of Pentecostal religion in sub-Saharan Africa. In Ghana's capital, Accra, the charismatic churches dominate the religious scene. By "charismatic" (or "Neo-Pentecostal") I mean specifically those churches that have emerged in Africa (and elsewhere) since the late 1970s and that are identified by a fluid but nonetheless common set of characteristics. These include an emphasis on "conversion": the moment that a believer rejects his or her old life and is born again; a belief in the power and presence of the Holy Spirit, which is often manifested in spirit baptism and "speaking in tongues"; the centrality of the Bible, as both an object of power and a living prophetic text; and the prolific use of modern media and technology, including print, radio, television and, increasingly, the Internet. These churches are also grouped according to a shared set of theological themes or "motifs." The first is the prominence given to concepts of "success," "victory," "winning ways," and the power of the miraculous. Faith is symbolized by "abundance" and "fruitfulness," and born-again Christians can expect to enjoy material success in this world. The second is the persistence of "deliverance thinking," which attributes poverty, sickness, and an inability to achieve in life to the influence of demons and evil spirits. Demonic influence may persist even after Christian rebirth and must be expelled by prayer, Bible study, and the prophetic powers of a man or woman of God. The third, then, is the increasing importance of the spiritual powers of individual preachers and pastors. A moment of connection with one of Ghana's chosen prophets can turn someone's life from a path of failure and disappointment to one of significance and success (and often this can all take place with little or no reference to God at all).

My fieldwork was conducted in three of Accra's charismatic churches, all of which had branches in other parts of Ghana, as well as overseas in Europe and the United States. They were Action Chapel International, founded by Nicholas Duncan-Williams in 1979 (making it one of the first of Ghana's charismatic-type churches); Alive Chapel International, founded in 1994 by Elisha Salifu Amoako; and Solid Rock Chapel International, one of the few charismatic churches in Accra founded by a woman, Christie Doe Tetteh, also in 1994. Action Chapel was the largest of the three, with a regular membership of three thousand or more. Alive Chapel attracted about half this number to its Sunday services, and Solid Rock Chapel was much smaller, with a probable membership of fewer than one thousand. Of particular relevance to this chapter are the Women's Fellowships and Women's Conventions organized by these churches, which I attended during two research trips. The Women in Action prayer meeting of Action Chapel International was led by Francisca Duncan-Williams, then the founder's wife, who had also established the Pastors' Wives and Women in Ministry Association, a support group for the wives of charismatic pastors. At Alive Chapel International the "Women for Jesus" fellowship was frequently addressed by the prophet Salifu's wife, Moha Amoako, while Christie Doe Tetteh, founder of Solid Rock International, was rarely present at the "Daughters of Zion" women's fellowship. She was, however, a key celebrity figure at many of the annual Women's Conventions organized by these and other churches that I attended. Women's Conventions are usually weeklong events that require months of planning and intensive fundraising and advertising. Most host churches print special cloth to be worn by convention participants and organize musicians and guest speakers (often from overseas, ideally the United States), as well as public transport to ferry people home after lengthy late-night sessions. Women's Conventions are large, intense, time-consuming affairs. The titles of the conventions speak for themselves: "The Real Woman," "Women of Worth," "Women of Destiny," "Women in Higher Places." It is from these conventions—alongside my attendance at women's fellowships; interviews with pastors, pastors' wives, and church members; and analysis of a large number of religious books, pamphlets, and magazines—that many of my conclusions in this chapter are drawn.

WOMEN AND (NEO-)PENTECOSTALISM IN THE GLOBAL SOUTH

Research into the social effects of Pentecostal and charismatic Christianity on women living in the global South paints a common picture. Pentecostal and charismatic Christianity is said in some sense to "empower" its female adherents. It undermines dominant male-centered cultures and encourages women to embrace individuation in a way that challenges the boundaries of their traditional roles. I have identified three main threads that distinguish the attitude to women of the new charismatic churches from the older, more established churches. First is the removal of traditional barriers to women's leadership and the exercise of official authority by women in the churches' organizational structures (Brusco 2010; Green 1993; Wolfe 2003). Second is a message of social change and social renewal, important elements of which are directed toward changing men's behavior that may be damaging to women (Brusco 1995; Gill 1990; Marshall 1993)—notably, domestic violence and sexual promiscuity. Third is the emphasis on the personal development of individuals, especially women, which includes the importance of encouraging women to build their self-confidence and self-esteem (Philip Jenkins 2006; Wolfe 2003, 2004). A recent study from Kenya suggests that, for a woman, being born again leads to "a revaluing of the self in relation to God" in such a way that "undermines patriarchal public culture" (Paristau 2011: 143). A study from Brazil suggests that, as women's primary responsibility shifts away from spouses and families to God, they are transformed into "active, responsible agents" (Mariz and Machado 1997: 110).

In Ghana, recent studies have highlighted the role of the charismatic churches in supporting gender equality and empowering local women (Asamoah-Gyadu 2005; Kalu 2008; Sackey 2006). Through an innovative gender ideology that encourages the emergence of powerful female leaders and a new Pentecostal theology that mobilizes the spiritual gifts of its vast female laity, the charismatic movement, studies suggest, might provide not only "a strong forum for social change" (Sackey 2006: viii) but also "an exit from the shackles of patriarchy" (Kalu 2008: 161). Women's organizations represent "sustainable female power in religion" (Sackey 2006: 196) and empower "women's capacity to confront society" (Kalu 2008: 154). While dual leadership between pastor husbands and wives helps in "bridging the gender gap" (Sackey 2006: 173), the presence of female founders empowers other women within the charismatic movement (Kalu 2008: 149). By democratizing charisma (Asamoah-Gyadu 2005: 130), the charismatic churches in Ghana empower women pneumatologically, transforming both the individual and the society.

In this chapter I use my empirical research to examine some of these assertions about the power and agency of women in Ghana's charismatic churches. I do this under three main headings: "Discursive Womanhood," "Female Religiosity and Leadership" and "Women and Power."

DISCURSIVE WOMANHOOD

The "spiritual equality" of believers is a cornerstone of the charismatic discourse on women. This is expressed in the commonly heard phrases, "God is no respecter of persons" and "In Christ there is neither male nor female." While the equality of men's and women's spiritual experiences was recognized almost a century ago by the early Pentecostal and Holiness movements (Lawless 1988; Powers 1999), Ghana's new churches take this a step further. In addition to removing traditional barriers to female religious authority, they argue that, in terms of worldly success—with which this form of Christianity is so concerned—there is no difference between male and female believers. That is to say, "success" and "prosperity" do not depend on gender. It should not be assumed, however, that the spiritual and material equality of believers undermines inherent biological and psychological differences between women and men, or that it fundamentally disrupts the rules governing social relations between them. In marriage, a woman is to "submit" to her husband (Ephesians 5:22–24). There is an important point of departure, however, because in Ghana's new churches, women's "submission" is inextricably linked to charismatic concepts of "success" and "victory." In contrast to the older Pentecostal churches, in charismatic Christianity submission is not simply a feminine virtue but equally a strategy for achieving personal success. Pastors' wives are the embodiment of this type of thinking.

The doctrine of conjugal submission tends to figure prominently in their public personas. The motto of the Pastors' Wives and Women in Ministry Association, for example, is "Helpmeet! By his side!" and the advice given by a member of the association to a group at Action Chapel's "Women of Worth" convention—"Your husband is your Abraham. Bless your Abraham"—is typical.

For many female pastors and pastors' wives, however, this sort of public rhetoric is largely just that: rhetorical. In practice, female leaders in the charismatic movement exercise considerable authority over both their female and male congregants. Francisca Duncan-Williams is an excellent example of this. In her account of her nine-month separation in 2001 from her husband, Nicholas, Francisca blamed the breakdown of the marriage primarily on her own shortcomings as a suitable "helpmeet" to her husband. "I realized that the way I was looking at things was wrong," she wrote. "I was seeing my husband from a certain angle, when as a helpmeet, my duty was to follow his vision and not the other way round" (Duncan-Williams 2002: 54). By employing such rhetoric, however, she was both protecting her own sphere of influence, which to a large extent depends on her closeness to the founding father of the charismatic movement in Ghana and gained necessary endorsement from her pastor husband—in one instance, the public gift of a new Mercedes-Benz. Like the wives of other prominent charismatic men, Francisca Duncan-Williams, by being seen to submit to one man, her husband, gains in return female-like submission from many other men within the ranks of the movement.

Many of the most prominent elements of this discourse of personal success, in fact, parallel the concerns and objectives of Ghanaian state feminism and the international Women in Development (WID) agenda.[1] Thus, charismatic preachers and writers advocate, in particular, the necessity of encouraging the education of female children so that girls will have the chance to overcome the "myths" and "misconceptions" that prevent them from becoming the "highfliers" of society (Darko 1999: 17). In a similar vein, they criticize customary law, which is blamed for giving women an "inferiority complex" and to which much of Ghana's gender inequality is attributed (Darko 1999: 15; Doe Tetteh 2003: 56). The work of women's rights organizations, such as the Commission on Human Rights and Administrative Justice (CHRAJ) and the International Federation of Women Lawyers (FIDA), are also commended in the numerous books and pamphlets produced by local charismatic writers and pastors on the issue of women in church and society.

This is not a straightforward counterculture critique. After all, in one sense the churches are simply echoing the current political consensus, which has adopted the international gender development discourse as its own.[2] Like the political rhetoric it parallels, charismatic Christianity largely contains its critique of local gender norms within a discourse of gender complementarity, which celebrates women's essential difference from men and values them for their inherent feminine qualities, such as mildness, nurturing, and support. Nonetheless, it is a social critique of sorts that explicitly challenges women to confront the status quo and assert themselves in both religion and society.

The charismatic discourse on womanhood prioritizes "self" and women's individuation in a way that is not seen in the classical Pentecostal and mission-style churches. As "children of God," born-again women are encouraged to develop their own self-esteem and build a positive "self-image" by spending time on themselves and even on their personal appearance (Darko 1999: 95–97; Doe Tetteh 2003: 20–21). In some popular pamphlets, even their sexuality comes under scrutiny as one aspect of a life lived in Christ. While women are given the right to demand pleasure and intimacy in sexual relations with their husbands, men are instructed on the intricacies of the clitoris and on the styles that are likely to please their partners (Adjabeng 1991; Jenkins 1996; Onwumere 2003). In a series of sermons for a radio broadcast called "Marriage 101," Mensa Otabil of the International Central Gospel Church—and one of Ghana's most prominent pastors—was explicit on this issue:

> Women like affirmation and words of encouragement more than sex. Am I right women? [*Laughter and applause from the congregation.*] So if you are a man who thinks you are a macho man and you really know how to satisfy your wife, you may know how to satisfy a prostitute, but that is different from satisfying your wife; it's a different thing. You need to be patient; no under the cover, rushing, before you realize it you're on top of her. No, you don't do things like that.... And some men think they have sexual experience: "I have experience." I mean, what experience? You were doing it under the chicken coop, under the mango tree; you have no idea how to handle a woman. You don't

know anything. . . . If a man is not understanding toward a woman, there is no way he can satisfy her sexually. All the styles you know, you can put into practice but it won't satisfy her, because what she wants, it's not just an act. It's a relationship. We don't do it in the animal way. We do it the human way, and that means you must understand your woman.³

This type of rhetoric is heavily influenced by recent trends within North American evangelicalism, where personal development, sexual satisfaction, and just plain "feeling good" have been given a prominence quite unknown by previous generations (Wolfe 2003, 2004).⁴ In many ways, then, the local discourses of Ghana's charismatic churches echo what is in fact a transnational shift in virtues from self-denial (epitomized by earlier forms of evangelicalism) to self-affirmation and the promotion of the individual self.

Discourse however, is rarely the whole picture and must always be viewed in conjunction with structure, which is what I do in the next section. I discuss two dimensions of female religiosity within the charismatic movement in Ghana: the role of the pastor's wife and women's leadership in a female-founded church.

FEMALE RELIGIOSITY AND LEADERSHIP

The pastor's wife is a surprisingly under-researched figure in the charismatic movement, given that the ever present, well-dressed, self-confident and loyal spouse may be said to be as integral to the charismatic package as the finely cut suit and Mercedes-Benz.⁵ It is welcome, therefore, that her role has begun to be recognized in recent analyses, more often than not as a source of empowerment for other women. In one study the pastor's wife is described as a "nodal power point for mobilizing and deploying female evangelical power" (Kalu 2008: 153), and in another, the leadership position of Francisca Duncan-Williams is called "an awakening and revolution of women in [African Initiated Churches] in Ghana" (Sackey 2006: 168). Kalu and Brigid Sackey make two further points about the prominence of pastors' wives, which need examining: first, that the male-and-female dual leadership model of the charismatic churches demonstrates "male encouragement for gender equality" and helps "in bridging the gender gap" by "giving due recognition to women's potentials and capabilities" (Sackey 2006: 173); and second, that if one of the keys to Africa's poor governance is the exclusion of women from political leadership, which allows male politicians to assume a "patriarchal power that disdains accountability," then the partnership of men and women suggested by the dual leadership of the charismatic churches may represent a model for the reform of Africa's big-man politics (Kalu 2008: 162).

In this section I examine the role of Francisca Duncan-Williams, who until recently was probably the most prominent spouse of any charismatic pastor in Ghana.[6] I return later to the issue of her divorce, but for now I want to make two points. First, the behavior displayed by Duncan-Williams illustrates the parallels that exist between the wives of charismatic pastors and the wives of political men. And second, her primary role as a source of spiritual power was intrinsically linked to her relationship with her husband, Nicholas Duncan-Williams.

According to a study by Lisa Aubrey (2001), in both Ghana and Nigeria the state structures responsible for delivering the provisions of state feminism—namely, the women's wings of governing political parties—have been dominated by what she calls "First Lady Syndrome." Aubrey (2001: 105) describes these so-called femocracies as "systems in which female autocracies parallel and serve male dictatorships while advancing conservative gender ideologies to the detriment of democracy and gender equality." Under the regime of Jerry Rawlings in the 1980s and early 1990s, for example, the WID agenda was controlled and monopolized by the female elite of the December 31 Women's Movement (in effect, the women's wing of the ruling Provisional National Defence Council [PNDC]), over which the president's wife, Nana Konadu Agyeman Rawlings, exercised considerable personal control. Gender development initiatives were often constrained by the interests of the state, and the movement's relationship with the governing party was prioritized over the advancement of gender equality. In fact, the movement did more to consolidate the class interests of a small group of privileged women, whose own interests were served by maintaining the power of a male political elite, than it did to open up a democratic space for the wider female electorate. As the main power base of the president's wife, the December 31 Women's Movement represented the "careful calculated political manipulations for women's space in public life without disturbing patriarchal and middle-class interests" (Aubrey 2001: 103).

Comparatively, during my fieldwork the women's activities of Action Chapel were strongly influenced by the personal authority of the bishop's wife and, like the women's wing of the PNDC, both Women in Action and the Pastors' Wives and Women in Ministry Association functioned as networks of patronage for a predominantly female clientele. The importance of Francisca Duncan-Williams's personal involvement in the women's prayer meeting was highlighted by the Reverend Clive Mold, the pastor in charge of Action Chapel, who implied in an interview that the Monday meetings would probably diminish considerably without her presence: "For some reason she has not been able to keep the fire blazing in her absence. For some strange reason, when she is not here the fellowship is not as if she were here." In fact, the public affirmation of Francisca Duncan-Williams was a prominent part of both the regular Monday prayer meetings and special events such as women's conventions. The question, "How many of you love this woman of God?" was put to the congregants on many occasions and was always greeted with the same enthusiastic response of hand clapping and wild shouting and cheering. When Duncan-Williams announced at the "Women of Worth" convention in June 2003 a forthcoming all-night women's prayer meeting that she would lead, she asked the crowd, "Do you love me for doing that for you? Then tell me you love me." In response, the women cried out, "Mummy, we love you!"

For the wives of other established pastors, Duncan-Williams's role was usually described as one of support and general encouragement, but with key figures such as Rita Korankye-Ankrah of Royal House Chapel International and Dora Tackie-Yarboi of Victory Bible Church International (both substantial churches) bestowing the honorific title of "Mother" on Duncan-Williams, allusions to a female charismatic dynasty were certainly evident. As Duncan-Williams herself claimed of her more junior counterparts, "Some of them were nobodies until they met me."[7] In fact, the women's prayer meetings and the Pastors' Wives and Women in Ministry Association functioned primarily as patron-client networks, with a small minority of women—those married to prominent charismatic men—receiving direct material patronage (such as overseas travel, gifts, and financial support for their projects) in exchange for public endorsement of Duncan-Williams's social and spiritual status.

It is therefore my contention that, in this sense, the structures that create and sustain the "First Lady" of the charismatic movement in Ghana are broadly similar to the structures of state feminism in which a female elite benefit from the patronage of a First Lady of politics. In both Ghanaian politics and charismatic Christianity, it is unclear whether ordinary women are empowered by or benefit from the same networks of patronage. When drawing conclusions about the empowering role of the charismatic churches, therefore, it is necessary to recognize the differences among born-again women so that the experiences of the majority are not misrepresented by the minority experiences of a female elite.

For most of her female congregants Francisca Duncan-Williams was a source not of social or material empowerment but of spiritual empowerment, and it is from her "spiritual patronage" that the vast majority of women attending Action Chapel hoped to gain. Her popularity and authority within the charismatic movement seemed to rest primarily on her ability to demonstrate privileged access to the spiritual forces that are believed to govern the lives of her congregants. Perceptions of her power in this regard, however, stemmed first and foremost from her close relationship with the "Man of God": her husband, Nicholas Duncan-Williams. Like other models of dual leadership in Ghana's social and political worlds (the political model embodied by the Rawlings, as mentioned earlier), the pastors' wives of the charismatic movement access authority primarily through their relationships with powerful men, and the charisma (on which their authority depends) is proportional to the charismatic power of their pastor husbands. Duncan-Williams's need to maintain this link between her husband's spiritual gifts and her own may account for her uncharacteristically submissive stance in her account of their separation and (temporary) reunion (see Duncan-Williams 2002), in which she blamed herself almost entirely for misunderstanding a wife's role as a helpmeet to her husband.

When I returned to Ghana a year after the publication of the book, however—and perhaps in recognition of the fragility of their reunion[8]—Duncan-Williams seemed to be trying to stretch the boundaries of her role as a pastor's wife by pursuing a spiritual and charismatic status independent of her husband's. In accordance with this prophetic mode, she was increasingly presenting herself as a point of contact between her congregants and the spirit world, either through her own physical presence or through objects she had touched or "blessed." The handkerchiefs and headscarves specially printed for the women's convention and worn by the convention participants became a source of "miracles" because they had been "anointed" by Duncan-Williams. The collection boxes made especially for the convention offerings were handed to the ushers by Duncan-Williams personally so that the "blessing" in each of the boxes would be transferred to them. "Let me give it to you," she said in June 2003. "It is filled with anointing."

Whatever the prophetic claims of Francisca Duncan-Williams, it is far from clear that either her spiritual gifts or her position of leadership within the charismatic movement in Ghana is sustainable outside her relationship with Nicholas Duncan-Williams. If, as Sackey (2006: 173) argues, the leadership positions attained by the wives of charismatic pastors are a sign of "male encouragement for gender equality" and demonstrate "that religion can be a most effective tool in bridging the gender gap and giving due recognition to women's potentials and capabilities," then there should be some indication that these positions are independent and autonomous of their husbands' authority. If not, the leadership role of pastors' wives in the charismatic movement is little more than a reflection of a discredited political model in which the first ladies of governing parties attain positions of status, but only by supporting a conservative gender ideology that sustains their relationships with the men on whom their own status depends. After the Duncan-Williamses's second divorce, Nicholas married the African American businesswoman Rosa Whitaker. As this occurred quite recently, the full implications of Francisca's ejection from Christian Action Faith Ministries are yet to be really seen, although in much of the local press coverage she has largely been vilified as a bossy and adulterous wife, even by her own children.

The Reverend Christie Doe Tetteh is almost certainly the most renowned charismatic female preacher and church leader in Ghana. Although her church is quite small in contrast with a mega-church such as Action Chapel,[9] her reputation within the movement, and her larger-than-life personality, far outweigh her fairly modest congregation. Her congregants and pastors (who are predominantly women) are in awe of her presence, and alongside salutations to her painted on colorful banners, images of Doe Tetteh dominate the interior of her church buildings. In most personal encounters with her, congregants and pastors (female and male) kneeled at her feet while being addressed or, more often, admonished. During references to Doe Tetteh in Solid Rock services, her name could be prefixed by as many as five titles, including Right Reverend, Doctor, Pastor, Bishop, and Mama. A single mention of any of these titles brought enthusiastic, even raucous, responses from her congregants—evidence, perhaps, of a view endorsed by Kalu (2008: 149, citing Olanyinka 2000) that Doe Tetteh and female founders like her are powerful and inspirational role models for other women in the charismatic movement and in society as a whole.

Without doubt, Doe Tetteh's religious authority is innovative to some extent. In contrast to the position of some traditional priestesses and of female founders of older African instituted churches, her femaleness is presented as a source of her authority rather than a distraction from it. Doe Tetteh is not thought of as an "honorary male," and her womanhood is positively celebrated by both herself and her followers. Her male counterparts gladly introduced her as "the only woman general overseer" and "the First Lady of Ghana's charismatic circle," and she often comments positively on her femaleness by saying, "Be glad that your pastor is a woman, your mother, your sister" and "Thank God he used a woman. I have no regrets God made me a woman." On one occasion, she said, "Don't let anyone tell you, 'Don't go to a woman's church.' If a woman was a dentist, you'd go there. What I am doing is more than a dentist, a gynecologist. We're saving souls." Among the congregants I spoke to, many were attracted to Solid Rock Chapel initially because it was led by a woman. One woman said that, on her first visit to the church during a three-day prayer and fasting session, the way Doe Tetteh "did things, the way she prayed, it touched me. I told myself, how can a woman go to that extent, because in our culture it's like women are not usually allowed into certain things. When I realized she was a woman but she was doing those things, I said, 'Wow, I will join this training,' and I became part of Solid Rock Chapel." Another remarked, "That woman is so precious to the Lord. What the woman is doing I don't think any man can do. This woman is a kind of person that, when you live with her for a long time, or when you give yourself to her, you achieve a lot."

Doe Tetteh's presence on the public stage thus was perceived by other women as both unusual and inspiring. As two different female market traders told me at Solid Rock Chapel in 2003:

If I told you the names people called this woman, ... you would be surprised. When you look at the things she has gone through. If she had listened to what people say and she had had that mentality—that mentality that "I am a woman, I can't make it"—then she would have stopped. We would all be lost souls by now.

One thing I can say I have benefited immensely from Mama Christie: ... this woman has made me believe that there are so many barriers men are crossing, so women, too, can cross. She has broken those barriers. So if she, being a woman, has broken them, why should I not break them? Let me tell you, some of the things of this woman has given me some kind of strength. We are made to believe that women are even not allowed to preach.... There are certain things that, without the strength of God, you can't stand publicly and say them, but it will be of benefit for you and those people around you. But because of that mentality—African mentality of we the women—you will fear to say those things, and because of that some women have been put in the dark. But this woman! "My dear," she will say, "go for it! It will do you good. Go for it." So because of that, you will look back and see somebody behind you, and definitely it will work for you. I saw this woman as a woman of God.... When I obey the rules and regulations of the Bible and follow in her footsteps, I know I'll make Heaven. And the strength she gives women—I can say that is why I'm a member of Solid Rock.

Furthermore, and in contrast to her classical Pentecostal and African Initiated Church predecessors (Lawless 1988; Powers 1999; Sackey 1997), Doe Tetteh is not presented to her congregants as simply a feminine "mouthpiece" of the Lord or a "vessel" of the Holy Spirit.[10] She is far more than just a medium of God's power. In fact, at times, she seemed to be taking the prophetic mode of charismatic leaders to a new level by creating ambiguity between the power of God and her own esoteric abilities. An account given by her Muslim driver during one of Solid Rock Chapel's deliverance services is illustrative of this development. (Deliverance sessions are popular meetings in which people are liberated from the demonic forces that cause misfortune and failure.) One morning, he gave a testimony to the assembled crowd that, since he began working for Mama Christie and attending Solid Rock Chapel, he had purchased his own car.

He implied that it was not his faith in the Christian God that enabled him to become a car owner ("As for me, I can't go into Christianity," he said) but, rather, his relationship with Doe Tetteh. If he, a Muslim, had been so "profited" by her, then "What about you, the Christian?" he asked. In the case of Christie Doe Tetteh, then, her charisma is not linked to her marital status, but neither, it seems, is it always linked directly to her relationship to God. This may not be quite what Asamoah-Gyadu had in mind when he labeled the gender ideology of the charismatic movement "innovative." But clearly the nature of Doe Tetteh's power and authority represents something of a departure from earlier models of women's religious leadership and demonstrates the distinctive gender neutrality of much charismatic practice in Ghana.

What, however, does the success of Christie Doe Tetteh tell us about the "power" and "agency" of women in the charismatic movement in Ghana? It is my contention that while Doe Tetteh's religious authority is innovative in many ways, the model on which her authority is based parallels the authoritarianism and neo-patrimonialism of "big-man" politics and male charismatic leadership. Elsewhere, I have described Doe Tetteh as a "big woman" and her congregants as "small girls" (Soothill 2007: 137). This relationship is the defining dynamic of Solid Rock Chapel, and one theme dominates her preaching: the importance of service and loyalty to Doe Tetteh in pursuit of worldly success. She is first and foremost a patron figure, and her status as a "big woman" depends primarily on her ability to access the power of the spirit world.

Female congregants are drawn to Doe Tetteh, as they were to Francisca Duncan-Williams, primarily for her spiritual rather than her material patronage. In recognition, perhaps, of her rather unusual position as a female but unmarried and childless charismatic leader, cures for infertility (the prime cause of which many believe to be witchcraft) and the provision of miracle babies seemed to be particularly prominent features of her ministry. Testament to this was the number of "Christians" and "Christines" running around Solid Rock Chapel, and the church magazine *Solid Rock News* was littered with examples of women who, with Doe Tetteh's help, had defied medical opinion to produce healthy children. In one instance, her miraculous intervention stretched beyond the provision of a child to the determination of its sex. "I got on a plane for her naming ceremony [another Christine]," "I told the father, 'It is a girl.'

He said a boy. I said, 'Even if it's a boy, when I get to the house, God will change it into a girl.'"

On a more explicit level, the spiritual power of Christie Doe Tetteh is accessed through direct physical contact with her. When, for example, she offered a hug to anyone presenting an offering during a deliverance service, everyone in the crowd clamored for a chance to be touched by the woman of God. On another occasion, she described the effects of her physical presence in more mundane situations, saying, "Every time [my hairdresser] washed my hair, she's falling down [slain in the spirit]. I say, 'No, I have to get another person.' Some people came to me house to wash my [laundry]. As soon as I handed them the things, they started falling. Every time they touched one of my things, they fell.... That's the anointing."

In whatever way Doe Tetteh's spiritual power is approached, access to it is determined by an individual's willingness to submit herself or himself to her spiritual and social authority and thus to enter into a new social hierarchy and a new relationship of patronage. These new networks are not defined by age, kinship, or gender, but they do reinforce a hierarchical relationship between this "big woman" and her many "small girls." Even her book *Celebrating Womanhood* (Doe Tetteh 2003) devotes considerable space to the importance of service to God's prophets and the necessity of sustaining a close personal relationship with Christie Doe Tetteh to maintain access to God's blessings. And she has issued warnings to potential dissenters that her power to heal can also be used to harm. "If you are in this church and you decide to be ashamed to associate with me, you are treading on dangerous ground," I heard her say in August 2003. "I'm very sharp; you may be standing a long way from me, but I'm hearing what you are saying. You are either for me or against me. If you're for me, that's good. If you're coming here and you're not for me, you are treading on dangerous ground. I know what I'm saying.... God will deal with you."

While Christie Doe Tetteh's presence on Ghana's charismatic scene may be an example of the "democratisation of charisma" (Asamoah-Gyadu 2005: 130)—after all, the exercise of her charismatic gifts is not defined or limited by gender[11]—it is less clear that the rise of this female founder is representative of the movement's capacity to empower women more generally.

WOMEN AND POWER

In this chapter, I have considered the discursive influence of charismatic (Neo-Pentecostal) churches on cultural attitudes toward women and the structural dynamics of women's religious leadership, but I have said very little thus far about the vast female laity of the charismatic movement. What about the women in the pews (or more often, plastic chairs) who go to church two, three, sometimes four times a week and participate in service after service, deliverance after deliverance, prayer meeting after prayer meeting? They are mothers, grandmothers, housewives, office workers, market traders, students, and professionals. What do these women have to say about "power" and "agency" in charismatic Christianity in Ghana?

In this section, I present case studies of three born-again women—Alice, Becky and Ama Nana—to explore and document how they perceive and experience the pneumatological power of charismatic (Neo-Pentecostal) Christianity in their everyday lives. They are representative of the many women with whom I had contact during my fieldwork. I use their stories to show how women in particular are drawn to the charismatic movement because of its perceived control over the powers of the spirit world. It is my contention that women seek spiritual power through charismatic practices to explain, predict, and sometimes control their gendered relationships.[12] Overwhelmingly, it was the domestic situations of female converts that had led them away from the Methodist, Presbyterian, and Catholic mission churches in which they had grown up and to the exuberance of the born-again ministries.

ALICE

Alice, age thirty-two, was a casual market trader, a divorced mother of two (her children reside with their father's family in his hometown), and a member of Solid Rock Chapel, where she was also a chorister. She attended church four or five times a week. Alice entered into a customary marriage with the father of her children when she lived in the Asante region of Ghana. Her husband was violent toward her and had many extramarital affairs so, on the advice of her mother-in-law, Alice left the marriage and moved to Accra. Alice had relationships with various men ("because of the financial strain") before moving in with a new "husband," to whom she was not legally or customarily married. When her business collapsed, she found herself in extreme financial difficulty, and the man she was living with refused to help, she made her first visit to Solid Rock Chapel, which was holding a three-day fast and prayer session. Alice said:

> That was the day that Mama Christie returned from her journey. Immediately when she entered the church—that was Wednesday morning—she took the microphone, came straight to me, and [said], "All that I have, every trouble that has been locked inside, I set you free. Everything that has been dropped inside of you, I set you at liberty in the name of Jesus." [At] that time, I had never experienced falling under the anointing because I was new to this charismatic movement, and everything around me was new. So before I realized, I was falling on the ground. *What is happening to me?* I thought. When I got up, I realized I had become light. It was like, *What is happening? This is strange; this is something else.* This is what I kept telling myself.

Following this experience, Alice joined Solid Rock and started attending Doe Tetteh's Bible college. Once she was born again, Alice felt uncomfortable sleeping with a man to whom she was not married, so she suggested that they perform the necessary rites to become legally married, but her partner refused. "So one day I had a dream," she said:

> I was living with this guy. Then I heard this squeaking of the door. I wouldn't say it was a dream, because it was too real. When I heard the squeaking of the door, I think I woke up—it was like in the dream—I woke up to see who was entering into the room. Then I realized it was Mama Christie. I ask[ed] her, "Mama what do you want here?" She said, "No, this is not where you should sleep. Who told you you belong here?" I said, "No, he's my husband." She said, "No, this guy is not your husband. Leave this place and come." I said, "No, I won't come." So she shouted, "I said, get up you! Get away from where you are sleeping!" And something just lifted me from the bed and dropped me down on the ground. Then I saw straight after that she had collected water, and she started pouring the water on me. Then when the water got on me, it was turning to oil. I was shocked, and my nightgown was wet, but she didn't mind me. So when I was struggling that she should leave me with the water she'd thrown on me, she started kicking me all over:

"Why are you doing this to yourself? You don't belong to this place, leave this place, blah, blah, blah." When I woke up, around 4 or 4.30, this guy woke up, got hold of me and just let me go: "Eh! What's happening? What has been smeared on your body? It's like oil." And when you look at it you can see that oil was in his palms. So I remembered the dream, and for about two weeks it was playing back. Every thirty minutes the thing would just recount back. It was giving me some sort of frustration, so I decided I wouldn't sleep with the guy again. But he didn't understand. So I came back one day, and he left.

After the man left her, Alice went to church in tears:

Mama Christie just walked into the room, passed by me, and said, "Won't you thank God he set you free from the cage you were in? Can't you see you've been liberated? Can't you see you've now gained freedom?" And it was like, Wow! What is this woman trying to tell me? I knew if I had been with this guy up to today, I wouldn't have gone [to Solid Rock], because when he saw me dressing up for church, that is when he wanted food. "Come and prepare food for me; come and do this thing for me," he'd say. You see? So I sat down and asked myself, "If I had been with this guy, would I be free to be coming to church like I'm doing?" I say, no. "Don't you think, this guy would have cut your anointing short?" I said, yes. Well, the questions were coming, and I was answering them myself. I remembered sometimes when [I was] going to pray, he'd say, . . . "I want sex first. I want sex before you go and pray." It was like, this guy was always asking for sex when I was still with him under this same roof. If I didn't do it, he would force me . . . , and [yet] he wasn't ready to legalize our marriage. So, in fact, I thank God. God has his own way of doing things. God understands, and he knows much better.

As a born-again Christian, Alice learned that her family had a curse that was causing the women to have unstable marriages and children with multiple men. If she was not careful about praying, the same curse would afflict Alice:

What I believe in, I always pray this thing, the family curses, because in our tradition, in our country, every family has some god, some small god, under it. So as for me, I normally pray to retreat myself from those family curses. I think they are the ones that are working against me, because since that thing has been there from times of old, it has been the protector of the family. When you belong to that family and you decide not to bow to it, and you decide to go in for another god, by all means it will work against you. But I believe my God is the Almighty God.

Marriage also was no longer a goal for Alice:

> They say a woman with no husband in our African system is like . . . it's like, you are useless. That is what we think. So some women think, without having a husband they can't achieve their aims. But I've seen many women flopping to the ground because of their husbands. So what is the sense of you saying [that] because you don't have a husband, you can't achieve your aims? As for me, I've made up my mind that I know with God I can achieve what I want. Since I know God is going to help me I don't think I should put any man first. I'm not going to put any man first.

BECKY

Becky was a fifty-one-year-old housewife and mother of six children, some of whom were grown up. She lived with her younger children and her husband, a former employee of Ghana Airways, who was frequently violent and abusive. She joined Solid Rock in 1996 and attended church up to four times a week. Prior to that, Becky had attended the Church of Pentecost, but she left when the church refused to give her a baptism card because her husband made it difficult for her to attend services regularly. Originally, Becky was a Presbyterian, but she stopped attending that church when a fellow (married) chorister made sexual advances toward her.

Becky's husband was a Methodist, but he rarely attended church. She had been in a customary marriage with her husband for twenty-nine years, and the marriage was abusive from the beginning. Early on, for example, Becky and her husband were going home in a taxi when her husband ordered her out of the car. "I followed him, because I don't know the area," she said. "That night this man [her husband] used me. I couldn't believe myself. He used me seven times. . . . So in the morning when I woke up and was going home, I couldn't walk. That was my first time sleeping outside. I haven't done anything of that sort in my life again." Becky had experienced frequent violence throughout her marriage, but she rarely spoke about it. "If my husband does something to me that hurts me," she said, "I just sit down quietly. I won't talk. But every time he used to beat me, my eyes would be swollen up." Becky described another instance of abuse close to the time of our interview that occurred when she and her husband were alone in the house:

> What the man did, I was shocked! He said I shouldn't put on anything else; I should be moving in the house naked. Even when I'm trying to work, prepare food, you see? He say, no, my food is not needed.... I was shivering. I said, "Do you want to kill me? Look, if you do not stop, I will run away," not knowing that he has locked the whole place. I couldn't do anything. So because of that I am now weak. I will say, now even when he come near me, maybe he wants [sex] ... a second time. If I can't again, that brings a quarrel between the two of us. For the last three days, he don't talk to me. I can't give what he wants from me. And it isn't my fault. Do you get me? I think what I'm saying, you get me? Is it my fault? So [he says that] I have to understand, if I won't give myself to him, I should go. He will go outside and chase women. [He says] I am a stupid woman. Is it fair to use that word on me?

In response to the abuse of her mother, Becky's twenty-three-year-old daughter reported her father to the Ghanaian police. The father was sent an official notice by the Women and Juvenile Unit, a specialist unit for dealing with cases of domestic violence. A friend had told the husband that there was something wrong with the daughter and that she should be sent to a fetish priest. "I was there when he said we should dress up, we are going to some place," Becky said. "When we go, we are called to a room. I see gods, and I say, 'I don't like this place.' So I go to my husband, and I beg him we should leave. They left my daughter [with the fetish priest. When] they brought my daughter [home], it was around 2 AM. [She was] moving like somebody who was bruised, and she was annoyed with me, but I don't have money to be doing that thing! If I have money, I'll be using it to do something good; not giving it to a fetish man."

Becky blamed her mother-in-law for many of the problems in her marriage. "[My] mother-in-law never liked the marriage," she said. "She [quarrels] with me all the time, and even my sister-in-law will come and abuse me. I haven't done anything to her." A Neo-Pentecostal pastor told Becky that her mother-in-law was a witch who had married her son to a spirit. The pastor also told Becky that the spirits would kill her if she left her husband. "Because of the kids, I should try to ignore things that he do to me," she recounted. "If the mother is a witch, then maybe she has been disturbing him since an infant, so this is what the guy will be." Becky was also having deliverance sessions with a Solid Rock pastor to break a connection to an ancestral stool on her father's side, which was contributing to her marital problems. Now that her children were growing up, however, Becky was looking to leave the marriage. "Maybe this thing that is crossing us now is opening some doors for me," she said. "I don't know. . . . What I have passed through in my life is enough for me. I have to be under the wings of my Savior. Now that I don't have to produce [children] anymore, God will help me out of the marriage. I'm praying God will help me out of it and give me one who is understanding me and I am understanding him, and live until the Maker will call us. That is my dream every day."

AMA NANA

Ama Nana, forty-two, was a market trader, the mother of three children, and a member of Alive Chapel International, which she attended three to four times a week. She joined the church in 1998. Ama Nana was raised Presbyterian but had attended various charismatic ministries since she was born again in 1990. She had been in a customary marriage to her husband, who did not attend any church, for seventeen years. At the time of our interview, Ama Nana's husband had entered into a customary marriage with another woman and was in the process of divorcing Ama Nana. He was also in a customary marriage to another woman when he married Ama Nana. Until her husband told her he wanted a divorce, Ama Nana was a cloth trader at Makola Market in central Accra, but she stopped trading because, she said, "he collected all the money from me. He told me that I should lend him some money to do a business, so I don't know that he has planned to divorce me. So I give all the money to him. After that, he said he is not going to give it back to me." Once she was divorced, she said she would start trading again.

Ama Nana described her husband as a womanizer:

In fact, my husband is a difficult man. That is why I don't have any helper in the house, because if you go in for a helper—I mean a maid—he like to sleep with the maid always. So this started me and him quarrelling about our marriage. So in fact I stopped giving myself to him. I went and had an AIDS test, . . . and by God's will, I don't have it. But I told him he should go for an AIDS test, because now he has been sleeping with girls, women, and . . . it's too much. But he said no, so I stopped sleeping with him about one year [ago].

Initially Ama Nana sought the advice of the Women and Juvenile Unit, who suggested she leave her marriage, but she also felt there was a spiritual dimension to her domestic problems. "In Africa here there is so many witches," she said, "so if something happens, then we blame the witches in the family. Papa [the prophet Salifu, the founder of Alive Chapel] called me and told me that my marriage was [the fault of] my husband's mother. That is why they want us to separate—so she can get the man." Ama Nana prayed to protect her husband from witches in the family, but, she said, he often curtailed her prayers: "If at times I'm praying, he will stop me, that I'm disturbing him. So there's no control on him."

Ama Nana also felt that a generational curse was affecting her family, because both her husband's father and his senior brother were sleeping with multiple women. "It's like a curse or something," she said. "That's why I always pray. I don't want it to come to my children. The eldest one is not attending church, because when I started born-again, my husband told me that I should not bring his children. So four years now this boy has not been attending church. Now he's doing what the father is doing. So I believe this thing is coming from the family."

Once she was divorced, Ama Nana did not intend to marry again. She said:

At first, I [will] think a lot. I can sit down from morning to evening without stop. I mean, even my hair started removing one by one. But now I think I'm OK. Reading Bible, listening to preaching, I think I'm OK. Because if I said I would think of this man, I would stop church. I have to forget him because of [what] he is doing. If I say I will follow him, we will always fight. So I want to give myself to God. I have to put all my mind in Christ, because now I have my children. If I say I will not marry again, I will be OK. So I have to give myself to God and worship him.

DISCUSSION

What do these narratives tell us about women, power, and agency in charismatic Christianity in Ghana? First, they reveal a shared experience of the conjugal relationship. Alice's, Becky's, and Ama Nana's marriages and domestic relationships have been characterized by abuse, violence, extramarital sex, financial dependence, insecurity, and marital instability. Alice and Ama Nana in particular spoke of their husbands as "womanizers" and highlighted the propensity of their husbands to sleep with other women as an overriding concern. Alice went as far as to characterize the majority of men—born-again, as well as non-born-again—as untrustworthy and womanizing:

> Of these men I'm tired. Today this man will tell you [that] if he doesn't see you, he can't sleep. Tomorrow that same man will tell you [that] you are disturbing him, so get out of his room and let him be. As I sit here, I know about four pastors who say they love me. So if he is a pastor, as he stands on the pulpit, and I know he's told me that he loves me, what do you think would be my impression about him? And being pastors, they can't marry two [women]. So if they are married and they are telling me I'm lovely, I am beautiful, ... what do you think it is they want from me? It is sex. When you sit down with ten women—married women—for nine of them, their problem will be men womanizing.

Second, the three narratives share an explanation for the state of gendered relationships. In each case, forces from within the spirit world were found to be wielding influence on the behavior of those in the material world. In Alice's case, a family curse was thought to be the reason that the women in her family had children with multiple partners. For Becky, it was through her mother-in-law's witchcraft that her husband had been married in the spirit world. The behavior of Ama Nana's husband also was thought to be caused by her mother-in-law's witchcraft, but an additional generational curse was believed to be afflicting both her husband and her husband's eldest sons. Participation in a charismatic ministry and being born again had revealed these forces, thereby providing an explanation for the gendered experiences of Alice, Becky, and Ama Nana.

Third, the narratives illustrate the ways in which born-again women harness the power of charismatic practices to exert control over the spiritual forces that are perceived to be shaping their gendered relationships. For the most part, Alice, Becky, and Ama Nana appealed to the power of prayer, but specific deliverance sessions were also employed to free them from family curses and witchcraft. In Alice's account of her dream, it was the prophetic power of Christie Doe Tetteh herself that changed the trajectory of her domestic relationship. The power of prophets over the conjugal bond could be used in other ways, too. For example, Ama Nana said, "If you go to some churches, they will just put something on salt, and you take the salt and cook for your husband so that your husband will love you more or give you money." And Alice distinguished clearly between the powers of prophets and the power of fetish priests:

> When you read the Bible, the Books of the Prophets, there are certain directions God gave them. When I take your handkerchief and I pray over it, "Lord let your spirit take over this handkerchief," I didn't do anything extraordinary. I prayed in the name of Jesus. Those who go to the fetish priest, they're working in a different way. When you pray, "God let this man, my husband, love me," you will know that when you are around the husband that the love between you is normal. But those with the fetish priest, you go to a woman's house, the man will wash, cook, do all the household chores. Sometimes when you go to those houses, sometimes you wouldn't know the difference between the husband and the maidservant. But if I pray in the name of Jesus that my husband should be understanding to me, my husband will still act like a man. When they are under possession, they don't even know they are men.

Thus, through the pneumatological practices of the charismatic ministries, women assert control over their conjugal relationships while conforming to social expectations of gendered behavior.

However, the stories of Alice, Becky, and Ama Nana also show that women's pneumatological power can sometimes be limited or constrained by their domestic relationships. All three women, at one time or another, had been prevented from attending church by their husbands. Alice's account in particular illustrates how women's access to spiritual power can be constrained by the social expectations of their male partners: when

Alice wanted to pray, her partner's demands for sex or food came first. These narratives thus reveal a complex dialectic between social agency and spiritual power; between the agency of women and the power of spirits; and between women's pneumatological power and the sociocultural structures of gendered relationships.

"POWER" AND "AGENCY": SOME CONCEPTUAL DIFFICULTIES

Ghanaian charismatic Christians, like most Ghanaians, inhabit a conceptual world in which the social and the spiritual are inextricably linked. Religion and the supernatural are part of the social fabric of everyday life. How, then, are we to approach the issues of "power" and "agency" in a way that makes sense both to the researcher and to the women researched? How are we to engage with the social implications of charismatic Christianity when, for most of the born-again women I spoke to, it was the quest for spiritual power that shaped their religious choices. For them, the appeal of the new churches lay not in their social teaching but in their ability to use the power of the spirit world to explain, predict, and sometimes control their gendered relationships (Soothill 2007: 12). When asked whether it was the churches' attitude toward the empowerment of women and the acceptance of female leaders that had attracted them to the charismatic movement, most of them simply said no. The attraction, according to a small selection of my female informants, was the power of charismatic prayer:

> What attracted me to the charismatic church is the way they pray. They are very aggressive in prayer. They pray with force; they pray with vibrancy, OK? And they demand what they want and then take it by force. (Student, Action Chapel, 2003)

> In other churches—the Presbyterian and this—they don't pray a lot. But in this church, we pray. We pray a lot, [which makes me feel] strong [and] happy. (Market seller, Alive Chapel, 2003)

> When you pray, you feel release. You will not feel heaviness, but if you don't pray, always you feel heaviness in you. Or fear. But orthodox churches, some of them don't have [the] Holy Ghost to lead them, so they pray amiss. (Food seller, Action Chapel, 2003)

If she is empowered by the Holy Spirit, it is much more better. When the woman is being empowered, he gives her both spiritual and physical resource. That is the way we look at empowerment. (Participant at "Daughters of Destiny" women's convention, 2003)

These comments are reflected in the analyses by Kalu and Asamoah-Gyadu, both of whom emphasize the relevance of spiritual power to understanding the religious experience of Africa's charismatic Christians, especially women. Echoing Allan Anderson's (1991) description of "enabling power," Asamoah-Gyadu writes about "the pneumatological empowerment of the believer," which can transform the individual, and he dismisses any analysis that ignores the spiritual dimension of the charismatic movement as "reductionist" (Asamoah-Gyadu 2005: 139, 141). Similarly, Kalu (2008: 164–65) urges analysts of the new churches to pay more attention to the ability of the Holy Spirit to "empower" female believers and calls on female African theologians, in particular, to explore "the power of prayer" as "a tool for hope" for African women. In stark contrast, Mercy Amba Oduyoye, the most prominent of Africa's female theologians and a Ghanaian, has been deeply critical of the charismatic movement. In an interview in 2003, she told me that the charismatic churches "have created a need that they are now fulfilling. They've created the need to get rid of demons and witches and so on, and now they are delivering people from them. Everything has to be demons and witches. So they all flock to these churches who have declared that we can help you deal with them." She accuses the charismatic churches of reaffirming the activities of the spirit realm while ignoring (or reinforcing) the social and cultural structures that limit the life choices of most African women (Oduyoye 1998; see also Pemberton 2003: 85). When Oduyoye articulates the empowering role of religion in women's lives, she speaks of its theological and institutional capacity to challenge and reconstruct Africa's political, economic, and social worlds. When Kalu (2008: 163) writes about the empowering role of charismatic Christianity, he highlights the "potency of feminine spirituality" and the ability of women to access power through the exercise of spiritual gifts.

Both of these positions, it seems to me, present real difficulties. To dismiss the spiritual dimension of Africa's social and political worlds, as Oduyoye does, is to ignore the actual constraints that many born-again women feel in their own lives. After all, it is often spiritual constraints that lie behind women's involvement in the charismatic movement. But conflating pneumatological power with social power, as Kalu and Asamoah-Gyadu seem to do, is equally problematic. While women in the charismatic movement may exercise spiritual "agency," they do so within a set of institutional and discursive structures that limit and constrain their actions. As spirit-filled individuals, they exist always in relation to a complex set of social structures and constraints that shape, and sometimes limit, their actions and experiences (Soothill 2007: 29).

I find Dorothy Hodgson's work on female Catholic converts among the Maasai to be of some benefit here. She questions how, as researchers, we are to assess the relative significance of one domain of power over another. The problem, she writes, is "how to reconcile the moral world with the material one, how to incorporate and analyze spiritual forms of power with political and economic ones, and how to understand the relationship of spirituality to the production, reproduction, and transformation of gender relations" (Hodgson 2005: x). A possible solution, she concludes, is "careful, empirical studies that probe and problematize" the possibilities of spirituality without universalizing a female religious essence (Hodgson 2005: 258). This is the challenge for current research on gender and agency in Pentecostal and charismatic Christianity, not just in Ghana, but across the global South: to examine the ways in which different categories of experience—the social and the spiritual—interact, and to explore in more depth what their interaction may tell us about the social and cultural significance of changing patterns of female religiosity.

NOTES

Permission to draw on previously published material has been graciously granted by Brill and Edinburgh University Press. See my *Gender, Social Change and Spiritual Power: Charismatic Christianity in Ghana* (Leiden: Brill, 2007) and "The Problem with 'Women's Empowerment': Female Religiosity in Ghana's Charismatic Churches," *Studies in World Christianity* 16, no. 1 (March 2010): 82–99.

1   Since its launch during the United Nations Decade for Women (1975–85), the WID agenda has been broadly criticized for limiting the scope of women's involvement in post–Cold War African politics to healthcare and social welfare projects. Amina Mama (1996) has argued that the WID agenda has allowed itself

to be co-opted and manipulated by national governments that have little interest in reforming gender politics.

2. The incorporation of the gender development discourse into Ghanaian national politics has allowed successive governments to contain the issue of gender reform within the non-governmental sector:, which has left assumptions about the natural roles of women unchallenged: "Women numerically dominating the NGO sector fits squarely with the notion of the apolitical woman interested more in the domesticity of the private sphere, and uncomfortable and unefficacious in the highly politicized environment of the public sphere" (Aubrey 2001: 94).

3. "Marriage 101," pt. 5. A series of taped sermons purchased in 2003 from a back street bookshop in Accra by the author. In author's possession.

4. Wolfe (2004: 133) summarizes the distance of current trends within North American evangelicalism from earlier Pentecostal forms: "A religious movement that once preached abstinence and restraint, now conducts classes in the best way to achieve orgasm."

5. Anna Adams (2002: 103) does note the important role of *la pastura* (the pastor's wife) among Catholic converts to Pentecostalism in Latino communities in the United States.

6. That is, until her divorce from Nicholas Duncan-Williams in 2006.

7. These female dynasties can become sites of contestation. At the "Women of Worth" convention, Francisca Duncan-Williams took credit for the success of Rita Korankye-Ankrah ("After I spoke over her, she started to travel"). However, a few months later, at Solid Rock's "The Real Woman" convention in August 2003, a similar claim was made by Christie Doe Tetteh: "When she saw me in Nigeria, she said: 'One day I want to be like this woman.' Look at her now, traveling all over the waters."

8. Brigid Sackey (2006: 171) hints that the formation of the Pastors' Wives and Women in Ministry Association may have represented an attempt by Francisca to create a role for herself outside Christian Action Faith Ministries. Nicholas and Francisca Duncan-Williams were married but separated during my fieldwork. Nicholas founded the international charismatic ministry Christian Action Faith Ministries, which has branches in Ghana, the UK, and the United States. Action Chapel is the ministry's headquarters in Accra. The Pastors' Wives and Women in Ministry Association was started by Francisca and based at Action Chapel. However, it incorporated wives and women pastors from across the charismatic community in Accra.

9. Kalu (2008: 152) suggests that Solid Rock Chapel attracts about two thousand people to its regular services, though in my experience the number was much smaller, perhaps three hundred to five hundred people, and far fewer at weekday services.

10. Christie Doe Tetteh did occasionally refer to herself as a vessel of the Holy Spirit and a simple instrument of God, but this was largely a rhetorical device.

11 The "democratisation of charisma" may not be quite as gender-neutral as Asamoah-Gyadu (2005: 131) implies, however, and neither are the gifts of the spirit necessarily free from "dynastic succession," as he also argues. It is difficult, for example, to separate the success of Doe Tetteh within the charismatic movement in Ghana from her connection with the founder of the movement in West Africa, Benson Idahosa. She attended his Bible school in Nigeria and served as his personal secretary throughout the 1980s. In her preaching, Doe Tetteh made frequent references to her connection with the Idahosa "lineage," through which, according to her head pastor, she enjoys "supernatural favor." She also emphasized repeatedly her close relationship with a number of prominent charismatic men in the international movement, including Matthew Ashimolowo and Morris Cerullo, in order, it seemed, to confirm her authority within what remains an essentially male dynasty.

12 Elsewhere I have written in some detail about the changing nature of gendered relationships in Ghanaian society from the early colonial period through the present day, including the shift away from kin relationships toward the conjugal bond with increased urbanization; the impact of economic collapse on urban relationships; and, especially, women's growing financial dependence on conjugal relationships that are increasingly unstable (Soothill 2007: 91–93).

BLESS US WITH CHILDREN — 8

Pregnancy, Prosperity, and Pragmatism in Nigeria's Christ Apostolic Church

LAURA PREMACK

Scholars of Pentecostalism are accustomed to considering the promise of prosperity one of the religion's main attractions. But just what is prosperity? In southwestern Nigeria, where Yoruba culture dominates, there is a proverb that says, "The person who has children has prospered." Another proverb asks, "What can one use one's money to buy that would be more precious than children?" Here, prosperity has as much to do with fertility as it does with finances.

This is true because one of the most important values in traditional Yoruba culture is *alafia*. Narrowly defined, "alafia" means peace. More broadly understood, "alafia" encompasses health, success, and prosperity—wealth not only in material goods, but also wealth in people. Typical Yoruba prayers from the nineteenth century, for instance, were for "peace, health, and children," often expressed as requests to "lengthen our lives, bless us with money and children, and deliver us from danger" (Peel 2000: 91). Having children has always been central to the pursuit of alafia.

Children are valuable. Furthermore, *not* having children can be costly. When a childless woman dies, she will have no one to give her a proper burial and to annually feast her spirit. She will be more likely to be accused of witchcraft. Her spirit will never have the opportunity to be reborn in one of her descendants. It is not a stretch to say that, not only in Yorubaland but across sub-Saharan Africa, having children is often understood as the very best kind of prosperity.

Nineteenth-century missionaries encountered this, discovering, to their dismay, that the women they ministered to considered having children far more important than achieving eternal life in heaven. As J. D. Y. Peel, a historian of Yoruba religion and culture, has written, "A barren woman could not really enjoy *alafia*, and her desire for children was likely to surpass all other needs" (Peel 2000: 91). Decades later, in the 1950s, Yoruba people continued to view childbearing as a woman's primary task and barrenness as a fate to be avoided at all costs (Peel 2000).

Infertility has persisted as a central concern for Yoruba women up through the present day. In 2010, for example, at an all-night Pentecostal prayer service that drew some 2 million participants to a stadium near Lagos, the line that drew the single greatest response was the pastor's promise that "a river that has dried up will run again."[1] For the hundreds of thousands of women who were at the service to seek spiritual healing of infertility, it seemed he was speaking directly to them.

Religions that address the problem of childlessness have always been well positioned to attract Yoruba women. Those who have become Christians—whether when missionaries first arrived in the mid-nineteenth century; with the explosion of indigenous, prophet-led churches in the 1930s and '40s; or during the Pentecostal boom of the late twentieth century—have, more often than not, been led to the churches' doors by their "pragmatic search for personal *alafia*" (Peel 2000: 227). Millions of them have become Pentecostal. Now Nigeria is one of the most Pentecostal countries in the world.[2]

Nigeria's largest Pentecostal church is the Christ Apostolic Church (CAC).[3] It was founded in the 1930s, and its first, critical decades of growth coincided with the final decades of colonialism. (Nigeria became independent from the United Kingdom in 1960.) This chapter tells the story of how fertility, pregnancy, and childbirth came to be central to the CAC during this (crucial and generally overlooked) period. Because CAC historians have paid extraordinarily little notice to women—most of the church's histories are written by men and about men—this is a story that has not been told.

This chapter argues that by sponsoring maternity centers and midwife training programs in the mid-twentieth century, the CAC pursued a pragmatic strategy that allowed it to attract and maintain female members; to support the autonomy of male leaders; and to lessen the interfering influence of the colonial state. Women who had been tempted to leave the church were convinced to stay when offered the opportunity to receive pre- and postnatal care from trained midwives. Male church leaders who supported initiatives to train and place these new midwives found themselves liberated from pressures put on them by government officials, who had been concerned by the church's commitment to faith healing alone. In other words, women's bodies provided a site where the power of the colonial state in the religious sphere could be negotiated.

WOMEN, HEALING, AND THE ALADURA MOVEMENT

To begin, we need to consider the origins of the Christ Apostolic Church, paying careful attention to the participation of women and the salience of the divine healing message. The CAC emerged from the Aladura (prophet-healing, literally "praying people") movement, launched by the prophet Joseph Babalola in the 1930s. Archival evidence makes it clear that, since its beginnings, the Aladura movement attracted mainly women.

Of the many accounts of the predominance of women, one comes from the assistant district officer for Ilesha, the site of the prophet Babalola's earliest revivals. In a confidential report to his superior in 1930, the officer wrote, "Recently I have been spending much time in road work on the Ijebu-Ijesha road and I have been very struck by the extraordinary numbers of people, mostly women, who are pouring into Ilesha and returning home with bottles of holy water." Many of these women, he reported, were "very aged cripples." When he asked around in Ijebu, he learned that "the men regard the whole thing as a nuisance as it has unsettled their women and they keep running into Ilesha," a distance of about ten miles. Women were coming from other areas, as well; the officer reported, "It is the same on the other roads, and the market is chock-a-block with lorries which have brought passengers in from a distance."[4]

The Resident of Oyo province made a similar report to the secretary of the southern provinces shortly after, stating that "thousands of persons from these Western Provinces and Lagos continue to pour into Ilesha to see [Babalola]," although the men the Resident spoke to were less disparaging. He reported that "the Owa and Chiefs, and in fact everyone to whom I have spoken on this subject, are greatly impressed by the cures

[Babalola] is able to effect." According to the Resident's account, some were so impressed that "they say God has come to Ilesha."⁵

Babalola's cures were the main draw for these crowds of people. As the assistant district officer stated in his report, "He preaches out of the Bible and claims to have the power of faith healing, and it is this which causes his great popularity." When the assistant district officer disguised himself to attend one of Babalola's sessions, which typically began after sundown and lasted until midnight, he "found a crowd of many hundreds of people, including a large contingent of the halt and lame and blind." The highlight of the prayer meeting came when everyone present stood in a half-circle and held their bottles of water above their heads while Babalola, from his position on a raised dais, held out his hands and blessed the water. Afterward, hymns were sung, and "the sick afterward received spiritual attention inside the Church."⁶ Healing was the center point of each meeting.

At this time, Babalola was still associated with the Faith Tabernacle of Philadelphia, and he circulated its pamphlets at his meetings.⁷ (The association with the Faith Tabernacle began in the early 1900s and continued until 1926. After parting ways with the Americans, the Nigerians invited missionaries from the British Apostolic Church to come work with them. This relationship lasted until 1940, when a schism led to the establishment of the entirely Nigerian Christ Apostolic Church.⁸) The most popular of these pamphlets, "Seven Principles of Prayer," taught that the keys to having one's prayers answered are repentance, forgiveness, surrender, belief, obedience, steadfastness, and love. It said that no matter what kind of "victory" one desired—spiritual, physical, or financial—effective prayer was the means to achieve it.⁹ And while the Faith Tabernacle pamphlets emphasized personal prayer, the prayer meetings demonstrated a more typically Yoruba approach, with Babalola serving as the conduit, the power of transformation resting in his hands (see Barber 1981). The people came; he blessed the water; they drank it; and, ostensibly, they were cured. Indeed, according to Peel (1968: 127–28), "The main occasion for the emergence of the Aladura churches [was] to cure people of sickness."

Of what were they cured? Everything. One denominational history of Babalola includes this remarkable list:

Some of the miracles witnessed at Ilesa include among others—safe delivery for women with prolonged pregnancies, instant healing for stomach aches, headaches, sicknesses and diseases, leprosy, goiter, gonorrhea, barreness [sic], issue of blood, ulcer, rheumatism, groin fungal infection, early morning weakness, malignancy, hernia, conjuctivitis [sic], backaches, pile, multifarious infant diseases (most of which cannot be named), sleeplessness, joblessness, poverty, hypolasia [sic] of the breast, impotence, lose [sic] of appetite, epilepsy, weariness, blindness, seizure of menstruation in women and a host of other numberless diseases which cannot be named here and for which there were no names: the raising of the dead, deliverance from familiar spirit, etc. (Ojo 1988: 69–70)

The catch was that women and men who sought Apostolic faith healing were forbidden from seeking healing elsewhere.

As the church historians Olubunmi and Abiodun Adeloye (2001: 52) explain, in the CAC, as in the Faith Tabernacle, the use of medicine was seen as showing a lack of faith in God: "The emphasis on divine healing [therefore] is a practical application of the belief that God is to be trusted in all things rather than man." This was the primary message of Babalola and the other Aladura prophets. It was also the main purpose of the original British Apostolic Church missionaries, who, when they arrived, had informed the Ibadan police that "they had been sent to Nigeria to co-ordinate the various faith healing movements."[10] When the elders of Christ Church, the Church Mission Society (CMS) church in Ekiti, wrote to the district officer expressing their concerns about the Aladuras, one of their main points of complaint was that "they refuse people from going to any doctor for treatment, and [make] them rely on water only, by that people die of slight sickness which the Doctors can cure in a moment."[11] Archdeacon Henry Dallimore echoed this concern in his own letter, stating that five Aladura followers died in a single day because "they were not allowed to take any medicine whatever, but only to drink water." He noted not only that Western medicine was prohibited, but also that "their own simple medicine," which probably "would have saved their lives," was forbidden, as well.[12] What did this mean specifically for women? It meant that women who chose to join the CAC relinquished the options of visiting shrines, consulting herbalists, seeing medical doctors, and taking medicine of any kind to get pregnant and carry pregnancies to term.

There is evidence that Babalola and other Aladura prophets addressed concerns about pregnancy and childbirth directly from the very beginning. For example, J. O. Ositelu, one of Babalola's contemporaries who went on to found the Church of Our Lord (Aladura), made prophecies in the early 1930s concerning pregnancy. One prophecy addressed the Yoruba belief that it is possible for witches and wizards to lock pregnancies inside wombs: "People who have been carrying long term pregnancies shall be freed from the bondage they have been put in by the wicked people of the world."[13] Babalola also recalled treating pregnant women. Early in his ministry, even before he became associated with the CAC, he healed a woman who had been pregnant for more than four years by giving her water to drink. Although he does not say so directly, he must have healed her, as the next day she returned with all of her relatives, "shouting for joy," until a group of two thousand had assembled and listened to Babalola "preach holiness and divine healing," as the voice of his visions directed him to do. Shortly after, he healed another pregnant woman, who was about to give birth and "in great agony," simply by placing his hands on her head.[14] Part of Babalola's success in gaining followers and growing the church was due to his ability to heal pregnant women and help deliver babies. Ministering to pregnant women was part of the Aladura mission from the beginning, which makes sense, given that most Nigerian health and healing initiatives at this time were aimed at helping women have babies; it was a major concern.

A decade later, after Babalola's revivals had been institutionalized into the CAC, healing still stood at the center of church activities. Of all of the Aladura churches, the CAC in particular "lay great emphasis on [its] belief in the power of prayer to cure all sickness"—so much so that its official doctrine forbade all cures other than prayer and *omi iye* (water of life). This was the original instruction given to the prophet Joseph Babalola in his first vision, when he was told to take a bell and preach that water will cure all illnesses, and all native medicines (e.g., herbs) should be destroyed. Other Aladura churches had adopted a more liberal attitude toward this instruction by the 1960s, but the CAC continued to hold complete reliance on divine healing as "its most treasured belief" (Peel 1968: 128).

As the movement matured, the CAC continued to attract more women than men. In his delightful memoir of his childhood in the 1940s, the neurosurgeon Adelola Adeloye offers a few reasons that women were drawn to the Aladura movement. He says that in his home village, Ikole, the former seat of the Ekiti North Division, women were attracted to the churches because they were tired of going to staid churches where they were forbidden to dance and because they liked Brother Sowedo, the tall, elegant, approachable, and unmarried pastor of Ikole's Christ Apostolic Church (Adeloye 2009: 109).[15] Sowedo had met the prophet Babalola in Oshogbo during World War II, decided to become a CAC minister, and found immediate success when he returned home to start a church. As Adeloye recalls, "He gave his audience the impression that through him and by attendance in his makeshift place of worship, . . . he could, and would solve all problems." In particular, he gave women this impression. In Adeloye's memory, "like a magnet," Brother Sowedo "attracted women in their hundreds to his new creed" (Adeloye 2009: 110).

Blessed water was still central to the CAC's practices. Adeloye's own mother was one of the women who attended Sowedo's church, and Adeloye has memories of how he, as a ten-year-old boy in 1946, used to go with her to "sing lustily and dance vigorously." They would bring home water blessed by Sowedo. His mother used to make him fast on Saturdays, a new practice that she said would cleanse his soul. His grandmother did not attend the church and did not fast, but she did not mind the practice as long as her grandson broke his fast with the food she prepared. He always did so, washing it down with Brother Sowedo's water (Adeloye 2009: 100).[16]

ESTABLISHING THE CAC MATERNITY CENTER

Since 1939, the Christ Apostolic Church had provided women with an alternative to shrines, hospitals, and traditional healers by offering pregnant women care throughout the course of their pregnancies by *iya aladura* (prayer women) who helped them by overseeing their hygiene, meals, exercise, and prayers (Alokan 1991: 220). The first training center for these women was established in Ede in 1944 (Crumbley 2008b: 38).[17] However, as the government began to take a greater interest in public health and medical services in southwestern Nigeria after World War II,[18] these prayer women turned out not to be enough. There were two main problems. One was that women were leaving the CAC to seek other medical options. By the early 1960s, there was a long-standing discussion in the CAC about the problem of the "temptations" faced by "our pregnant women" to follow advice to see medical doctors for biweekly checkups at hospitals and clinics throughout the course of their pregnancies.[19] This was strictly forbidden by the church's divine healing doctrine, which prohibited any treatment other than prayer. The other problem was that government officials began to interfere with the CAC's religio-medical practices in the interest of protecting public health. The CAC dealt with these increasing postwar pressures by establishing its first maternity center at Ede in Oyo State in 1959 (Alokan 1991: 220).

Adeware Alokan, a retired educator who held several positions in the CAC's national leadership, wrote briefly about the center in his denominational history. After the center was founded, it became a hub of revival and evangelism where barren women became pregnant; cursed women gave birth safely; half-human and half-animal babies were born without surgery; long overdue women were finally delivered; and women who continually miscarried were healed (Alokan 1991: 222–23). Another center was built in Olugbode, Ibadan, in 1963, and specific examples of its work were given in a 1964 issue of the *Onward Christian*, a CAC magazine. One success reported was the case of Mrs. Maria Babalola from Ilesha, who, swollen "from head to toe," admitted that she would rather die than give birth. After praying for many hours, however, she gave birth to a set of twins and lived. Another was Mrs. Limota Lasupo of Oke-Foko, Ibadan, who was taken to the maternity center after having visited most of the hospitals in Ibadan, where she had been X-rayed and told "they could only see something like a stone and not a babe in her womb." But "through relentless prayers for her," the article reported, "God again ascertained His supremacy over the doctors of the world and she gave birth to a Fairy, which died immediately," though the mother lived. A third, Mrs. Abigail Adejumo of Olugbode, Ibadan, gave birth to a dead child, who after three days of prayer returned to life. Another woman, Mrs. Florence Adeleye of Alaho, Ibadan, gave birth to a baby with six arms. The child died, but the mother lived. "If the woman were with [a] native doctor," the article warned, "she would have been asked to bring what might have caused her poverty, for the doctor would insist that sacrifices must be made [of animals the woman would have had to purchase]." But she did not have to pay a kobo for the care she received, as "all healings are freely given in CAC."[20]

As word of these healings spread, people began going to the maternity center for help with others kinds of problems. It became the site of a monthly revival called Olorun Gbogbonse, which means "The Lord is all problem-solving" (Alokan 1991: 223).[21] In other words, the CAC's reported success at healing fertility-related problems led other women and men to seek out its prayer-based solutions, as well. The maternity center became instrumental in spreading the CAC's divine healing mission and growing the church. In Alokan's assessment, "The importance of the establishment of maternity centre[s] in C.A.C. throughout Nigeria cannot be overemphasized." While he devotes only a few pages of his book to them, he argues that it is this system of centers and midwives that "has successfully sustained one of the pillars on which the C.A.C. is built—Divine Healing" (Alokan 1991: 224). It was the maternity center's success that led the church leaders to decide to start sponsoring women to attend midwife-training courses, aiming to expand its healing ministry.[22] The response to this project was slow at first because it required each CAC district to budget money for it—much of it raised by female church members (Crumbley 2008b)—but as the first midwives completed their training and opened centers, and as villagers began to see how valuable having a trained midwife in the community could be, a "healthy rivalry among districts, towns and villages" soon developed, and the number of trained CAC midwives continued to rise (Alokan 1991: 224).

There is an interesting irony in the CAC's decision to found a maternity center to keep women in the church. During the height of the Aladura revivals, Henry Dallimore, the CMS archdeacon who served in Ekiti district from 1929 until 1947, had done the same thing: he established a hospital in Ado-Ekiti to stem the flow of women leaving the CMS for the Aladuras. It was a personal project; he and his wife raised the money themselves. We know this because Oba Aladesanmi II of Ado-Ekiti explained it in the speech he gave at Dallimore's burial ceremony. Speaking directly to the deceased, the oba recalled, "After the [march] of the Aladura healing parade in 1929, when Joseph Babalola claimed that God could cure sickness through him, this claim, coupled with the sight of the sick flocking to Joseph Babalola for cure, led you, Dallimore, and your wife to attempt medical work in Ekiti in sheer sympathy for the people, realising that people needed bodily healing as well as spiritual healing you latter [sic] solicited for money in England and you founded 'Our Saviour's Hospital' in Ado-Ekiti."[23] The hospital opened in 1937 and is now known as the Ile-Abiye Maternity Hospital. Brigadier R. A. Adebayo, the military governor who spoke at the ceremony, selected the establishment of this hospital as Dallimore's single most important achievement. He cited the center, "which is today thriving and has received national acclaim for its work among our pregnant women and sick people," as the model for "the maternity centres which are now built in every town and village."[24] Dallimore established the center as a response to Babalola's revivals; later, the CAC, which grew out of those same revivals, established its own health clinic focused on serving the needs of pregnant women for the very same reason: to stem the flow of women from the church.

Opening the maternity center and training midwives was not just a response to women's health needs. It was also a means of responding to government officials' concerns. As the CAC expanded, it lost the protection that had been afforded by its affiliations with foreign missionaries, and as interest in public health increased, the care offered by the prayer women was not enough to satisfy local authorities. Thus, the decision to invest in maternal and child health was in large part a response to tension between the CAC and the colonial government. It was, in Alokan's words, a response to "unyielding persecutions from the detractors of the church" (Alokan 1991: 220), who most likely consisted of an assortment of mainline Protestant and Apostolic church leaders and missionaries and their native and colonial government allies.[25]

Thus, the founding of the first maternity center in 1959 was a solution to two problems at once: the problem of women leaving for other medical options, as discussed earlier, and the ongoing institutional problems of government persecution. In other words, the CAC leaders decided to found a maternity center and fund midwife training in large part to get the government off their backs. As their network of midwives expanded, according to Alokan, the "harrowing experiences of government officials threatening the Church [was] reduced to the barest minimum" (Alokan 1991: 224).[26] Indeed, these women's health initiatives may have been *the* central ingredient in freeing the CAC from governmental interference. The initiatives allowed the CAC to continue to compete, on its own terms, in an increasingly crowded religio-medical marketplace—one centered on maternal health—in which "apostolic faith healers" were a viable alternative to traditional healers and government and missionary hospitals and clinics. Women's health issues were at the very center of the CAC's growth from its beginnings, when women flocked to Babalola's revivals in the 1930s, into the 1940s and 1950s and beyond.

AGENCY AND PRAGMATISM

There is a tension between the way Pentecostals—men and women—have both embraced and relinquished agency in the practice of their faith. The choice to become Pentecostal is an embrace of the agency afforded by a direct, unmediated relationship with God. The Holy Spirit provides a direct connection to the divine; there is no need for gatekeepers or intermediaries. Choosing Pentecostal practices, such as praying for healing, can be seen as a real rejection of the clientelist ethos of Yoruba culture and the intercessory nature of traditional African religions: it becomes possible for ordinary people to circumvent the so-called big men and their networks and get what they want by going directly to the biggest man of all.

Yet at the same time, the choice to practice Pentecostalism is also a relinquishing of agency. All of the power to make change happen is in the hands of God. There are now Pentecostal tracts that encourage students to pray rather than study to attain academic success (see, e.g., Madueke 2017). By putting their achievement in the hands of God, they accept that they can only do so much alone, recognizing and even celebrating just how limited their own agency is and just how powerful is God's. Another example of this way of thinking is exemplified by the name of the Ibadan-based God-Will-Do-It Ministries. The belief that "God is going to solve your problems for you," as one Nigerian business leader put it, is widespread.[27]

In the era examined in this chapter, one can argue that agency was at play in two different ways. The first way is the most obvious one: the decisions made by the women who chose the CAC maternity centers over other options for dealing with fertility-related concerns. Instead of *babalawos* (traditional priests), shrines, or medical clinics, some women chose CAC midwives and prayer. However, some of these women may have been pressured—by their families or by their financial situations—to "choose" the CAC option. In circumstances where lack of access to healthcare is more common than not, people work with what is available to them. Thus, even though an argument for the agency of the women who chose CAC care for their pregnancies is tempting, it is not entirely convincing.

More persuasive is the argument to be made for the agency male leaders (they were—and still are—all male) achieved by establishing maternity centers and training midwives. By building these centers, CAC leaders aimed to prevent pregnant women from leaving, to attract new pregnant women to their congregations, and to entice both men and women to their maternity center-based monthly revivals. In other words, the decision to invest in establishing and staffing places for women to bear children was a decision to invest in a strategy to grow church membership. This is not a surprising decision; establishing medical clinics and schools is a long-standing missionary strategy. What is more interesting is the way that investing in these centers served as a strategy to gain a measure of freedom from government interference, as discussed in the previous section.

Yet given that both the men and the women described in this chapter were reacting to certain pressures—whether from their families, their finances, or the state—is agency really the best interpretive framework for considering the development of the CAC maternity centers? On the one hand, yes. Such a zero-sum understanding of agency is faithful to Pentecostal understandings of how power works. Individuals have the power to manage their human affairs and to choose to put their faith in the Father, the Son, and, especially, the Holy Spirit; only God has the ultimate power to heal, provide, and protect. Power, at every level, has a sovereign source. This understanding of agency aligns with the colonial and postcolonial circumstances of the early Pentecostals discussed here.

On the other hand, agency may not be the best lens for evaluating the significance of the CAC maternity centers for the development of Nigerian Pentecostalism. In recent years, historians and other scholars have rightfully questioned just how useful agency is as a category of analysis (see, e.g., Johnson 2003). The zero-sum model of thinking about power tends to obscure the more complex dynamism of "relative agency." It also discourages thinking about power as an operational force. The presumption that real agency is found only when an agent is able to choose without any outside pressure fails to reckon with Foucauldian notions of power as something that is circulated rather than possessed.

While the concept of agency has helped us understand the particulars of the development of the CAC maternity centers, at this point it may be more helpful to return to the pragmatic considerations that were introduced in this chapter's opening discussion of alafia, the Yoruba concept of peace as health, wealth, and children. Pragmatism considers how power is *used*. It focuses on collaborations and compromises. It rests not on a model of one sovereign individual making her own decisions but, rather, on the model of many interdependent individuals operating in relationship with one another. Pragmatists may be guided by ideology, but they are rarely limited by it. Above all else, they are interested in what works.

In what ways are Pentecostalism, pragmatism, and alafia linked? A quick detour to the present day helps us begin to answer this question. Consider the predicament of Chinasa Ugoala, author of the memoir and inspirational tract *Overcoming This Monster Called Fibroid: Let God Sort It Out* (2008). The book describes the Pentecostal Ugoala's experience with uterine fibroids, a common and dangerous condition among Nigerian women that can cause infertility. Ugoala's predicament was to decide whether to rely on God to heal her, as her faith taught, or seek medical intervention. She faced the dilemma of deciding, to quote from her pastor's foreword to the book, "What should a good Christian do when confronted with sickness?" Should she "go to a doctor or call for prayers?" And "if prayers fail, does it mean God has not answered?" (Ugoala 2008: 8).

Ugoala ultimately decided to do both: to pray *and* to have surgery. And she found a way to think about it that let her reconcile her belief in divine healing with her decision to seek medical care. Both were central to her pursuit of alafia. Her pastor encouraged this reconciliation, advising her that a successful operation "would translate to a miracle from God" (Ugoala 2008: 38). She had wanted a healing without surgery, but instead, "He had it His own way, still to His glory" (Ugoala 2008: 70). In other words, the way that God wanted her to be healed was through surgery.

Ugoala also conceived of divine healing not as a gift—which how it is typically categorized, as one of the *charismata*—but as a right. "Like a creditor," Ugoala recalls, "I reminded God of the debt of restoration of my health and the healing of the wounds He owed me." She made demands of God using the language of rights: "I meant to let my Maker realize I did know my right, as a daughter, not a bondwoman" (Ugoala 2008: 56).

In Ugoala's insistence that she receive the healing that was rightfully hers as a born-again Christian, we see that she viewed healing as a matter of will. God may have held the power to heal, but she held the power to demand that healing. Ugoala's advice to readers of her evangelistic memoir thus is never to take no for an answer. "I have strongly considered God's willingness to give you a miracle and it is unequivocally clear that His willingness is guaranteed," she promises (Ugoala 2008: 44). "Nevertheless, your will is also of great importance" (Ugoala 2008: 98). Healing is a right that one has to claim.

CONCLUSION

The desire to have children has attracted women to native priests and foreign missionaries, to prophet healers and Pentecostal churches, to medicine men and medical doctors. They have sought help from whatever sources might work—traditional, medical, "magical," Christian, or some alchemic mix of them all. In the mid-twentieth century, the story of these women found a parallel in the story of Yoruba men challenging the colonial hierarchy and growing their own religious and political institutions. Focusing on fertility illuminates the direction and development of the earliest Pentecostal churches in Nigeria by showing how concerns about childbearing were central to the growth of the most significant of these churches, motivating membership and shaping governance.

A focus on fertility also illuminates one of Africanist scholars' favorite debates: the periodization question. Briefly put, African historians typically presume three periods: precolonial, colonial, and postcolonial. Revisionist historians have questioned whether these changes in political organization actually had such long-standing influence and have concluded that colonialism was not a point of rupture but, rather, simply an interruption: the "colonial parentheses" is one way to describe it (Cooper 2002: 15). This chapter's investigation into fertility supports the revisionist conclusion. In broad terms, conventional wisdom holds that while maternity and reproduction were central to politics in precolonial Africa, colonization achieved the separation of government and reproduction. The conclusions presented here, however, show that politics and childbearing remained intertwined during the colonial period. Having children mattered to Yoruba women before, during, and after colonialism. The most successful institutions responded to that concern.

Indeed, this kind of pragmatism is nearly axiomatic of many African traditional religions. A religion is worthwhile only if it provides material results: health, money, children. These material concerns are what drew all of those women with their bottles and buckets of water to the prophet Babalola's revivals in the 1930s. It is what convinced many of them to join the Christ Apostolic Church in the 1940s, '50s, and '60s. And, extending far beyond the loose borders of Yorubaland, it was one of the motivating factors of Nigeria's incredible Pentecostal boom in the last decades of the twentieth century.

Gazing across the Atlantic, we can see a similar dynamic: religious affiliation not as static and fixed but as shifting and fluid; religious practices providing options to fill each individual's spiritual toolbox; the pragmatism of the "whatever works" approach; the privileging of phenomenology over theology. This could very well be a result of the influence of African spiritual thinking on diasporic cosmologies. Although this chapter has looked specifically at Nigeria, given the influence of Yoruba culture on the Americas (especially those parts, like Brazil, that continued to import enslaved Africans though the nineteenth century, when the bulk of the trade was with communities on the coast of what is now Nigeria), the discussion may have broader interpretive significance. It is common to think of contemporary Pentecostalism in the global South as evidence of a rupture with "traditional" and "local" religions, but there are just as many continuities as changes. For various reasons responding to various pressures, seeking recourse to various tools and resources, women and men have turned to Pentecostalism as a matter of pragmatism. They continue to seek to improve their health, their well-being, and the material conditions of their lives. They continue to seek alafia.

NOTES

This chapter was researched and written with support from the Andrew W. Mellon Foundation, the Gerda Henkel Foundation, the US Department of

Education, and the Graduate School of the University of North Carolina, Chapel Hill. I am grateful to the late Dorcas Akintunde, Randy Browne, Judith Casselberry, Deidre Crumbley, David Gordon, Lisa Lindsay, and Elizabeth Pritchard for their helpful comments and insights, and to Chief (Mrs.) Ade-Ajayi, Chris Bankole, Bolaji Bateye, and David Ogunbile for their many kindnesses during my fieldwork.

1 Pastor E. A. Adeboye, General Overseer, Redeemed Christian Church of God, in a sermon delivered at the Special Holy Ghost Service, Redemption Camp, Lagos-Ibadan Expressway, Nigeria, March 5, 2010.
2 Nigeria, the most populous country in Africa, also has the largest Christian population in Africa, estimated at more than 80 million people. Nearly 60 million of these Christians are Protestants, broadly defined (see Pew Research Center Forum on Religion and Public Life 2011). The vast majority of Protestant churches in Nigeria, even those that are not officially considered Pentecostal, engage in at least some Pentecostal practices, such as praying for divine healing, holding all-night prayer services, receiving prophecies, and exorcising evil spirits. (In Nigeria, as in most of the global South, Pentecostalism is not necessarily characterized by speaking in tongues.)
3 While some scholars insist on marking a separation between Aladura and Pentecostal churches, I see this typological distinction as more political than phenomenological, and I consider the CAC Pentecostal. In this view I am supported by the current leadership of the CAC, who refer to their church in some recent promotional literature, as being "the first Pentecostal church in Africa."
4 Assistant District Officer, Ilesha, to District Officer, Ife, August 13, 1930, "Appendix II: Copies of Archival Material from the Nigerian National Archives, University of Ibadan," in Fatokun 2005: 304.
5 Resident, Oyo Province, to Secretary, Southern Provinces, Enugu, August 25, 1930, "Appendix II," in Fatokun 2005: 307.
6 Assistant District Officer, Ilesha, to District Officer, Ife, August 13, 1930, 304, 306.
7 Assistant District Officer, Ilesha, to District Officer, Ife, August 13, 1930, 304–5.
8 For a more detailed account of this early history, see Premack 2005.
9 Elder J. Wesley Ankins, "Seven Principles of Prevailing Prayer," n.d., Faith Tabernacle Congregations, Philadelphia, in the personal collection of Adam Mohr.
10 Assistant Commissioner of Police, Oyo-Ondo Province, Ibadan, to Resident, Oyo Province, October 29, 1931, "Appendix II," in Fatokun 2005: 315.
11 Christ Church Elders, Efon Alaye, to District Officer, Ekiti Division, April 7, 1931, in "EKITI DIV 1/1," Nigerian National Archives, Ibadan, Nigeria.
12 Henry Dallimore to District Officer, Ekiti, July 10, 1931, in "EKITI DIV 1/1," Nigerian National Archives, Ibadan, Nigeria.
13 J. O. Ositelu, "Awon Asotele," trans. Ayodele Olofintuade, Nigerian Pamphlets, 1867–1964, Collection, African Collection, Yale University Library, New Haven, CT (hereafter, African Collection), reel 14, item 329.

14 *The History and Works of the Prophet Joseph Babalola* (Ibadan: Ilare), 6, 9, in African Collection, reel 10, item 249.
15 Also discussed with Adelola Adeloye, personal conversation, December 31, 2009.
16 Adeloye, personal conversation.
17 Deidre Crumbley has studied the state of these centers in the late twentieth century and early twenty-first century. Her former graduate student Charles Omosehin was engaged in researching the history of these centers when he was killed in a motorcycle accident. Much is still to be learned about the fundraising efforts for and administrative oversight of these centers.
18 University College Hospital in Ibadan was founded in 1952, as were dozens of clinics funded through the Social Welfare Department. While funding was never substantial, there was a significant propaganda effort in many parts of Africa with the purpose of improving maternal health in the years after World War II. On the expansion of government maternity services in the 1950s, see, e.g., Hunt 1999.
19 *Onward Christian*, no. 2, August 1964, in African Collection, reel 7, item 193.
20 All cases from "What a Friend We (C.A.C.) Have in Jesus?" in *Onward Christian*, no. 2, 10. There may have been additional centers at this time; research into the exact numbers, locations, and years of establishment still needs to be done. According to Deidre Crumbley (personal communication, April 22, 2012), there are records of the deliveries overseen at all of the CAC centers going back at least to the 1950s, which are available at the CAC headquarters in Lagos. As my interest in this topic did not emerge until after I completed my fieldwork, I have not yet tracked down and consulted them.
21 Alokan gives no date for when these revivals began.
22 The church's extreme position on medicine did permit learning midwifery skills, as "common-sense treatments" were allowed (see Peel 1968: 133).
23 "Funeral Oration by Oba Aladesanmi II at the Burial Ceremony of Archdeacon Henry Dallimore at Ado-Ekiti on Saturday, 18th July, 1970," personal papers of Adelola Adeloye, Ibadan, Nigeria.
24 "Funeral Oration at the Graveside of the Late Venerable Archdeacon Henry Dallimore as delivered by His Excellency Brigadier R. A. Adebayo, IDC, PSC, the Military Governor of the Western State at Ado-Ekiti on Saturday, 18th July, 1970," personal papers of Adelola Adeloye, Ibadan, Nigeria.
25 Most Apostolic Church missionaries resented the Nigerian Christ Apostolic Church leaders for having broken off and established their own church, taking most of the church buildings and members with them.
26 Though, to be fair, those threatening experiences may have become less harrowing on their own with Nigerian independence in 1960.
27 Christopher Kolade, Chairman, Cadbury Nigeria, quoted in Onayiga 1999: 29.

REFERENCES

ADAMS, ANNA. 2002. "Perception Matters: Pentecostal Latinas in Allentown, Pennsylvania." In *A Reader in Latina Feminist Theology: Religion and Justice*, edited by Maria Pilar Aquino, Daisy L. Machado, and Jeanette Rodriquez, 98–113. Austin: University of Texas Press.

ADELOYE, ADELOLA. 2009. *My Salad Days: The Primary School Years*. Ibadan, Nigeria: BookBuilders.

ADELOYE, OLUBUNMI, and ABIODUN ADELOYE. 2001. *A Treatise of the Early Apostolic Churches in Nigeria*. Ilorin, Nigeria: Corporate Office Max.

ADJABENG, JOSHUA. 1991. *Sex, Friendship and Marriage*. Accra: Pentecost Press.

ALEXANDER, ESTRELDA Y. 2011. *Black Fire: One Hundred Years of African American Pentecostalism*. Downers Grove, IL: InterVarsity.

ALOKAN, ADEWARE. 1991. *The Christ Apostolic Church: CAC 1928–1988*. Lagos: Ibukunola Printers.

ALVES, JAIME. 2012. "Macabre Spatialities: The Politics of Race, Gender and Violence in a Neoliberal City." PhD diss., University of Texas, Austin.

ANDERSON, ALLAN. 1991. "Pentecostal Pneumatology and African Power Concepts: Continuity or Change?" *Missionalia* 1: 65–74.

ANDERSON, ALLAN. 2001. *African Reformation: African Initiated Christianity in the 20th Century*. Trenton: Africa World Press.

ANDERSON, ALLAN. 2004. *An Introduction to Pentecostalism: Global Charismatic Christianity*. Cambridge: Cambridge University Press.

ANDERSON, ALLAN. 2013. *To the Ends of the Earth: Pentecostalism and the Transformation of World Christianity*. Oxford: Oxford University Press.

ANIJAR, KAREN. 1999. "Jewish Genes, Jewish Jeans: A Fashionable Body." In *Religion, Dress, and the Body*, edited by Linda B. Arthur, 181–200. New York: Berg.

APPADURAI, ARJUN, ed. 2001. *Globalization*. Durham, NC: Duke University Press.

ARNFRED, SIGNE. 2011. *Sexuality and Gender Politics in Mozambique: Rethinking Gender in Africa*. Suffolk, UK: James Currey.

ARTHUR, LINDA B. 1999. "Dress and the Social Control of the Body." In *Religion, Dress, and the Body*, edited by Linda B. Arthur, 1–6. New York: Berg.

ASAD, TALAL. 1997. "Remarks on the Anthropology of the Body." In *Religion and the Body*, edited by Sarah Coakley, 42–52. Cambridge: Cambridge University Press.

ASAMOAH-GYADU, J. KWABENA. 2005. *African Charismatics: Current Developments within Independent Indigenous Pentecostalism in Ghana*. Leiden: Brill.

ASAMOAH-GYADU, J. KWABENA. 2013. *Contemporary Pentecostal Christianity: Interpretations from an African Context*. Eugene, OR: Wipf and Stock.

AUBREY, LISA. 2001. "Gender, Development, and Democratization in Africa." *African and Asian Studies* 36, no. 1: 87–105.

AUSTIN-BROOS, DIANE J. 1997. *Jamaica Genesis: Religion and the Politics of Moral Orders*. Chicago: University of Chicago Press.

AUSTIN-BROOS, DIANE J. 2001. "Jamaican Pentecostalism: Transnational Relations and the Nation-State." In *Between Babel and Pentecost: Transnational Pentecostalism in Africa and Latin America*, edited by Andre Corten and Ruth Marshall-Fratani, 142–58. Bloomington: Indiana University Press.

AYMER, PAULA. 1997. *Uprooted Women: Migrant Domestics in the Caribbean*. Santa Barbara: Praeger.

BAILEY, STANLEY. 2009. *Legacies of Race: Identities, Attitudes, and Politics in Brazil*. Stanford, CA: Stanford University Press.

BALDWIN, JAMES. 1989. *Conversations with James Baldwin: 1924–1987*. Edited by Fred L. Standley and Louis H. Pratt. Jackson: University Press of Mississippi.

BALLARD, ALLEN B. 1984. *One More Day's Journey: The Story of a Family and a People*. New York: McGraw-Hill.

BARBER, KARIN. 1981. "How Man Makes God in West Africa: Yoruba Attitudes toward the 'Orisa.'" *Africa* 51: 724–45.

BARROW, CHRISTINE. 2011. "Mating and Sexuality in Carricou: Social Logic and Surplus Women." In *M. G. Smith: Social Theory and Anthropology in the Caribbean and Beyond*, edited by Brian Meeks, 148–64. Kingston, Jamaica: Ian Randle.

BARTON, BRUCE E., general ed. 1989. *Life Application Study Bible*. Wheaton, IL: Tyndale House.

BASTIAN, JEAN-PAUL. 2006. "The New Religious Economy of Latin America." *Social Compass* 53, no. 1: 65–80.

BECKER, DANA. 2005. *The Myth of Empowerment: Women and Therapeutic Culture in America*. New York: New York University Press.

BELL, CATHERINE M. 1992. *Ritual Theory, Ritual Practice*. New York: Oxford University Press.

BERLANT, LAUREN. 1997. *The Queen of America Goes to Washington City: Essays on Sex and Citizenship*. Durham, NC: Duke University Press.

BEST, FELTON O. 1998. "Breaking the Gender Barrier: African-American Women and Leadership in Black Holiness-Pentecostal Churches, 1890–Present." In *Flames of Fire*, edited by Felton O. Best, 153–68. Lewiston, NY: Edwin Mellen.

BEST, WALLACE. 2005. *Passionately Human, No Less Divine: Religion and Culture in Black Chicago, 1915–1952*. Princeton, NJ: Princeton University Press.

BEST, WALLACE. 2006. "The Spirit of the Holy Ghost Is a Male Spirit: African American Preaching Women and the Paradoxes of Gender." In *Women and Religion in the African Diaspora*, edited by R. Marie Griffith and Barbara Dianne Savage, 101–27. Baltimore: Johns Hopkins University Press.

BLACKING, JOHN. 1977. "Toward an Anthropology of the Body." In *The Anthropology of the Body*, edited by John Blacking, 1–28. New York: Academic Press.

BORIS, EILEEN, and RHACEL SALAZAR PARREÑAS, eds. "Introduction." In *Intimate Labors: Cultures, Technologies, and the Politics of Care*. Stanford, CA: Stanford Social Sciences, 2010.

BOYER, HORACE CLARENCE. 1979. "Contemporary Gospel Music." *Black Perspective in Music* 7, no. 1: 5–58.

BRAVO, EVA FERNANDEZ, YVONNE B. DRAKES, and DELORIS SEIVERIGHT. 2001. "Across the Waters: Practitioners Speak." In *Nation Dance*, edited by Patrick Taylor, 17–24. Bloomington: Indiana University Press.

BROUWER, STEVE, PAUL GIFFORD, and SUSAN D. ROSE. 1996. *Exporting the American Gospel: Global Christian Fundamentalism*. London: Routledge.

BROWN, CANDY GUNTHER, ed. 2011. *Global Pentecostal and Charismatic Healing*. New York: Oxford University Press.

BROWN, ELSA BARKLEY. 1994. "Negotiating and Transforming the Public Sphere: African American Political Life in Transition from Slavery to Freedom." *Imprint Public Culture* 7: 107–46.

BROWN, MICHAEL JOSEPH. 2004. "Constructing a Doctrine for the Ecclesia Militans." In *Loving the Body: Black Religious Studies and the Erotic*, edited by Anthony Pinn and Dwight N. Hopkins, 53–72. New York: Palgrave.

BRUSCO, ELIZABETH. 1995. *The Reformation of Machismo: Evangelical Conversion and Gender in Colombia*. Austin: University of Texas Press.

BRUSCO, ELIZABETH. 2010. "Gender and Power." In *Studying Global Pentecostalism: Theories and Methods*, edited by Allan Anderson, Michael Bergunder, Andre F.

Droogers, and Cornelis van der Laan, 74–92. Berkeley: University of California Press.

BULTMANN, RUDOLPH. 2007. *Theology of the New Testament*. Waco, TX: Baylor University Press.

BURDICK, JOHN. 1998. *Blessed Anastácia: Women, Race, and Popular Christianity in Brazil*. New York: Routledge.

BURDICK, JOHN. 1999. "What Is the Color of the Holy Spirit? Pentecostalism and Black Identity in Brazil." *Latin American Research Review* 34, no. 2: 109–31.

BURDICK, JOHN. 2013. *The Color of Sound: Race, Religion and Music in Brazil*. New York: New York University Press.

BUSS, DORIS, and DIDI HERMAN. 2003. *Globalizing Family Values: The Christian Right in International Politics*. Minneapolis: University of Minnesota Press.

BUTLER, ANTHEA D. 2007. *Women in the Church of God in Christ: Making a Sanctified World*. Chapel Hill: University of North Carolina Press.

BUTLER, JUDITH. 2002. "Mbembe's Extravagant Power." *Public Culture* 5, no. 1: 68–71.

BYRD, AYANA, and LORI THARPS. 2002. *Hair Story: Untangling the Roots of Black Hair in America*. New York: St. Martin's Griffin.

CABRITA, JOÃO. 2000. *Mozambique: The Tortuous Road to Democracy*. New York: Palgrave.

CANNON, KATIE G. 2004. "Sexing Black Women." In *Loving the Body: Black Religious Studies and the Erotic*, edited by Anthony Pinn and Dwight N. Hopkins, 11–31. New York: Palgrave.

CARAWAN, GUY, with CANDIE CARAWAN. 1995. "Singing and Shouting in Moving Star Hall." *Black Music Research Journal* 15, no. 1: 17–28.

CARBINE, ROSEMARY P. 2006. "Ekklesial Work: Toward a Feminist Public Theology." *Harvard Theological Review* 99, no. 4: 433–55.

CARBY, HAZEL V. 1992. "Policing the Black Woman's Body in an Urban Context." *Critical Inquiry* 18, no. 4: 738–55.

CARDOSO, CRISTIANE. 2009. *Melhor do que comprar sapatos, várias mensagens*. Rio de Janeiro: Unipro.

CARPENTER, DELORES. 1989–90. "Black Women in Religious Institutions: A Historical Summary from Slavery to the 1960s." *Journal of Religious Thought* 46, no. 2: 7–27.

CARROLL, CHARLES. 1900. *The Negro a Beast, or, In the Image of God*. St. Louis: American Book and Bible House.

CASANOVA, JOSÉ. 1994. *Public Religions in the Modern World*. Chicago: University of Chicago Press.

CASIMIRO, ISABEL. 2004. *"Paz na terra, guerra em casa": Feminismo e organizações de mulheres em Moçambique*. Maputo: Promédia.

CASSELBERRY, JUDITH. 2013. "The Politics of Righteousness: Race and Gender in Apostolic Pentecostalism." *Transforming Anthropology* 21, no. 1: 72–86.

CASSELBERRY, JUDITH. 2017. *The Labor of Faith: Gender and Power in Black Apostolic Pentecostalism*. Durham, NC: Duke University Press.

CAVALLO, GIULIA. 2013. "Curar o passado: Mulheres, espíritos e "caminhos fechados" nas igrejas Zione em Maputo, Moçambique." PhD diss., Lisbon University.

Centre for African Studies, Forum Mulher, and Southern African Research and Documentation Centre-Women In Development Southern Africa Awareness. 2000. *Beyond Inequalities: Women in Mozambique*. Maputo: Centre for African Studies, University Eduardo Mondlane, Forum Mulher and Southern African Research and Documentation Centre–Women In Development Southern Africa Awareness.

CESAR, WALDO. 2001. "From Babel to Pentecost. A Social-Historical-Theological Study of the Growth of Pentecostals." In *Between Babel and Pentecost: Transnational Pentecostalism in Africa and Latin America*, edited by Andre Corten and Ruth Marshall-Fratani, 22–40. Bloomington: Indiana University Press.

CHANG, HAE-KYUNG. 2007. "The Christian Life in a Dialectical Tension? Romans 7:7–25 Reconsidered." *Novum Testamentum* 49, no. 3: 257–80.

CHARLES, CAROLLE. 1995. "Gender and Politics in Contemporary Haiti: The Duvalierist State, Transnationalism, and the Emergence of a New Feminism (1980–1990)." *Feminist Studies* 21, no. 1: 135–64.

CHATTERJEE, PIYA. 2009. "Transforming Pedagogies: Imagining Internationalist/Feminist/Antiracist Literacies." In *Activist Scholarship: Antiracism, Feminism, and Social Change*, edited by Margo Okazawa-Rey and Julia Sudbury, 131–48. Boulder, CO: Paradigm.

CHOSA, JIM, and FAITH CHOSA. 2004. *Thy Kingdom Come Thy Will Be Done in Earth: A First Nation Perspective on Strategic Keys for Territorial Deliverance and Transformation*. Yellowstone, MT: Day Chief Ministries.

Church of God. 1951. *Doctrinal Points of the Church of God (7th Day Apostolic) Reorganized 1933*. Salem, WV: Church of God.

CICALO, ANDRÉ. 2012. *Urban Encounters: Affirmative Action and Black Identities in Brazil*. New York: Palgrave Macmillan.

CLARK, JAMES I., JR. 2001. "The Role of Christian Religious Education in Transforming the African American Apostolic Pentecostal Church's World View and Mission." PhD diss., Teacher's College, Columbia University, New York.

CLARKE, EDITH. 1966. *The Mother Who Fathered Me: A Study of the Family in Three Selected Communities in Jamaica*. London: George Allen and Unwin.

CLARK-LEWIS, ELIZABETH. 1994. *Living In, Living Out: African-American Domestics and the Great Migration*. Washington, DC: Smithsonian Institution.

COLE, JENNIFER. 2010. *Sex and Salvation: Imagining the Future in Madagascar*. Chicago: University of Chicago Press.

COLEMAN, SIMON. 2000. *The Globalisation of Charismatic Christianity: Spreading the Gospel of Prosperity*. Cambridge: Cambridge University Press.

COLLIER-THOMAS, BETTYE. 1998. *Daughters of Thunder: Black Women Preachers and Their Sermons, 1850–1979*. San Francisco: Jossey-Bass.

COLLIER-THOMAS, BETTYE. 2010. *Jesus, Jobs, and Justice: African American Women and Religion*. New York: Alfred A. Knopf.

COLLINS, PATRICIA HILL. 2008. *Black Feminist Thought: Knowledge, Consciousness, and the Politics of Empowerment*. 3rd ed. New York: Routledge.

COMAROFF, JEAN, and JOHN COMAROFF. 1999. "Occult Economies and the Violence of Abstraction: Notes from the South African Postcolony." *American Ethnologist* 26, no. 3: 279–301.

CONE, JAMES. 1972. *The Spirituals and the Blues*. New York: Orbis.

COOPER, FREDERICK. 2002. *Africa since 1940: The Past of the Present*. Cambridge: Cambridge University Press.

COOPER, VALERIE C. 2011. "Laying the Foundations for Azusa: Black Women and Public Ministry in the Nineteenth Century." In *Afro-Pentecostalism: Black Pentecostal and Charismatic Christianity in History and Culture*, edited by Amos Yong and Estrelda Y. Alexander. New York: New York University Press.

COPELAND, M. SHAWN. 2010. *Enfleshing Freedom: Body, Race, and Being*. Minneapolis: Fortress.

CORTEN, ANDRE. 2001. "Transnationalised Religious Needs and Political Delegitimisation in Latin America." In *Between Babel and Pentecost: Transnational Pentecostalism in Africa and Latin America*, edited by Andre Corten and Ruth Marshall-Fratani, 106–23. Bloomington: Indiana University Press.

CORTEN, ANDRÉ, and RUTH MARSHALL-FRATANI. 2001. "Introduction." In *Between Babel and Pentecost: Transnational Pentecostalism in Africa and Latin America*, edited by André Corten and Ruth Marshall-Fratani, 1–21. London: Hurst.

COSTA, ANA BÉNARD. 2007. *O preço da sombra: Sobrevivência e reprodução social entre famílias de Maputo*. Lisbon: Livros Horizonte.

COX, EDWARD L. 1994. "Religious Intolerance and Persecutions: The Shakers of St. Vincent, 1900–1934." *Journal of Caribbean History* 28, no. 2: 208–42.

COX, HARVEY. 1995. *Fire from Heaven: The Rise of Pentecostal Spirituality and the Reshaping of Religion in the Twenty-First Century*. Reading, MA: Addison-Wesley.

CRAIG, MAXINE LEEDS. 2002. *Ain't I a Beauty Queen? Black Women, Beauty, and the Politics of Race*. Oxford: Oxford University Press.

CRENSHAW, KIMBERLÉ W. 1989. "Demarginalizing the Intersection of Race and Sex: A Black Feminist Critique of Antidiscrimination Doctrine, Feminist Theory and Antiracist Politics." *University of Chicago Legal Forum* 140: 139–68.

CRUMBLEY, DEIDRE. 2008a. "From Holy Ground to Virtual Reality: Aladura Gender Practices in Cyberspace—an African Diaspora Perspective." In *Christianity in Africa and the African Diaspora: The Appropriation of a Scattered Heritage*, edited by Afe Adogame, Roswith Gerloff, and Klaus Hock, 126–39. London: Continuum.

CRUMBLEY, DEIDRE. 2008b. *Spirit, Structure, and Flesh: Gendered Experiences in African Instituted Churches among the Yoruba of Nigeria*. Madison: University of Wisconsin Press.

CRUMBLEY, DEIDRE. 2012. *Saved and Sanctified: The Rise of a Storefront Church in Great Migration Philadelphia*. Gainesville: University Press of Florida.

CRUZ E SILVA, TERESA. 2003. "Mozambique." In *Les nouveaux conquérants de la foi: L'Église Universelle du Royaume de Dieu (Brésil)*, edited by André Corten, Jean-Pierre Dozon, and Ari Pedro Oro, 109–17. Paris: Karthala.

CUCCHIARI, SALVATORE. 1990. "Between Shame and Sanctification: Patriarchy and Its Transformation in Sicilian Pentecostalism." *American Ethnologist* 18: 687–707.

CUMBI, ALBERTO. 2009. "Mulheres com formação superior e emprego remunerado: Mulheres emancipadas?" *Outras Vozes* 27 (June): 7–12.

DARKO, EVELYN OBENG. 1999. *Womanhood: Blessing or Curse?* Accra: Journagrafx.

DAVIS, ADRIENNE. 2002. "Don't Let Nobody Bother Yo' Principle: The Sexual Economy of American Slavery." In *Sister Circle: Black Women and Work*, edited by Sharon Harley, 103–27. Piscataway, NJ: Rutgers University Press.

DAVIS, ANGELA Y. 1981. *Women, Race and Class*. New York: Random House.

DAVIS, ANGELA Y. 1998. *Blues Legacies and Black Feminism: Gertrude "Ma" Rainey, Bessie Smith, and Billie Holiday*. New York: Pantheon.

DAYAN, JOAN. 1994. "Erzulie: A Women's History of Haiti." *Research in African Literatures* 25, no. 2: 5–31.

DELEUZE, GILLES, and FÉLIX GUATTARI. 1987. *A Thousand Plateaus: Capitalism and Schizophrenia*. Minneapolis: University of Minnesota Press.

DILL, BONNIE THORNTON. 1994. *Across the Boundaries of Race and Class*. New York: Garland.

DINERMAN, ALICE. 2006. *Revolution, Counter-Revolution and Revisionism in Postcolonial Africa: The Case of Mozambique, 1975–1994*. London: Routledge.

DODSON, JUALYNNE E., and CHERYL TOWNSEND GILKES. 1995. "'There's Nothing like Church Food': Food and the U.S. Afro-Christian Tradition: Re-membering Community and Feeding the Embodied S/spirit(s)." *Journal of the American Academy of Religion* 43, no. 3: 519–36.

DOE TETTEH, CHRISTIE. 2003. *Celebrating Womanhood*. Accra: Journagrafx.

DOUGLAS, KELLY BROWN. 2004. "The Black Church and the Politics of Sexuality." In *Loving the Body: Black Religious Studies and the Erotic*, edited by Anthony Pinn and Dwight N. Hopkins, 345–62. New York: Palgrave.

DOUGLAS, MARY. 1966. *Purity and Danger: An Analysis of the Concepts of Pollution and Taboo*. London: Routlege and Kegan Paul.

DRAKE, ST. CLAIR. 1987. *Black Folk Here and There: An Essay in History and Anthropology*. Vol. 2. Los Angeles: Center for Afro-American Studies, University of California.

DUNCAN-WILLIAMS, FRANCISCA. 2002. *Reflections: The Untold Story*. Accra: Action Faith.

EDMONDS, ENNIS B., and MICHELLE A. GONZALEZ. 2010. *Caribbean Religious History*. New York: New York University Press.

ELLISON, RALPH. 1980. *Going to the Territory*. New York: Random House.

EVENSON, SANDRA LEE, and DAVID J. TRAYTE. 1999. "Dress and Interaction in Contending Cultures: Eastern Dakota and Euroamericans in 19th Century Minnesota." In *Religion, Dress, and the Body*, edited by Linda B. Arthur, 95–116. New York: Berg.

FATOKUN, SAMSON ADETUNJI. 2005. "Pentecostalism in Southwestern Nigeria with Particular Emphasis on the Apostolic Church, 1931–2003." PhD diss., University of Ibadan, Nigeria.

FESSENDEN, TRACY. 2000. "The Sisters of the Holy Family and the Veil of Race." *Religion and American Culture: A Journal of Interpretation* 10, no. 2: 187–224.

FISCHER, GAYLE VERONICA. 1999. "The Obedient and Disobedient Daughters of the Church." In *Religion, Dress, and the Body*, edited by Linda B. Arthur, 73–94. New York: Berg.

FLOYD, SAMUEL A., JR. 1995. *The Power of Black Music: Interpreting Its History from Africa to the United States*. New York: Oxford University Press.

FOUCAULT, MICHEL. 1981. "Two Lectures." Translated by Colin Gordon, Leo Marshall, John Mepham, and Kate Soper. In *Power/Knowledge: Selected Interviews and Other Writings, 1972–1977*, edited by Colin Gordon, 78–108. New York: Pantheon.

FOUCAULT, MICHEL. 2003. *"Society Must Be Defended": Lectures at the Collège de France, 1975–76*. Edited by Mauro Bertani and Allesandro Fontana; translated by David Macey. New York: St. Martin's.

FRANKLIN, ROBERT MICHAEL. 1989. "Church and City: Black Christianity's Ministry." *Christian Ministry* 20: 17–19.

FRASER, NANCY. 1990. "Rethinking the Public Sphere: A Contribution to the Critique of Actually Existing Democracy." *Social Text* 25–26: 56–80.

FREDERICKS, MARLA. 2012. "Neo-Pentecostalism and Globalization." In *The Cambridge Companion to Religious Studies*, edited by Robert A. Orsi, 380–402. Cambridge: Cambridge University Press.

FRENCH, TALMADGE LEON. 2011. "Early Oneness Pentecostalism, Garfield Thomas

Haywood, and the Interracial Pentecostal Assemblies of the World (1906–1931)." PhD diss., University of Birmingham.

FRESTON, PAUL. 1994. "Popular Protestants in Brazilian Politics: A Novel Turn in Sect-State Relations." *Social Compass* 41, no. 44: 537–70.

FRESTON, PAUL. 1995. "Pentecostalism in Brazil: A Brief History." *Religion* 25: 119–33.

FRESTON, PAUL. 1998. "Pentecostalism in Latin America: Characteristics and Controversies." *Social Compass* 45, no. 3: 335–58.

FRESTON, PAUL. 2005. "The Universal Church of the Kingdom of God: A Brazilian Church Finds Success in Southern Africa." *Journal of Religion in Africa* 35, no. 1: 33–65.

FRY, PETER. 2000. "O Espírito Santo contra o feitiço e os espíritos revoltados: 'Civilização' e 'tradição' em Moçambique." *Mana* 6, no. 2: 65–95.

GIDDINGS, PAULA. 1984. *When and Where I Enter: The Impact of Black Women on Race and Sex in America*. New York: Bantam.

GIFFORD, PAUL. 2004. *Ghana's New Christianity: Pentecostalism in a Globalising African Economy*. London: Hurst.

GILKES, CHERYL TOWNSEND. 1985. "'Together and in Harness': Women's Traditions in the Sanctified Church." *Signs* 10, no. 4: 678–99.

GILKES, CHERYL TOWNSEND. 1986. "The Role of Women in the Sanctified Church." *Journal of Religious Thought* 43, no. 1: 24–41.

GILKES, CHERYL TOWNSEND. 1987. "Some Mother's Son and Some Father's Daughter: Gender and Biblical Language in Afro-Christian Worship Tradition." In *Shaping New Vision: Gender and Values in American Culture*, edited by Clarissa W. Atkinson, Constance H. Buchanan, and Margaret R. Miles, 73–95. Ann Arbor.: UMI Research Press.

GILKES, CHERYL TOWNSEND. 1994. "The Politics of Silence: Dual-Sex Political Systems and Women's Traditions of Conflict in African-American Religion." In *African-American Christianity*, edited by Paul E. Johnson, 80–109. Berkeley: University of California Press.

GILKES, CHERYL TOWNSEND. 1998a. "Plenty Good Room: Adaptation in a Changing Black Church." In "Americans and Religions in the Twenty-First Century," special issue, *Annals of the American Academy of Political and Social Science* 558 (July): 101–21.

GILKES, CHERYL TOWNSEND. 1998b. "The Sanctified Church and the Color-Line: Reorganization, Social Change, and the African-American Religious Experience." In *Religion in a Changing World*, edited by Madeleine Cousineau, 167–76. Santa Barbara, CA: Praeger.

GILKES, CHERYL TOWNSEND. 2001. *If It Wasn't for the Women: Black Women's Experience and Womanist Culture in Church and Community*. Maryknoll, NY: Orbis.

GILL, LESLEY. 1990. "'Like a Veil to Cover Them': Women and the Pentecostal Movement in La Paz." *American Ethnologist* 17 (4): 709–21.

GILROY, PAUL. 1991. "Sounds Authentic: Black Music, Ethnicity, and the Challenge of a 'Changing' Same." *Black Music Research Journal* 11, no. 2: 111–36.

GLAZIER, STEPHEN, ed. 1980. *Perspectives on Pentecostalism: Case Studies from the Caribbean and Latin America*. Lanham, MD: University Press of America.

GOLDSCHMIDT, HENRY, and ELIZABETH MCALISTER. 2004. *Race, Nation and Religion in the Americas*. New York: Oxford University Press.

GRANJO, PAULO. 2007. "The Homecomer: Postwar Cleansing Rituals in Mozambique." *Armed Forces and Society* 33, no. 3: 382–95.

GREEN, LINDA. 1993. "Shifting Affiliations: Mayan Widows and *Evangélicos* in Guatemala." In *Rethinking Protestantism in Latin America*, edited by Virginia Garrard-Burnett and David Stoll, 159–79. Philadelphia: Temple University Press.

GREGG, ROBERT. 1993. *Sparks from the Anvil of Oppression: Philadelphia's African Methodists and Southern Migrants, 1890–1940*. Philadelphia: Temple University Press.

GRIFFITH, R. MARIE. 1997. *God's Daughters: Evangelical Women and the Power of Submission*. Berkeley: University of California Press.

GRIFFITH, R. MARIE, and BARBARA DIANNE SAVAGE, eds. 2006. *Women and Religion in the African Diaspora: Knowledge, Power, and Performance*. Baltimore: Johns Hopkins University Press.

GROES-GREEN, CHRISTIAN. 2011. "'The Bling Scandal': Transforming Young Femininities in Mozambique." *Young* 19, no. 3: 291–312.

GROSZ-NGATE, MARIA, and OMARI H. KOKOLE, eds. 1997. *Gendered Encounters: Challenging Cultural Boundaries and Social Hierarchies in Africa*. London: Routledge.

HARDESTY, NANCY. 1999. *Women Called to Witness: Evangelical Feminism in the Nineteenth Century*. 2nd ed. Knoxville: University of Tennessee Press.

HARDING, RACHEL. 2006. "*E a senzala*: Slavery, Women, and Embodied Knowledge in Afro-Brazilian Candomblé." In *Women and Religion in the African Diaspora*, edited by R. Marie Griffith and Barbara D. Savage, 3–18. Baltimore: Johns Hopkins University Press.

HARKINS-PIERRE, PATRICIA. 2005. "Religion Bridge: Translating Secular into Sacred Music: A Study of World Christianity Focusing on the U.S. Virgin Islands." In *Changing Face of Christianity: Africa, the West, and the World*, edited by L. O. Sanneh and J. A. Carpenter, 21–44. New York: Oxford University Press.

HAYES, KELLY E. 2008. "Wicked Women and Femmes Fatales: Gender, Power and Pomba Gira in Brazil." *History of Religions* 48, no. 1: 1–21.

HENDERSON, KATHARINE RHODES. 2006. *God's Troublemakers: Women of Faith Are Changing the World*. New York: Continuum International.

HERVIEU-LÈGER, DANIÈLE. 2000. *Religion as a Chain of Memory*. Translated by Simon Lee. New Brunswick, NJ: Rutgers University Press.

HERZFELD, MICHAEL. 2001. *Anthropology: Theoretical Practice in Culture and Society*. Malden, MA: Blackwell.

HIGGINBOTHAM, EVELYN BROOKS. 1992. "African-American Women's History and the Meta-Language of Race." *Signs* 17, no. 7: 251–74.

HIGGINBOTHAM, EVELYN BROOKS. 1993. *Righteous Discontent: The Women's Movement in the Black Baptist Church, 1880–1920*. Cambridge, MA: Harvard University Press.

HODGES, MELVIN. 1986. "A Pentecostal's View of Mission Strategy." In *Azusa Street and Beyond: Pentecostal Missions and Church Growth in the Twentieth Century*, edited by Grant L. McClung Jr., 82–89. Newberry, FL: Bridge Logos.

HODGSON, DOROTHY L. 2005. *The Church of Women: Gendered Encounters between Maasai and Missionaries*. Bloomington: Indiana University Press.

HONWANA, ALCINDA M. 2002. *Espíritos vivos, tradições modernas: Possessão de espíritos e reintegração social pós-guerra no sul de Moçambique*. Maputo: Promédia.

HONWANA, ALCINDA M. 2003. "Undying Past: Spirit Possession and the Memory of War in Southern Mozambique." In *Magic and Modernity: Interfaces of Revelation and Concealment*, edited by Birgit Meyer and Peter Pels, 60–80. Stanford, CA: Stanford University Press.

HOOD, ROBERT K. 1994. *Begrimed and Black: Christian Traditions of Black and Blackness*. Minneapolis: Fortress.

HOPKINS, DWIGHT D. 2004. "The Construction of the Black Male Body." In *Loving the Body: Black Religious Studies and the Erotic*, edited by Anthony Pinn and Dwight N. Hopkins, 179–97. New York: Palgrave.

HOPKINS, JOHN B. 1978. "Music and the Pentecostal Church." *Jamaica Journal* 42: 22–40.

HOPPER, MATTHEW S. 2008. *From Refuge to Strength: The Rise of the African-American Church in Philadelphia 1787–1949*. Preservation Alliance for Greater Philadelphia. Accessed June 18, 2016. http://www.preservationalliance.com/files/aachurches.pdf.

HUNT, NANCY ROSE. 1999. *A Colonial Lexicon of Birth Ritual, Medicalization, and Mobility in the Congo*. Durham, NC: Duke University Press.

HUNT, STEPHEN, ed. 2001. *Christian Millenarianism: From the Early Church to Waco*. Bloomington: Indiana University Press.

HUNTER, TERA W. 1997. *To 'Joy My Freedom: Southern Black Women's Lives and Labor after the Civil War*. Cambridge, MA: Harvard University Press.

HURBON, LAËNNEC. 1993. *Les mystères du Vaudou*. Paris: Gallimard.

HURSTON, ZORA NEALE. 1981. *The Sanctified Church*. New York: Marlowe.

IGREJA, VICTOR, BÉATRICE DIAS-LAMBRANCA, and ANNEMIEK RICHTERS. 2008. "Gamba Spirits, Gender Relations and Healing in Post-Civil War Gorongosa, Mozambique." *Journal of the Royal Anthropological Institute* 14, no. 2: 353–71.

Instituto Nacional de Estatística. 2009. *Sinopse dos resultados definitivos do 30 recenseamento geral da população e habitação—Cidade de Maputo*. Maputo: Instituto Nacional de Estatística.

JACOBS, LOUIS. 1997. "The Body in Jewish Worship." In *Religion and the Body*, edited by Sarah Coakley, 71–89. Cambridge: Cambridge University Press.

JACOBSEN, DOUGLAS, ed. 2003. *Thinking in the Spirit: Theologies of the Early Pentecostal Movement*. Bloomington: Indiana University Press.

JACOBSEN, DOUGLAS. 2006. *A Reader in Pentecostal Theology: Voices from the First Generation*. Bloomington: Indiana University Press, 2006.

JENKINS, DANIEL. 1996. *How to Have an Enjoyable Marriage*. Accra: Altar International.

JENKINS, PAUL. 2006. "Image of the City in Mozambique: Civilization, Parasite, Engine of Growth or Place of Opportunity?" In *African Urban Economies: Viability, Vitality or Vitiation?*, 107–30. New York: Palgrave Macmillan.

JENKINS, PHILIP. 2006. *The New Faces of Christianity: Believing the Bible in the Global South*. Oxford: Oxford University Press.

JENKINS, PHILIP. 2011. *The Next Christendom: The Coming of Global Christianity*. Oxford: Oxford University Press.

JOHNSON, PAUL C. 2007. "On Leaving and Joining Africanness through Religion: The 'Black Caribs' across Multiple Diasporic Horizons." *Journal of Religion in Africa* 37, no. 2: 174–211.

JOHNSON, WALTER. 2003. "On Agency." *Journal of Social History* 37, no. 1: 113–24.

JONES, ARTHUR C. 2004. "Black Spirituals, Physical Sensuality, and Sexuality: Notes on a Neglected Field of Inquiry." In *Loving the Body: Black Religious Studies and the Erotic*, edited by Anthony Pinn and Dwight N. Hopkins, 235–46. New York: Palgrave.

JOSEPH, MAXO. N.d. *Vision pour Haiti et pour le monde*. Port-au-Prince: Vision Pour Haiti et Pour le Monde.

JULES-ROSETTE, BENNETTA. 1975. *African Apostles: Ritual and Conversion in the Church of John Maranke*. Ithaca, NY: Cornell University Press.

JUNGR, BARB. 2002. "Vocal Expression in the Blues and Gospel." In *The Cambridge Companion to Blues and Gospel Music*, edited by Allen F. Moore, 102–15. Cambridge: Cambridge University Press.

KALU, OGBU. 2003. "Introduction: Anatomy of an Explosion." *Christian History* 79: 7–9.

KALU, OGBU. 2008. *African Pentecostalism: An Introduction*. Oxford: Oxford University Press.

KEANE, WEBB. 2007. *Christian Moderns*. Berkeley: University of California Press.

KELLEY, ROBIN D. G. 1993. "'We Are Not What We Seem': Rethinking Black Working Class Opposition in the Jim Crow South." *Journal of American History* 80, no. 1: 75–112.

KIRK-DUGGAN, CHERYL. 2004. "Salome's Veiled Dance and David's Full Monty: A Womanist Reading on the Black Erotic in Blues, Rap, R&B and Gospel Blues." In *Loving the Body: Black Religious Studies and the Erotic*, edited by Anthony Pinn and Dwight N. Hopkins, 217–33. New York: Palgrave.

KLASSEN, PAMELA E. 2004. "The Robes of Womanhood: Dress and Authenticity among African American Methodist Women in the Nineteenth Century." *Religion and American Culture* 14, no. 1: 39–82.

LAMBEK, MICHAEL. 2003. "Rheumatic Irony: Questions of Agency and Self-Deception as Refracted through the Art of Living with Spirits." *Social Analysis* 47, no. 2: 40–59.

LAWLESS, ELAINE J. 1988. *Handmaidens of the Lord: Pentecostal Women Preachers and Traditional Religion*. Philadelphia: University of Pennsylvania Press.

LAWSON, ROBERT C. [1925] 1969. *The Anthropology of Jesus Christ Our Kinsman (Dedicated to the Glory of God and to the Help of Solving the Race Problem)*. New York: Church of Christ.

LEVINE, LAWRENCE W. 1977. *Black Culture and Black Consciousness: Afro-American Folk Thought from Slavery to Freedom*. New York: Oxford University Press.

LEVITT, PEGGY. 2013. "Religion on the Move: Mapping Global Cultural Production and Consumption." In *Religion on the Edge: De-centering and Re-centering the Sociology of Religion*, edited by Courtney Bender, Wendy Cadge, Peggy Levitt, and David Smilde, 159–77. Oxford: Oxford University Press.

LEWIS, PETER M., PEARL T. ROBINSON, and BARNETT R. RUBIN. 1998. *Stabilizing Nigeria: Sanctions, Incentives, Support for Civil Society*. New York: Center Foundation Press.

LINCOLN, C. ERIC, and LAWRENCE H. MAMIYA. 1990. *The Black Church in the African American Experience*. Durham, NC: Duke University Press.

LLEWELLYN, HENRY BYRON. 1997. "A Study of the History and Thought of the Apostolic Church in Wales, in the Context of Pentecostalism." Master's thesis, University of Wales, Cardiff.

LOFORTE, ANA MARIA. 2003. *Género e poder entre os Tsonga de Moçambique*. Lisbon: ElaporEla.

LUNDIN, IRAÊ BAPTISTA. 2007. *Negotiating Transformation: Urban Livelihoods in Maputo Adapting to Thirty Years of Political and Economic Changes*. Göteborg: Department of Human and Economic Geography, Göteborg University.

MACAGNO, LORENZO. 2008. "Multiculturalism in Mozambique? Reflections from the Field." *Vibrant* 5, no. 2: 223–46.

MACAMO, ELÍSIO S. 2005. "Denying Modernity: The Regulation of Native Labour in Colonial Mozambique and Its Postcolonial Aftermath." In *Negotiating Modernity: Africa's Ambivalent Experience*, 67–97. London: Zed.

MACEDO, EDIR. 2000. *Orixás, caboclos and guias: Deuses ou demônios?* Rio de Janeiro: Editora Gráfica Universal.

MACROBERT, IAIN. 1997. "The Black Roots of Early Pentecostalism." In *African-American Religion: Interpretive Essays in History and Culture*, edited by Timothy E. Fulop and Albert J. Raboteau, 295–309. New York: Routledge.

MADUEKE, PRAYER M. 2017. *Deliverance from Academic Defeats*. N.p.: Self-published.

MAGAIA, LINA. 1988. *Dumba Nengue, Run for Your Life: Peasant Tales of Tragedy in Mozambique*. Trenton, NJ: Africa World Press.

MAHMOOD, SABA. 2005. *Politics of Piety: The Islamic Revival and the Feminist Subject*. Princeton, NJ: Princeton University Press.

MAHUMANE, JONAS ALBERTO. 2016. "'Marido espiritual': Possessão e violência simbólica no sul de Moçambique." PhD diss., Lisbon University.

MAMA, AMINA. 1996. *Women's Studies and Studies of Women in Africa during the 1990s*. Dakar: Council for the Development of Social Science Research in Africa.

MARIZ, CECILIA LORETO, and MARIA DAS DORES CAMPOS MACHADO. 1997. "Pentecostalism and Women in Brazil." In *Power, Politics and Pentecostals in Latin America*, edited by Edward L. Cleary and Hannah Stewart-Gambino, 41–54. Boulder, CO: Westview.

MARSHALL, RUTH. 1993. "'Power in the Name of Jesus': Social Transformation and Pentecostalism in Western Nigeria 'Revisited.'" In *Legitimacy and the State in Twentieth Century Africa*, edited by Terence Ranger and Olufemi Vaughan, 213–46. London: Macmillan.

MARSHALL, RUTH. 2009. *Political Spiritualities: The Pentecostal Revolution in Nigeria*. Chicago: University of Chicago Press.

MARSHALL-FRATANI, RUTH. 2001. "Mediating the Global and Local in Nigerian Pentecostalism." In *Between Babel and Pentecost: Transnational Pentecostalism in Africa and Latin America*, edited by Andre Corten and Ruth Marshall-Fratani, 80–105. Bloomington: Indiana University Press.

MARTIN, BERNICE. 1995. "New Mutations of the Protestant Ethic among Latin American Pentecostals." *Religion* 25: 101–17.

MARTIN, BERNICE. 1998. "From Pre- to Postmodernity in Latin America: The Case of Pentecostalism." In *Religion, Modernity and Postmodernity*, edited by Paul Heelas, David Martin, and Paul Morris, 102–46. Oxford: Blackwell.

MARTIN, BERNICE. 2001. "The Pentecostal Gender Paradox: A Cautionary Tale for the Sociology of Religion." In *The Blackwell Companion to Sociology of Religion*, edited by Richard K. Fenn, 52–66. Oxford: Blackwell.

MARTIN, DAVID. 2002. *Pentecostalism: The World Their Parish*. Oxford: Blackwell.

MASSEY, DOREEN. 1994. *Space, Place, and Gender*. Minneapolis: University of Minnesota Press.

MAULTSBY, PORTIA K. 1990. "Africanisms in African-American Music." In *Africanisms in American Culture*, edited by Joseph E. Holloway, 185–210. Bloomington: Indiana University Press.

MAY, VIVIAN A. 2015. *Pursuing Intersectionality, Unsettling Dominant Imaginaries*. New York: Routledge.

MBEMBE, ACHILLE. 2001. *On the Postcolony*. Berkeley: University of California Press.

MCALISTER, ELIZABETH. 2000. "Love, Sex, and Gender Embodied: The Spirits of Haitian Vodou." In *Love, Gender, and Sexuality in the World Religions*, edited by Joseph Runzo and Nancy M. Martin, 128–45. Oxford: Oneworld.

MCALISTER, ELIZABETH. 2002. *Rara! Vodou, Power, and Performance in Haiti and Its Diaspora*. Berkeley: University of California Press.

MCALISTER, ELIZABETH. 2011. "Listening for Geographies: Music as Sonic Compass Pointing towards African and Christian Diasporic Horizons in the Caribbean." In *Geographies of the Haitian Diaspora*, edited by Regine O. Jackson, 207–28. New York: Routledge.

MCALISTER, ELIZABETH. 2012. "From Slave Revolt to a Blood Pact with Satan: The Evangelical Rewriting of Haitian History." *Studies in Religion/Sciences Religieuses* 41, no. 2: 187–215.

MCCLINTOCK, ANNE. 1993. "Family Feuds: Gender, Nationalism and the Family." *Feminist Review* 44: 61–80.

MEYER, BIRGIT. 1998. "'Make a Complete Break with the Past': Memory and Postcolonial Modernity in Ghanaian Pentecostal Discourse." *Journal of Religion in Africa* 28, no. 3: 316–49.

MEYER, BIRGIT. 2008. "Powerful Pictures: Popular Christian Aesthetics in Southern Ghana." *Journal of the American Academy of Religion* 76, no. 1: 82–110.

MEYER, BIRGIT. 2009. "Introduction: From Imagined Communities to Aesthetic Formations: Religious Mediation, Sensational Forms, and Styles of Binding." In *Aesthetic Formations: Media, Religion, and the Senses*, edited by Birgit Meyer, 1–29. New York: Palgrave Macmillan.

MEYER, BIRGIT. 2012. "'Religious' and 'Secular,' 'Spiritual' and 'Physical' in Ghana." In *What Matters? Ethnographies of Value in a Not So Secular Age*, edited by Courtney Bender and Ann Taves, 86–118. New York: Columbia University Press.

MODERN, JOHN LARDAS. 2011. *Secularism in Antebellum America*. Chicago: University of Chicago Press.

MOHLER, R. ALBERT, JR. 1996. "'Evangelical': What's in a Name?" In *The Coming Evangelical Crisis*, edited by John H. Armstrong, 29–44. Chicago: Moody.

MOLTMANN-WENDEL, ELISABETH 1995. *I Am My Body*. New York: Continuum.

MONSON, INGRID. 2007. *Freedom Sounds: Civil Rights Call Out to Jazz and Africa.* New York: Oxford University Press.

MONTEITH, ANDREW. 2010. "The Light and the Night: An Ethnographic Examination of Spiritual Warfare." Master's thesis, Memorial University of Newfoundland, St. John's.

MORRISON, TONI. 1987. *Beloved.* New York: Vintage.

MURRELL, NATHANIEL SAMUEL. 2010. *Afro-Caribbean Religions.* Philadelphia: Temple University Press.

NASH, GARY B. 2006. *First City: Philadelphia and the Forging of Historical Memory.* Philadelphia: University of Pennsylvania Press.

NEWITT, MALYN. 1997. *A History of Mozambique.* London: Hurst.

NIEHAUS, ISAK. 1997. "'A Witch Has No Horn': The Subjective Reality of Witchcraft in the South African Lowveld." *African Studies* 56, no. 2: 251–78.

NORRIS, PIPPA, and RONALD INGLEHART. 2012. *Sacred and Secular: Religion and Politics Worldwide.* Cambridge: Cambridge University Press.

NORRIS, REBECCA SACHS. 2001. "Embodiment and Community." *Western Folklore* 60, nos. 2–3: 111–24.

NOVAES, REGINA. 1985. *O negro evangélico.* Rio de Janeiro: Instituto de Estudos da Religião.

ODUYOYE, MERCY AMBA. 1998. "Women, Culture and Theology: A Foreword." In *Women, Culture and Theological Education*, edited by Protus O. Kemdirim and Mercy Amba Oduyoye, 31–37. Enugu, Nigeria: West African Association of Theological Institutions.

OJO, JOHN ODUNAYO. 1988. *The Life and Ministry of Apostle Joseph Ayodele Babalola.* Lagos: Prayer Band.

OLANYINKA, BOLAYI OLUKEMI. 2000. "Female Leaders of New Generation Churches as Change Agents in Yorubaland." PhD diss., Obafemi Awolowo University, Ife, Nigeria.

O'LAUGHLIN, M. BRIDGET. 2000. "Class and the Customary: The Ambiguous Legacy of the 'Indigenato' in Mozambique." *African Affairs* 99: 5–42.

ONAYIGA, TOSIN. 1999. "What Matter of Talkshop." *Redemption Light* 5, no. 3 (May).

O'NEAL, GWENDOLYN S. 1999. "The African-American Church, Its Sacred Cosmos and Dress." In *Religion, Dress, and the Body*, edited by Linda B. Arthur, 117–34. New York: Berg.

O'NEILL, KEVIN LEWIS. 2009. *City of God: Christian Citizenship in Postwar Guatemala.* Berkeley: University of California Press.

ONWUMERE, EVANGELIST ISRAEL. 2003. *Great Practical Steps You Must Take to Achieve Total Success in Your Marriage.* Lagos: Israel Publishing Ventures.

OPOKU, KOFI ASARE. 1990. "A Brief History of Independent Church Movement in Ghana since 1862." In *The Rise of Independent Churches in Ghana*, 22–26. Accra: Asempa.

OPPENHEIMER, JOCHEN, and ISABEL RAPOSO. 2002. *A pobreza em Maputo: A cooperação direccionada para os grupos vulneráveis no contexto da concentração urbana acelerada/1*. Lisbon: Departamento de Cooperação, Ministério do Trabalho e Solidaridade.

OSHUN, C. O. 1983. "The Pentecostal Perspective of the Christ Apostolic Church." *Orita* 17: 105–14.

OSITELU, RUFUS OKIKIOLAOLU OLUBIYI. 2002. *African Instituted Churches*. New Brunswick, NJ: Transaction.

OWEN, HILARY. 2007. *Mother Africa, Father Marx: Women's Writing of Mozambique, 1948–2002*. Lewisburg, PA: Bucknell University Press.

PANDIAN, JACOB. 1985. *Anthropology and the Western Tradition: Toward an Authentic Anthropology*. Prospect Heights, IL: Waveland.

PARDUE, DEREK. 2008. *Ideologies of Marginality in Brazilian Hip Hop*. New York: Palgrave Macmillan.

PARISTAU, DAMARIS. 2011. "'Arise Oh Ye Daughters of Faith': Women, Pentecostalism and Public Culture in Kenya." In *Christianity and Public Culture in Africa*, edited by Harri Englund, 131–48. Athens: Ohio University Press.

PEDDE, V. 2002. "Etnia, religião e política: Relações e deslocamento de fronteiras." *Noticias de antropología y arqueología*.

PEEL, J. D. Y. 1968. *Aladura: A Religious Movement among the Yoruba*. Oxford: Oxford University Press.

PEEL, J. D. Y. 2000. *Religious Encounter and the Making of the Yoruba*. Bloomington: Indiana University Press.

PEMBERTON, CARRIE. 2003. *Circle Thinking: African Women Theologians in Dialogue with the West*. Leiden: Brill.

PENVENNE, JEANNE MARIE. 1995. *African Workers and Colonial Racism: Mozambican Strategies and Struggles in Lourenço Marques, 1877–1962*. Portsmouth, NH: Heinemann.

Pew Research Center Forum on Religion and Public Life. 2008. "U.S. Religious Landscape Survey: Religious Affiliation: Diverse and Dynamic." Report, February 1. Accessed June 9, 2014. http://www.pewforum.org/2008/02/01/u-s-religious-landscape-survey-religious-affiliation/.

Pew Research Center Forum on Religion and Public Life. 2009. "A Religious Portrait of African-Americans." Report, January. Accessed June 9, 2014. http://www.pewforum.org/2009/01/30/a-religious-portrait-of-african-americans.

Pew Research Center Forum on Religion and Public Life. 2011. "Global Christianity: A Report on the Size and Distribution of the World's Christian Popula-

tion." Report, December 19. Accessed July 26, 2013. http://www.pewforum.org
/Christian/Global-Christianity-Nigeria.aspx.

PIERCE, CHUCK. 2007. *God's Unfolding Battle Plan: A Field Manual for Advancing the Kingdom of God*. Ventura, CA: Regal.

PIERUCCI, FLAVIO. 2006. "Religião como solvente." *Novos estudos CEBRAP* 75: 111–27.

PINHEIRO, MARCIA. 1998. "O proselitismo evangélico: Musicalidade e imagem." *Cadernos de Antropologia e Imagem* 7, no. 2: 57–67.

PINHEIRO, MARCIA. 2003. "Experiências sonoras e inovações religiosas." Paper presented at the Symposium on Popular Religious Groups in Latin America, Ica, Chile.

PINHEIRO, MARCIA. 2004. "Produção musical: A periferia do meio evangélico." Paper presented at the Fifth Congress of the Latin American Section of the International Association for the Study of Popular Music. Rio de Janeiro, Brazil.

PINHEIRO, MARCIA. 2009. "Dinâmicas da religiosidade: Experiências musicais, cor e noção de sagrado." *Stockholm Review of Latin American Studies* 4: 61–72.

PINN, ANTHONY. 2003. "Black Bodies in Pain and Ecstasy: Terror, Subjectivity, and the Nature of Black Religion." *Nova Religio* 7, no. 1: 76–89.

PINN, ANTHONY. 2004a. "Embracing Nimrods' Legacy: The Erotic, the Irreverence of Fantasy, and the Redemption of Black Theology." In *Loving the Body: Black Religious Studies and the Erotic*, edited by Anthony Pinn and Dwight N. Hopkins, 157–78. New York: Palgrave.

PINN, ANTHONY. 2004b. "Introduction." In *Loving the Body: Black Religious Studies and the Erotic*, edited by Anthony Pinn and Dwight N. Hopkins, 1–8. New York: Palgrave.

PINN, ANTHONY. 2009. "Introduction: The Black Labyrinth, Aesthetics, and Black Religion." In *Black Religion and Aesthetics: Religious Thought and Life in Africa and the African Diaspora*, edited by Anthony Pinn, 1–17. New York: Palgrave Macmillan.

PITCHER, ANNE. 2006. "Forgetting from Above and Memory from Below: Strategies of Legitimation and Struggle in Postsocialist Mozambique." *Africa* 76, no. 1: 88–112.

POLOMA, MARGARET M. 1989. *The Assemblies of God at the Crossroads: Charisma and Institutional Dilemmas*. Knoxville: University of Tennessee Press.

POWERS, JANET EVERTS. 1999. "'Your Daughters Shall Prophesy': Pentecostal Hermeneutics and the Empowerment of Women." In *The Globalization of Pentecostalism: A Religion Made to Travel*, edited by Murray W. Dempster, Byron D. Klaus, and Douglas Petersen, 313–37. Oxford: Regnum.

PRANDI, REGINALDO. 2004. "Afro-Brazilian Identity and Memory." *Diogenes* 51, no. 1: 35–43.

PREMACK, LAURA. 2005. "Prophets, Evangelists, and Missionaries: Trans-Atlantic

Interactions in the Emergence of Nigerian Pentecostalism." *Religion* 45, no. 2: 221–38.

PRITCHARD, ELIZABETH. 2014. *Religion in Public: Locke's Political Theology*. Palo Alto, CA: Stanford University Press.

RABOTEAU, ALBERT J. 1978. *Slave Religion: The Invisible Institution in the Antebellum South*. New York: Oxford University Press.

RADANO, RONALD. 1993. "The Bounds of Black Musical Significance." Paper presented at the annual meeting of the Society for Ethnomusicology, Oxford, Mississippi, October 20.

RADANO, RONALD, and PHILIP BOHLMAN, eds. 2000. *Music and the Racial Imagination*. Chicago: University of Chicago Press.

RAI, AMIT. 2009. *Untimely Bollywood*. Durham, NC: Duke University Press.

RAMSEY, GUTHRIE P. 2004. *Race Music: Black Cultures from Bebop to Hip-Hop*. Berkeley: University of California Press.

RANSBY, BARBARA. 2001. "Behind-the-Scenes View of a Behind-the-Scenes Organizer: The Roots of Ella Baker's Political Passions." In *Sisters in the Struggle: African-American Women in the Civil Rights-Black Power Movement*, edited by Bettye Collier-Thomas and V. P. Franklin, 42–57. New York: New York University Press.

REAGON, BERNICE JOHNSON. 2001. *If You Don't Go, Don't Hinder Me: The African American Sacred Song Tradition*. Lincoln: University of Nebraska Press.

REITER, BERND. 2008. *Negotiating Democracy in Brazil: The Politics of Exclusion*. London: Lynne Rienner.

REITER, BERND, and GLADYS L. MITCHELL, eds. 2009. *Brazil's New Racial Politics*. London: Lynne Rienner.

RICOEUR, PAUL. 1984. "From Proclamation to Narrative." *Journal of Religion* 64, no. 4: 502–12.

RIGBY, PETER 1996. *African Images: Racism and the End of Anthropology*. Oxford: Berg.

ROBBINS, JOEL. 2004. "The Globalization of Pentecostal and Charismatic Christianity." *Annual Review of Anthropology* 33: 117–43.

ROBBINS, JOEL. 2007. "Continuity Thinking and the Problem of Christian Culture: Belief, Time, and the Anthropology of Christianity." *Current Anthropology* 48, no. 1: 5–38.

ROBERTS, DOROTHY. 1997. *Killing the Black Body: Race, Reproduction, and the Meaning of Liberty*. New York: Vintage.

RODRIGUES, CRISTIANO, and MARCO AURELIO PRADO. 2013. "A History of the Black Women's Movement in Brazil: Mobilization, Political Trajectory and Articulations with the State." In *Social Movement Studies* 12, no. 2: 158–77.

ROSENIOR, DERRICK. 2009. *Toward Racial Reconciliation: Collective Memory, Myth and Nostalgia in American Pentecostalism*. Saarbrücken, Germany: VDM.

ROUSE, CAROLYN MOXLEY. 2004. *Engaged Surrender: African American Women and Islam.* Berkeley: University of California Press.

SACKEY, BRIGID M. 1997. "'Don't Think of Me as a Woman Because He That Is in Me Is a Man': The Story of Sofo Mary Owusu of the Great I Am That I Am Church." In *Living Faith—Lebendige religiöse Wirklichkeit,* edited by Reiner Mahlke, Renate Pitzer-Reyl, and Juachim Süss, 125–37. Sonderdruck: Peter Lang.

SACKEY, BRIGID M. 2006. *New Directions in Gender and Religion: The Changing Status of Women in African Independent Churches.* Oxford: Lexington.

SANDERS, CHERYL. 1996. *Saints in Exile: The Holiness-Pentecostal Experience in African-American Religion and Culture.* Oxford: Oxford University Press.

SANNEH, LAMIN. 1990. *West African Christianity: The Religious Impact.* London: C. Hurst.

SCHUETZE, CHRISTY. 2010. "The World Is Upside Down: Women's Participation in Religious Movements and the Search for Social Healing in Central Mozambique." PhD diss., University of Pennsylvania.

SCOTT, JOAN. 2010. *The Politics of the Veil.* Princeton, NJ: Princeton University Press.

SCOTT, SHAUNNA. 1994. "'They Don't Have to Live by the Old Traditions': Saintly Men, Sinner Women, and an Appalachian Pentecostal Revival." *American Ethnologist* 21, no. 2: 227–44.

SELKA, STEPHEN. 2005. "Ethnoreligious Identity Politics in Bahia, Brazil." *Latin American Perspectives* 32, no. 1: 72–94.

SELKA, STEPHEN. 2007. *Religion and the Politics of Ethnic Identity in Bahia, Brazil.* Gainesville: University of Florida Press.

SELKA, STEPHEN. 2009. "Rural Women and the Varieties of Black Politics in Bahia, Brazil." *Black Women, Gender and Families* 3, no. 1: 16–38.

SELKA, STEPHEN. 2010. "Morality in the Religious Marketplace: Evangelical Christianity, Candomblé, and the Struggle for Moral Distinction in Brazil." *American Ethnologist* 37, no. 2: 291–307.

SERNETT, MILTON C. 1997. *Bound for the Promised Land: African-American Religion and the Great Migration.* Durham, NC: Duke University Press.

SERNETT, MILTON C., ed. 1999. *African American Religious History: A Documentary Witness.* Durham, NC: Duke University Press.

"Seven Standards of Excellence." 2003. Standards of Excellence in Short-Term Mission. Accessed September 6, 2018. https://soe.org/7-standards/.

SHARP, JOANNE R. 1996. "Gendering Nationhood: A Feminist Engagement with National Identity." In *BodySpace: Destabilizing Geographies of Gender and Sexuality,* edited by Nancy Duncan, 97–107. London: Routledge.

SHELDON, KATHLEEN E. 2002. *Pounders of Grain: A History of Women, Work, and Politics in Mozambique.* Portsmouth, NH: Heinemann.

SHELDON, KATHLEEN E. 2003. "Markets and Gardens: Placing Women in the History of Urban Mozambique." *Canadian Journal of African Studies* 37, nos. 2–3: 358–95.

SILVA, GRAZIELLA MORAES DA, and ELISA P. REIS. 2011. "The Multiple Dimensions of Racial Mixture in Rio de Janeiro, Brazil: From Whitening to Brazilian Negritude." *Ethnic and Racial Studies* 35, no. 3: 1–18.

SIMONE, ABDOUMALIQ. 2001. "On the Worlding of African Cities." *African Studies Review* 44, no. 2: 15–41.

SINGH, JAKEET. 2015. "Religious Agency and the Limits of Intersectionality." *Hypatia* 30, no. 4 (fall): 657–74.

SITOE, EDUARDO. 2003. "Making Sense of the Political Transition in Mozambique: 1984–1994." In *Community and the State in Lusophone Africa*, edited by Malyn Newitt, Patrick Chabal, and Norrie Macqueen, 15–34. London: Department of Portuguese and Brazilian Studies, King's College London.

SMITH, ABRAHAM. 2004. "The Bible, the Body, and the Black Sexual Discourse." In *Loving the Body: Black Religious Studies and the Erotic*, edited by Anthony Pinn and Dwight N. Hopkins, 73–90. New York: Palgrave.

SMITH, JONATHAN Z. 1980. "The Bare Facts of Ritual." *History of Religions* 20, nos. 1–2: 112–27.

SMITH, M. G. 1962. *West Indian Family Structure*. Seattle: University of Washington Press.

SNOWDEN, FRANK M. 1970. *Blacks in Antiquity*. Cambridge, MA: Harvard University Press.

SOARES, MARIA ANDREA DOS SANTOS. 2012. "Look, Blackness in Brazil! Disrupting the Grotesquerie of Racial Representation in Brazilian Visual Culture." *Cultural Dynamics* 24, no. 1: 75–101.

SOOTHILL, JANE E. 2007. *Gender, Social Change and Spiritual Power: Charismatic Christianity in Ghana*. Leiden: Brill.

SOUSA SANTOS, BOAVENTURA, and JOÃO CARLOS TRINDADE, eds. 2003. *Conflito e transformação social: Uma paisagem das justiças em Moçambique*, vol. 2. Porto, Portugal: Ediçoes Afrontamento.

SPIVAK, GAYATRI. 2012. *An Aesthetic Education in the Era of Globalization*. Cambridge, MA: Harvard University Press.

SPRONK, RACHEL. 2012. *Ambiguous Pleasures: Sexuality and Middle Class Self-Perceptions in Nairobi*. Oxford: Berghahn.

STARKE, BARBARA M. 1990. "US Slave Narratives: Accounts of What They Wore." In *African-American Dress and Adornment: A Cultural Perspective*, edited by Barbara M. Starke, Lillian O. Holloman, and Barbara K. Nordquist, 69–79. Dubuque, IA: Kendall Hunt.

STOKES, MELVYN. 2007. *D. W. Griffith's* The Birth of a Nation: *A History of the Most Controversial Motion Picture of All Time*. New York: Oxford University Press.

STUCKEY, STERLING 1987. *Slave Culture: Nationalist Theory and the Foundations of Black America*. New York: Oxford University Press.

SUMICH, JASON. 2008. "Ideologias de modernidade da elite moçambicana." *Análise Social* 43, no. 187: 319–45.

SUMICH, JASON. 2010. "Nationalism, Urban Poverty and Identity in Maputo, Mozambique." Working Paper no. 68. Crises States Research Centre, London School of Economics.

SUNDKLER, BENGT. 1971. *Bantu Prophets*. London: Oxford University Press.

SWARR, AMANDA LOCK, and RICHA NAGAR, eds. 2010. *Critical Transnational Feminist Praxis*. Albany: State University of New York Press.

SYNAN, VINCENT. 1997. *The Holiness-Pentecostal Tradition: Charismatic Movements in the Twentieth Century*. 2nd ed. Grand Rapids, MI: William B. Eerdmans.

TAYLOR, CHARLES. 2007. *A Secular Age*. Cambridge, MA: Harvard University Press.

TAYLOR, CHARLES. 2011. "Western Secularity." In *Rethinking Secularism*, edited by Craig Calhoun, Mark Juergensmeyer, and Jonathan VanAntwerpen, 31–53. Oxford: Oxford University Press.

TAYLOR, CLARENCE. 1994. *The Black Churches of Brooklyn*. New York: Columbia University Press.

THOMPSON, ALVIN O. 1976–77. "Race and Colour Prejudices and the Origin of the Trans-Atlantic Slave Trade." *Caribbean Studies* 16, nos. 3–4 (October–January): 29–59.

TINNEY, JAMES. 1971. "Black Origins of the Pentecostal Movement." *Christianity Today* 15: 4–6.

TORJENSEN, KAREN JO. 1993. *When Women Were Priests: Women's Leadership in the Early Church and the Scandal of Their Subordination in the Rise of Christianity*. San Francisco: HarperCollins.

TOULIS, NICOLE RODRIGUEZ. 1997. *Believing Identity: Pentecostalism and the Mediation of Jamaican Ethnicity and Gender in England*. Oxford: Berg.

TOUSSAINT, GREGORY. 2009. *Jezebel Unveiled*. Miami, FL: High Way.

TRIPP, AILI MARI, ISABEL CASIMIRO, JOY KWESIGA, and ALICE MUNGWA. 2009. *African Women's Movements: Transforming Political Landscapes*. Cambridge: Cambridge University Press.

TURNER, BRYANT S. 1997. "The Body in Western Society: A Social Theory and Its Perspectives." In *Religion and the Body*, edited by Sarah Coakley, 15–42. Cambridge: Cambridge University Press.

TWEED, THOMAS A. 2006. *Crossing and Dwelling: A Theory of Religion*. Cambridge, MA: Harvard University Press.

UGOALA, CHINASA. 2008. *Overcoming This Monster Called Fibroid: Let God Sort It Out*. Ibadan, Nigeria: Oluseyi.

URDANG, STEPHANIE. 1989. *And Still They Dance: Women, War, and the Struggle for Change in Mozambique*. London: Earthscan.

VAN DE KAMP, LINDA. 2011. "Converting the Spirit Spouse: The Violent Transformation of the Pentecostal Female Body in Maputo, Mozambique." *Ethnos* 76, no. 4: 510–53.

VAN DE KAMP, LINDA. 2012. "Afro-Brazilian Pentecostal Re-formations of Relationships across Two Generations of Mozambican Women." *Journal of Religion in Africa* 42, no. 4: 433–52.

VAN DE KAMP, LINDA. 2013. "South-South Transnational Spaces of Conquest: Afro-Brazilian Pentecostalism, 'Feitiçaria' and the Reproductive Domain in Urban Mozambique." *Exchange* 42, no. 4: 343–65.

VAN DE KAMP, LINDA. 2015. "Transatlantic Pentecostal Demons in Maputo." In *Evil in Africa: Encounters with the Everyday*, edited by William C. Olsen and Walter E. A. van Beek, 344–63. Bloomington: Indiana University Press.

VAN DE KAMP, LINDA. 2016. *Violent Conversion: Brazilian Pentecostalism and Urban Women in Mozambique*. Suffolk, UK: James Currey.

VAN DIJK, RIJK. 2010. "Social Catapulting and the Spirit of Entrepreneurialism: Migrants, Private Initiative, and the Pentecostal Ethic in Botswana." In *Traveling Spirits: Migrants, Markets and Mobilities*, edited by Gertrud Hüwelmeier and Kristine Krause, 101–17. London: Routledge.

VAN KLINKEN, ADRIAAN. 2013. "God's World Is Not an Animal Farm—or Is It?" *Religion and Gender* 3, no. 2: 240–58.

VESSEY, GWEN. 1952. *Looking at the West Indies*. London: Cargate.

VINES, ALEX. 1996. *Renamo: From Terrorism to Democracy in Mozambique?* London: James Currey.

Wailing Women Worldwide. 2004. *Training Manual*, vol. 1. Port Harcourt, Nigeria: Fidelity Press.

Wailing Women Worldwide. 2008. *5th National Conference 2008: Behold He Comes*. Unpublished conference program, Sheraton Hotel, Fort Lauderdale, FL.

WARD, LARRY. 1997. "Filled with the Spirit: The Musical Life of an Apostolic Pentecostal Church in Champaign-Urbana, Illinois." PhD diss., University of Illinois, Urbana-Champaign.

WARHURST, CHRIS, DENNIS NICKSON, ANNE WITZ, and ANNE MARIE CULLEN. 2000. "Aesthetic Labor in Interactive Service Work: Some Case Study Evidence from the 'New' Glasgow." *Service Industries Journal* 20, no. 3: 1–18.

WARNER, MICHAEL. 2002. *Publics and Counterpublics*. New York: Zone.

WATERSTON, ALISSE, and BARBARA RYLKO-BAUER. 2006. "Out of the Shadows of History and Memory: Personal Family Narrative in Ethnographies of Rediscovery." *American Ethnologist* 33, no. 2: 397–412.

WEST, HARRY G. 2005. *Kupilikula: Governance and the Invisible Realm in Mozambique*. Chicago: University of Chicago Press.

WILKERSON, ISABEL. 2010. *The Warmth of Other Suns: The Epic Story of America's Great Migration*. New York: Random House.

WILLIAMS, J. L. 2008. *Kingdom Leadership: A Special Study for National Leaders*. Burlington, NC: NDI Press.

WILLIAMS, MELVIN D. 1974. *Community in a Black Pentecostal Church: An Anthropological Study*. Groveland, IL: Waveland.

WILLIAMS-JONES, PEARL. 1975. "Afro-American Gospel Music: A Crystallization of the Black Aesthetic." *Ethnomusicology* 19, no. 3: 373–85.

WILSON, KEN B. 1992. "Cults of Violence and Counter-Violence in Mozambique." *Journal of Southern African Studies* 18, no. 3: 527–82.

WOLFE, ALAN. 2003. *The Transformation of American Religion: How We Actually Live Our Faith*. New York: Free Press.

WOLFE, ALAN. 2004. "Dieting for Jesus." *Prospect* Magazine (January): 52–57.

WOMACK, DAVID A. 1968. *The Wellsprings of the Pentecostal Movement*. Springfield, MO: Gospel.

WONG, DEBORAH. 2000. "The Asian American Body in Performance." In *Music and the Racial Imagination*, edited by Ronald Radano and Philip Bohlman, 57–94. Chicago: University of Chicago Press.

YONG, AMOS, and ESTRELDA Y. ALEXANDER, eds. 2011. *Afro-Pentecostalism: Black Pentecostal and Charismatic Christianity in History and Culture*. New York: New York University Press.

YUVAL-DAVIS, NIRA. 1997. *Gender and Nation*. London: Sage.

CONTRIBUTORS

Paula Aymer is an associate professor in the Department of Sociology, Tufts University, Medford, Massachusetts, and director of the undergraduate minor Africa and the New World. Her research and teaching areas are religion, immigration and labor migration, family cross-culturality, Caribbean studies, and racial/ethnic minorities. Her current book project is entitled *Evangelical Awakenings in the Anglophone Caribbean (1850–1950) and (1950s–Present)*. She has presented at numerous professional meetings; recent talks include "Heathen Stubbornness: Early Wesleyan Methodist Missions in Grenada, West Indies 1790s–1830s" and "Spiritual Warfare and the Restructuring of Caribbean Societies."

John Burdick is a professor and the chair of anthropology at the Maxwell School, Syracuse University, Syracuse, New York. His current research charts the causes and effects of a new religio-political movement in Brazil: an emerging network among evangelical churches uniting their faith to a Black consciousness and antiracist agenda. He is the author of numerous publications, including *Looking for God in Brazil* (1993), *Blessed Anastacia: Women, Race and Popular Christianity in Brazil* (1998), *Legacies of Liberation* (2004), and *The Color of Sound: Race, Religion and Music in Brazil* (2013).

Judith Casselberry is an associate professor of Africana studies at Bowdoin College, Brunswick, Maine. An interest in African American religious and cultural studies, with particular attention to gender, guides her research agenda. Her current ethnography, *The Labor of Faith: Gender and Power in Black Apostolic Pentecostalism* (Duke University Press, 2017), employs feminist labor theories to examine the spiritual, material, social, and organizational work of women in a New York–based Pentecostal denomination. A vocalist and guitarist, Casselberry was a member of the award-winning reggae duo Casselberry-DuPreé and currently performs internationally with Toshi Reagon and BIGLovely.

Deidre Helen Crumbley is an emeritus professor at North Carolina State University, Raleigh. She holds a master's degree in comparative religion from Harvard Divinity School and a doctorate in anthropology from Northwestern University. She is the author of *Spirit, Structure and Flesh: Gendered Experiences in African Instituted Churches among the Yoruba* (2008) and *Saved and Sanctified: The Rise of a Storefront Church in Great Migration Philadelphia* (2012).

Elizabeth McAlister is a professor and the chair of religion at Wesleyan University, Middletown, Connecticut. Her research focuses on Afro-Caribbean religions, transnational migration, the New Apostolic evangelical movement, and race theory, with a focus on Haiti. McAlister is the author of *Rara! Vodou, Power and Performance in Haiti and Its Diaspora* (2002) and coeditor (with Henry Goldschmidt) of *Race, Nation, and Religion in the Americas* (2004). She has produced three compilations of Afro-Haitian religious music: *Rhythms of Rapture*, *Angels in the Mirror*, and *Rara*, the CD that accompanies her first book. Her current research examines the rise of the New Apostolic Reformation, or Spiritual Warfare movement, and its global networks, particularly in the circuits between the United States and Haiti.

Laura Premack is a lecturer in global religion and politics in the Department of Politics, Philosophy, and Religion, Lancaster University, Lancaster, UK. Her research interests are fundamentally interdisciplinary; her work, which focuses on Brazil, Nigeria, and the larger Atlantic world, has been funded by the Gerda Henkel Foundation, Andrew W. Mellon Foundation, Fulbright-Hays Program, and US Department of State. She is currently writing a monograph on spiritual warfare in contemporary global Christianity.

Elizabeth A. Pritchard is an associate professor in the Department of Religion, Bowdoin College, Brunswick, Maine. She offers courses on Christianity, gender, secularization, and politics. She has published articles on the theological rhetoric of Marxist and radical democratic theorists, feminist theories of agency and mobility, and contemporary formations of religious publics. She is the author of *Religion in Public: Locke's Political Theology* (2014) and coeditor of the *Journal of Feminist Studies in Religion*.

Jane Soothill is a research associate at the School of Oriental and African Studies, London. She is the author of *Gender, Social Change and Spiritual Power: Charismatic Christianity in Ghana* (2007), which examines the gender implications of the fastest-growing movement in Africa's Christian sector.

Linda van de Kamp is an assistant professor in the Department of Sociology, University of Amsterdam. She has conducted research in Mozambique, Brazil, and the

Netherlands. She is the author of *Violent Conversion: Brazilian Pentecostalism and Urban Women in Mozambique* (2016). Her current project, titled "Yoga, Bingo and Prayer in Urban Regeneration Areas," was awarded a Veni grant from the Netherlands Organization for Scientific Research.

INDEX

Action Chapel International (Accra), 152, 159–70, 178n8; "Women of Worth" convention and, 155
Adeboye, E. A., 195n1
Adeloye, Abiodun, 184
Adeloye, Adelola, 186
Adeloye, Olubunmi, 184
adultery: demon of, 61; in Haiti, 61; as sin, 61
aesthetic labor, 128, 130–37, 143; of COOLJC women, 133–37; and end times, 131, 134; eschatology and, 143; singing as, 143. *See also* bodily practices; runners; singing; wailing; Wailing Women Worldwide
Africa: authentic, 9; cultural distance from, 69; destroying, 69; enchanted, 5; maternal health in, 196n18; meaning of, in postcolonial diasporic contexts, 9; Pentecostalism rates in, 195; rebranding, 9. *See also* Third Wave evangelicalism
African Americans: eros and, 100; Great Migration of, 93; white-controlled social agencies and, 99–100
African diaspora, 47, 98; in Greece and Italy, 105n4
African music and dance, 8; singing as predisposition, 29
Africanness: and Blackness, 50

African politics: exclusion of women in leadership in, 158, 177
African priestess, 58
Africans: in Bible, 37, 39, 40, 145n9; in leadership positions, 40; self-identification as negro, 42n4. *See also* negro
African social practices, 61
African spirituality, 52, 114; as demonic, 50, 51, 63, 69; Sanctified church and, 92, 104n1; and spirit spouses
African traditional religion, 9, 112; as demonic, 15, 50–51, 63, 68, 69; Great Awakening and, 98; intercession in, 190; pragmatism of, 194; and Wailing Women Worldwide, 125–26. *See also* pragmatism; Vodou
Afro-Brazilian: identity, 28; singers, 28
Afro-Brazilian religion, 15, 17, 27–43; as work of the Devil, 15
Afro-diasporic consciousness, 48
agency, 102, 151–77; authentic versus fake, 11; of Black women, 99; body and, 92–93; dangers of mislocated, 11; decolonizing politics and, 51; fertility-related concerns and, 190; healing and, 190; local, 50–51; male, 51; pragmatism and, 192; real, 192; relative, 191–92; relinquishing, 190

Aladura (prophet healing) movement, 182–84; appeal to women of, 186–88; Dallimore (Henry) and, 188; divine healing and, 185; ministry to pregnant women of, 185; miracles of, 184; Pentecostal churches and, 195n3; prayer as cure in, 185; pregnancy and, 185; refusal to use medicine, 184–85; women and, 182. *See also* Babalola, Joseph; Christ Apostolic Church; healing

alafia (peace), 21, 180; pragmatism and, 192

alcohol: as male domain, 69

Alive Chapel International (Accra), 152, 171–72

Alokan, Adeware, 187

American paradox, 138–39

ancestral spirits, 68, 75; as demonic, 68

Anderson, Allan, 176

anointing, 161; of church, 136; Doe Tetteh and, 165, 177; Duncan Williams and, 161; of financial offering, 161; of Holy Ghost, 136; men hampering, 168; of tongues, 130; of women, 132–33, 136, 144n3; women's song as, 36, 132

appearance (of men), 91

appearance (of women), 5, 91, 136, 156; biblical injunctions about, 90, 135, 146n9; in COGIC, 101, 136, 147n16; covering, 91, 103; dress codes, 5, 17, 18, 45, 56, 89, 91–92, 135, 147n14; Ephesians 5 and, 135; hair, 90; holiness and, 90–91, 145; perfect, 98n22; reasons for, 91, 147n14; white clothes, 89–91. *See also* body; dress codes; First Ladies; pastor's wife

armor of God, 82

Asamoah-Gyadu, J. Kwabena, 164, 176, 187, 179n11

ascetic individualism, 18

Ashimilowo, Matthew, 179n11

Asiedu, Mercy, 8–9, 23n10

assemblage: media, 7, 9; religious, 7

Assemblies of God: in Nigeria, 115; and Rhema Ministries, 115

atonement: Black women and, 132

Austin-Broos, Diane, 8, 23n8, 98, 103, 113

authority, 33n17, 165; blood-covered, 53; examples of, 54; gender and, 8, 12–14, 18, 20, 23n17, 61, 63, 64, 138, 153–55, 161, 164–65, 179n11; indigenous spiritual, 53–54; men's, 3, 8, 61, 63, 110, 124, 153, 164; of sons-of-the-soil, 63; spiritual-political, 55; women's, 61, 153–55, 159–64, 179n11; women's through men, 179n11. *See also* Doe Tetteh, Christie; Duncan-Williams, Francisca; Duncan-Williams, Nicholas; First Ladies; male headship; pastor's wife; Rawlings, Jerry

Aymer, Paula, 19, 109–27, 221

Azusa Street Church: Movement, 104; Pentecost Revival, 132

Babalola, Joseph, 182–86, 188–90, 194

Babalola, Maria, 182–90, 194

baptism: card, 169; in Holy Spirit, 132, 151; Jesus Only, 132; re-, 132; theology of spirit, 135

barrenness: as stigma, 181, 184, 187. *See also* infertility

Bell, Catherine M., 133

belting, 30, 38, 42. *See also* singing; voice

Berlant, Lauren, 3

Best, Wallace, 10, 23n12, 23n15, 94–95

Bible: Africa in, 29; centrality in Pentecostalism, 151; Scofield Reference, 146n12; Thompson Chain Reference, 146n12; women's leadership in, 32. *See also* Women's Bible Bands

Black evangelical movement. *See movimento negro evangélico*

Black gospel choir, 40

Black gospel music: definition of, 42n2; sales of, 42n2

Black gospel singers, 28–29, 40; Blackness and, 29, 34; building Black church, 40–41; civil rights and, 40–41; the Devil and, 29–32; emotion and, female, 35, 38–39; female, 40; male, 40; music of, 29; oppression and, 41; patriarchal masculinity, 38; physical strength of, 38; political views of, 40–41; power of, 35; race and, 13n14, 15, 38, 39, 41; racism and, 29, 34, 38, 40; real world change and, 39; slavery and,

40–41; as spiritual battle, 29–32, 39; suffering and, 38–39; US civil rights struggle and, 29; voices and, 29, 41
Black identity politics, 15, 28
Blackness, 41, 48–54; in Bible, 37–39; in Brazil, 42n6; demonic and, 97; denigration of, 105n4; hypersexuality and, 97, 105nn4–5; Jerome on, 105n5; in North America, 42n6; racial, 48, 50, 53–54; Satan and, 97; sin and, 50, 54, 97, 105n5; singing and, 15, 34–35, 40–42. *See also* Burdick, John
Black rebellion, 36–37
blessed water. *See* holy water
blood of animal, 52
blood of Jesus, 61–62, 141
blood pact, 54–55, 60
Blues women, 90, 139
bodily practices, 130; and end times, 131; of motion, 20. *See also* embodiment; labor; praying; running; singing; wailing
body: African/European tension about, 101; in COGIC, 101; color-coding of, 97; control of, 11; covering, 18, 89–103; denigrating, 96, 101; as divine vessel, 101; dualism, 96, 98; exclusion of female, 97; Great Awakening and, 98; Hellenism and, 96; incarnation and, 96; as matrix of memory, 98; Paul and, 96; Platonized Christianity and, 96; poor women and, 98; power and, 101; as provoking theology, 128; sanctification of, 101; Sanctified church and, 89–100; as savage, 97; sexual abuse of, 98–99; sexual potency of, 101; sin and female, 96; slavery and the, 98; rape of, 99
Bohlman, Philip, 34
Brazil, 28; gender in, 17, 28–41, 48, 69, 70, 75–76, 84–86, 153; gender equality in, 27; identity in, 28, 48; patriarchal masculinity in, 38; race in, 27; racial politics in, 28; skin color in, 28
Brazilian Pentecostals, 27–41; musicians, 27–41; rates of women among, 70. *See also* Afro-Brazilian
buffered self, 4, 10. *See also* self: enchanted
Burdick, John, 15, 23n14, 27–43, 48, 221
Butler, Anthea D., 23, 101, 103, 104n2

Caesar, Shirley, 100
Candomblé, 69
Carbine, Rosemary P., 145n5
Caribbean Christians: Assemblies of God, 113; citizenship of, 47; colonialism and, 112–13; diasporic consciousness of, 46–47; emotional displays among, 123–24; gender displays and, 123–24; Jerusalem and, 46–47; "magical charisma" and, 124; majority female membership of, 122; marriage practices among, 121–22; motherhood among, 122; Pentecostal, 113–14; religious choices of post-slavery, 112–13; women's leadership among, 123
Casselberry, Judith, 20, 128–48, 221–22
Cerullo, Morris, 179n11
"chains of utterance," 117; examples of in WWW, 117
Chang, Hae-Kyung, 145n5
change: of men's behavior, 153; social, 153
charisma: democratization of, 13, 21, 165, 179n11
charismatic churches: agency of women in, 154, 177; attitudes to women in, 153; criticisms of, 176; democratizing charisma in, 154; domestic situations of women in, 166; empowering women, 176; exuberance of, 166; female founders in, 154; as forum for social change, 153; gender equality in, 153–54; liberation and, 168; marriage and, 155, 166–67; pastors' wives in, 155, 157; rhetoric of, 155; spiritual constraints and, 177; spiritual equality in, 154; spiritual gifts and, 153, 176; submission and, 154–55; success and, 154; wife as helpmeet in, 155; women's authority in, 155
charismatic healing, 56
childbearing: growth of churches and, 193
childlessness. *See* infertility
children, 20; eternal life and, 181; prosperity and, 21, 180–82; witchcraft and, 180. *See also* maternity centers; midwife
Chosa, Faith, 53
Chosa, Jim, 53

Christ Apostolic Church (CAC) (Nigeria), 181; agency and, 191; church membership and, 191; dancing in, 186; fertility and pregnancy and, 181, 185; governmental public health services and, 187; government persecution and, 189; maternity centers of, 181, 186–87; medicine and, 187, 196n22; midwife training programs of, 181–82, 188; origins of, 182; as Pentecostal, 195n3; popularity with women of, 186; prayer women of, 186–87; pregnancy care of, 186; problem solving in, 186

Christian Action Faith Ministries, 161, 178n8

Christians: as diaspora, 47

church mother, 145n7

Clark, James I., Jr., 133, 144n5, 146n12

Collins, Dalon, 30

colonial-church relations, 22, 112–13

colonialism: in Africa, 113; intertwining of women's health and, 194; maternity, reproduction and, 193; separation of government and reproduction through, 193–94

color coding, 97

conversion: effects of on women, 70; Pentecostalism and, 151; tension from, 70

Cook, Glen, 132, 140–42

COOLJC: as denomination, 131; gender politics in, 133; majority female membership of, 132

Corten, Andre, 117

Crenshaw, Kimberlé Williams, 2

Crumbley, Deidre Helen, 17–18, 89–105, 196n17, 196n20, 196n222

curses, 168–69, 172–74, 187

Dallimore, Henry, 184, 188–89

Daughters of Zion women's fellowship, 152

death, 20; raising from, 187

deliverance, 33, 104, 163, 167, 174; Doe Tetteh and, 163; instructions for in WWW manual, 119; in Pentecostalism, 151; thinking, 151; wailing for, 118. *See also* demons; Doe Tetteh, Christie; Ezilis; spirit spouses; wailing; Wailing Women Worldwide; witchcraft

demonic influence, 151. *See also* demons; spirit spouses

demon possession, 59, 94, 114; African Pentecostalism and, 114–15; Caribbean Pentecostals and, 114

demons, 17, 31, 33, 44, 45, 49–56, 61, 79, 82; charismatic churches and, 176; female, 60, 63; fertility and, 17; in Nigeria, 117; Roman Catholicism and, 60; war and, 17; WWW and, 117. *See also* Ezilis; Jezebel

Devil, 15, 27, 29–34, 41, 50, 52, 53, 60, 68, 79–81, 105n5; as black, 105n5; emotions and, 30–32; and gender, 15–16, 32; interior versus exterior battle against, 32; men and, 32, 33, 34; as monster, 105n5; prayers against, 119; singing and, 29–33; women and, 29–32; WWW and, 114

Dezabiye Jezabel (Unveiling Jezabel), revival campaign, 60

diaspora: evangelical Christianity as, 47; Haiti and, 46–47; mobility and, 20; nostalgia and, 10

diasporic: identity, 47; imaginary, 47–48

discrimination: labor, 99

divine healing, 22n3; churches, 21–22. *See also* Aladura movement; Christ Apostolic Church

divorce, 171–72; of the Duncan-Williamses, 158, 161, 178n6

divorce ritual, 57

djab rasyal (family spirits), 56

"Doctrine Party," 118. *See also* "Experience Party"

Doe Tetteh, Christie, 152, 161–65, 167, 174, 178n7, 178n10, 179n11

domestic abuse, 153

Douglas, Kelly Brown, 96

Drake, St. Clair, 104n4

dress codes, 1, 17, 18, 89–105, 135; as allegiance to faith community, 101; Bible and, 135; Black women's experience reflected in, 103; as bolstering patriarchy, 101; commodification through, 103; of COOLJC women, 134; countering hypersexualized stereotypes, 135; of Dakota Native Americans, 104n2; economic power dynasties, female, 178n7;

as embodiment of holiness, 136; false consciousness and, 102; individual expression through, 103; of Jewish immigrants, 104n2; meanings of, 103–4; millenarianism, 103; politics of representation and, 135; rebellion of, 104n2; of runners, 134; after salvation, 136; as social capital, 104n2; spiritual power of, 104; of women, 23n8, 74–76. *See also* appearance; body; Mother Brown

Duncan-Williams, Francisca, 152, 155, 157, 158–61, 164, 178nn6–8

Duncan-Williams, Nicholas, 152, 155, 160–61, 178n6, 178n8

Dutty, Boukman, 52, 60

education: of girls, 155
ekklesia, 145
electronic media, 4; buffered self and, 4
Ellison, Ralph, 10
emancipation: mobility and, 10. *See also* diaspora
embodiment: ecstatic practices of, 147n15. *See also* tongues; wailing
emotional reformation, 14, 39. *See also* power
"empowering partnerships," 51, 162–63; local leadership and, 51
empowerment: of females, 21; in Ghana, 21, 151, 155–56, 161–64, 178n2; Women in Development (WID) and, 155, 177n1
end of times, 130; church teachings about, 133. *See also* rapture; Second Coming
eroticism: and women preachers, 23n15
eschatology, 131, 143; realized, 144n5; social justice and, 155
evangelicalism: trends in, 178n4
evil, 50; African deities as, 50, 52–53; God and, 119; idolatry, 50; indigenous spirits as, 50; powers, 76; racial Blackness and, 50; spirits, 69. *See also* spiritual warfare; Third Wave evangelicalism; Vodou
exorcism: singing as, 23n14; WWW Training Manual and, 114, 119. *See also* deliverance
"Experience Party," 118
Ezili Dantò, 58–59; Gran Ezili and, 59; as mother, 59; as Trinity, 59
Ezili Freda (spirit), 56–57, 58–59

Ezili Je Wouj (Ezili Red Eyes), 58; as lesbian whore, 59; as silenced, 59
Ezilis, 58–60; biblical references to, 59; creolized Catholic origins of, 60; as Jezebel Spirit; 59; slave revolution and, 60; Spiritual Warfare movement and, 59

Faith Tabernacle of Philadelphia, 183
family discord, 56–57, 77
family roles, 74–75. *See also* male headship
family: definitions of, 63; evangelical understandings of, 61, 63
fashion, 18. *See also* dress codes
fasting, 44, 68, 167, 186
Fatiman, Cecile, 52, 58, 60, 64n5
Fauset, Arthur, 3
female: sin of, 61; submission, 61
feminism: state, 158
femocracy, 158
fertility, 22; centers, 22; periodization and, 193–94
fetish priest, 170, 174
filmmaking, Ghanaian Pentecostal, 131
First Ladies, 21, 159–61; and pastors' wives, 21
"First Lady Syndrome," 158
flows, 23n11
Flynn, John, 45
Frelimo (Frente de Libertação de Moçambique), 72, 87n8
Friday: liberating evil powers on, 67; as men's day, 67

gender: agency and, 177; complementarity, 21, 23n17, 156; construction, 9, 69–70; equality, 18, 21, 23n17; integrity, 23n17; politics, 133; roles, 72–74. *See also* Asiedu, Mercy
gendered: behavior, 70, 76, 174; geography, 136–37; nationalisms, 57; relationships in Ghana, 179n11; singing, 29–35; space, 137
Ghanian church, 20, 151–79; in Accra, 20, 151–79; in Amsterdam, 7–8; charismatic churches in, 151; gender equality in, 153, 178; and national politics, 178; power and agency in, 20, 151–79, 153, 164

gifts of the Spirit: in Black Pentecostalism, 2, 3, 15, 20, 42n1, 56, 62, 93, 153, 160, 161, 165, 176, 179n11, 192. *See also* spiritual warfare
Gilkes, Cheryl, 12–13, 23n8, 48, 145n7, 147n17
Gilroy, Paul, 34
glossolalia (tongues), in British Caribbean before 1950, 94, 102, 112, 120
God: Caribbean images of, 119; as gentle lover, 119; judgmental Father, 119; Nigerian images of, 119; Sicilian images of, 119; vengeful, 119
God-Will-Do-It-Ministries, 190; relinquishing agency and, 190
gospel choir: in Brazil, 28
gospel music: Black identity politics and, 28; gender and, 28
gospel rap, 28–29, 42n2; hyper-masculinity and, 42n3
gospel samba, 27–28, 42n2; hyper-masculinity and, 42n3
Great Migration, 23n12, 91, 93–94, 99
Grenada, 19, 109–12, 122, 134n2
grief, 137–38; singing and, 138
Griffith, R. Marie, 3, 148n20

Haiti: as demonized, 44–45, 54–55; 2010 earthquake in, 45, 50, 52; evangelical movement in, 5; masculinity in, 58; national origins of, 51; as nation dedicated to Satan, 44–45, 51; Pentecostalism in, 16, 44–49; racialized demonization of, 55; 1791 slave revolution in, 51, 54, 57; women in, 58. *See also* Spiritual Warfare movement; Third Wave evangelicalism
Haywood, Garfield T., 132
head covering, 18, 56, 90, 93, 96, 134, 161
healing, 20, 62; Joseph Babalola and, 183–85; certainty of, 140; death and, 141; divine, 140; exclusivity of, 184; lack of, 139–40; medicine and, 147n20, 184, 192; prayer for, 56, 62, 130, 136, 139–42, 183, 185, 187, 189–90, 192, 195n2; as right, 192–93; women as agents of, 61, 153
Henderson, Katherine Rhodes, 125

hierarchy, 16; disrupting, 130; gender, 13; of governing structures, 13, 23n17; racialized, 63; women displacing, 137
Higginbotham, Evelyn Brooks, 147n15
Hodgson, Dorothy L., 12, 177
holiness: aesthetics of, 135, 147n15
Holy Spirit, 31, 33, 57, 62–63, 114, 132–37, 143, 151; and African spirit world, 98, 114; agency through, 175–76, 190–91; Azusa Street Church and, 132; citizenship and, 47; egalitarianism of, 13; Great Awakening and, 98; institutional church and, 39; as lending social capital, 98; Mother Brown and, 94; in Nigeria, 110, 118, 195n2; Pentecostal church and, 42, 81, 116; and spiritual war, 30–31, 33, 68, 81, 84, 114–15; Vodou spirits and, 61. *See also* Doe Tetteh, Christie
holy water, 182–83, 186, 194. *See also* Aladura movement
homegoing, 142
household roles (by gender), 63, 69–70, 73–74, 84
Hurston, Zora Heale, 100

Idahosa, Benson, 179n11
identity, 2, 5; Black, 15, 28; Black churchwomen, 48; Christian, 46–47; diasporic, 47–48; earthly indigenous, 53; extra-ethnic, 48; global, 48; group, 71; Haitian, 48–49, 53; intersections of, 63; mixed-race, 27; music and, 38; national, 5, 71; Pentecostal, 48; politics, 28; racial, 41; singers and, 28; spiritual immaturity and, 35; voice and, 34
indigenous: church leadership, 50–51, 114, 181; earthly identity, 53; spirits, 50
industrialization, 70
infertility, 181; religious response to, 181; uterine fibroids and, 192
Inglehart, Ronald, 10
integration: body-faith-, 95; body-spirit, 92; of US schools, 89–90
intersectionality theory, 2–3, 22, 57; evangelical theology and, 48; religion and, 2–3, 69

intimacy: collective public, 6; with God, demons, 31; with Jesus, 100; marital, 156; Pentecostal, 6

Jerome, 105n5
Jesus, 47, 90, 119; authority in, 63; blood of, 62, 132, 146n9; as burden bearer, 141; citizenship and, 47; feminine Pentecostal, 19; genealogy of, 156n9; Haitians and, 55; identity in, 137; as lover, 100–101; name of, 29, 56–57, 66–67, 81, 94, 116; Only, 132; as physician, 62, 140; Second Coming of, 133, 135, 143, 145; women and, 96. *See also* deliverance; Women for Jesus fellowship
Jezebel, 57–61; Father God and, 60; masculinity and, 60; spirit, 57–61, 124–25. *See also* Dezabiye Jezabel

Kalu, Ogbu, 113–14, 157, 162, 176–77
kin: distancing from, 74, 77, 81–85
Kingdom of God, 130; Africa as, 48; building through marriage, 45–47, 55; Caribbean understanding of, 47; song as bringing about, 37; Third Wave Evangelicalism and, 51–53. *See also* Mother Reeves
Kirk-Duggan, Cheryl, 100
knowledge: narrative, 14–15; nonlinear, 14–15; women's, 119, 136–37
Korankye-Ankrah, Rita, 159, 178n7
Kraft, Charles, 51
kraze alyans (break alliance/end relationship), 56; ritual of, 56–57

labor: of Haitians, 55, 64; for Kingdom of God, 55; prayer and, 49; sexual division of, 96; sharecropping, 99; spiritual, 5, 20; women's, 5, 20, 71, 73–74, 80, 81, 88n22; women as producers of labor, 98. *See also* aesthetic labor
laity: agency of, 166
language, 85; Africans as lacking, 105; chains of utterance, 117; about drawing down Holy Spirit, 31; gendered, 71; local, 75; of rights, 193; of WWW, 117

Lawson, Carrie F., 132
Lawson, Robert C., 131–32, 145n9
leadership: female, 18, 21, 93, 95, 101, 103, 110, 123–27, 146n7, 153–54; indigenous, 50–51; local, 51–54, 64n3, 113; male, 40–41, 61, 64n3, 113, 124; official positions of, 18–19; structural dynamics of, 157–66. *See also* Mother Brown; Wagner Leadership Institute; Wailing Women Worldwide; Women's Aglow Fellowship International; Women's Bible Bands
Levitt, Peggy, 7
liberation: Black, 48; bodily, 92; eros and, 100; from evil powers, 67–68, 163; gender and race, 138; from governmental rules, 182; from man, 167–68; Mozambican, 72; Pentecostal, 92; sessions in Mozambique, 67–68; theology, 100–101; women's, 14
literacy: Women's Bible Bands and, 23n16
liturgical space: gendered, 20. *See also* Casselberry, Judith
liturgy: as public service, 20; women's actions as, 20
lived religion, 6–7
Locke, John, 11–12

Macedo, Edir, 69
Madugba, Chinyere Gloria, 115
Madugba, Mosy, 115
male headship, 18–19, 61; as heroic, 63; as redemptive, 63
Man-Child Printing Press, 124
marido da noite (husband of the night), 68, 79
marido spiritual (spiritual husband), 68
marriage, 169–70, 178; abuse in, 179–80; customary (*lobolo*), 77, 87n17, 169, 171; deception and, 54; financial dependence and, 179n12; God's choice, 173; Haitian, 55–64; infidelity in, 172; nationality and, 57–58; Pentecostal, 55; problems with, 55, 77; as sanctifying, 46; spiritual, 77; violence in, 169–70. *See also* polygamy
Marshall-Fratani, Ruth, 6, 13–14, 127
Martin, Bernice, 18, 23n17

masculinity: in Brazil, 34, 38, 42n3; evangelical notions of, 124; in Haiti, 57–58; Jezebel/Ezili as threat to, 60; revolutionaries', 57; traditional West African, 120; women's, 19

materiality: in COOLJC, 133, 136. *See also* runners

maternal care: CAC in, 189; in Nigeria, 21–22

maternity centers, 22, 176–91; CAC, 22, 181, 196n18, 196n20; as freedom from government interference, 191; government expansion of, 196n18; as missionary strategy, 191. *See also* Christ Apostolic Church

Mbembe, Achille, 71

McAlister, Elizabeth, 15, 16, 44–64, 222

McClintock, Anne, 57

media: assemblages, 7; as contested production of sensation, 7; gender and, 9–10; holdings of Pentecostal churches, 1; migration and, 4; Neo-Pentecostal churches use of, 151; power and, 11–12, 112–13; Robertson and, 45, 52; use in Pentecostalism, 2–9, 112–13, 119, 151; Wailing Women Worldwide and, 124

medicine: dismissal of, 184–85; deaths from lack of, 184; healing and, 148; midwifery and, 196n22. *See also* Christ Apostolic Church; healing

mestiço (mixed), 28

methodologies, 28, 144n1

Meyer, Birgit, 131

midwife: medicine and, 196n22; training, 22, 181–82, 188–89. *See also* maternal care; maternity centers

migration, 10, 94; neoliberal capitalism and, 10; reasons for, 10; religion and, 10–11; subjectivity and, 4. *See also* Great Migration

miracles, 183–84; babies, 164; COOLJC and, 129–30, 148n20; headscarves and handkerchiefs and, 161; healing and, 148n20; Memphis, 104n1; in Pentecostalism, 151; surgery as, 192; testimony of, 116; Ugola, 192–93. *See also* Babalola, Joseph; Doe Tetteh, Christie; Ugoala, Chinasa

Mohler, R. Albert, Jr., 118

Mold, Clive, 159

moreno (brown), 28

Morrison, Toni, 33

Mother Brown, 17, 91–112, 104n3; beliefs and practices of, 95; Bible and, 95–96; bicameral power structure of, 96; church and world of, 95; "clean church" and, 102; dress of, 27, 91, 93–95, 96, 102–4; female leadership of, 95; gender and, 95–96; hair and, 96; values of, 94

motherhood: leverage of, 71–72; in Nigeria, 121; single Caribbean, 19, 122; status through, 122

Mother Reeves, 137–43

movement, 7–9; Azusa Street Pentecostal, 104; Black activism, 27; Black Baptist women's, 147n15; Black evangelical, 40, 111; bodily, 100; Brazil's Black, 41; charismatic, 153–57, 160–67, 175–79; of Christianity, 22n2; civil rights, 41, 89; counterculture, 89; diasporic, 10; Haiti evangelical, 50–51, 55, 63; Holiness, 93, 111, 134, 154; Jesus, 97; migration, 10, 48; Pentecostal, 111–13, 154, 118; of people, 10; physical, 124; pro-Black, 40; of religious bodies, 10; revival, 16; women's, 158. *See also* Aladura movement; Azusa Street Church; Duncan-Williams, Francisca; Duncan-Williams, Nicholas; running; Spiritual Warfare movement; Third Wave evangelicalism

movimento negro evangélico (Black evangelical movement), 40

Mozambique, 17, 67–87; "down with" policies in, 72; issues of societal development in, 71–72; rates of Pentecostal adherence in, 86n3; traditional versus modern practices in, 72–75

music, 8, 139; African, 9; anointing and, 144n3; Brazilian Black Gospel, 15, 27–43; church versus worldly, 100; in COOLJC, 129; Holiness Pentecostals and, 135; Mother Reeve and, 139; racial understandings of, 29; tasks of, 139; tradition and, 78 música negra, 27–28. *See also* Black gospel; rap gospel music; samba gospel music

negro (black), 15, 28–29, 34–42; atonement and, 132; Bible and, 146n9; flesh and, 101; spirituals, 100, 139
Neo-Pentecostalism, 21; characteristics of, 151; prosperity gospel and, 21; race and class among, 23n13; women and, 153–75
"New Issue" or "Jesus Only" doctrine, 132
Nigeria, 180–94, 195n2; Christians in, 126; churches in, 20–21, 180–94; Muslims in, 126; Pentecostal boom in, 194; Pentecostalism in, 13–14, 20–22, 181, 195n2; pregnancy and, 180–94; religious fears in, 126; warfare in, 126; women and WWW, 19, 109–27. *See also* Wailing Women Worldwide
Norris, Pippa, 10

objects in motion, 23n11
Oduyoye, Mercy Amba, 176
O'Neill, Kevin Lewis, 22n2
oppression: demon, 114–15; gender and race, 138; religion and, 3, 35–36; singing to resist, 35–36, 41
ordination: controlling, 23n8; COOLJC and women's, 136; power of, 23n8; women's, 132

parousia, 90, 133; COOLJC and, 133; Paul and, 96
pastor's wife, 152–61; among Catholic converts, 178n5; COGIC and, 18; dual leadership and, 154, 158, 160; images of, 157; gender equality and, 157–58; in Ghana, 157; influence of, 159; as leaders, 161; as mother, 159; political leadership and, 158; research on, 157; role of, 157, 178n5. *See also* Duncan-Williams, Francisca; spirit spouses
Pastors' Wives and Women in Ministry Association, 152, 155, 159, 178n8; as patron-client network, 159
patriarchy: dress codes and, 101; exit from, 154; in Pentecostalism, 18; race and, 39; set pieces of, 8; subversion of, 8–9, 32n8. *See also* dress codes
Peel, J. D. Y., 181, 183
Pentecostal: definition of, 42n1, 151
Pentecostal Christianity: in Africa, 151; alienation from kin and, 17; appeal to Black women, 2; beliefs and practice, 1; colonialism and, 2; continuities of, with traditional religions, 194; conversion rate in, 1; as coping strategy, 85; democracy and, 23n17; empowerment and, 21, 153; as force of change, 85; gender and, 40–41; gender equality and, 69, 153; in Ghana, 2, 7–9, 151–77; global reach of, 1–2, 22n2; growth of, 1; individuation in, 153; insecurity and, 14; international, 22n2; interpretations of spread of, 118; lifestyles of, 1; Nigerian, 13–14, 115, 127; political implications of, 3; politics and, 1; power and, 41; pragmatism and, 194; promotion of household, 69; proselytization and, 126; race and, 1, 41, 27, 63; racism and, 41; rates of women in, 1; stress and, 17; terminology of, 2; transnational, 22n2; women's autonomy and, 69. *See also* power
periodization, 193–94
personal development (of women), 153, 155, 158; in American evangelicalism, 157; through being born again, 153
Pinn, Anthony, 100, 131
Pliny, 105n4
polygamy: Brazilian Pentecostals and, 69; in Haiti, 60–61; Pentecostalism and, 69–70
Pombagira (Mistress of the Night): definition of, 79–80
possession: in African traditions, 98; female of priest, 58; gendered, 59; of medium, 61; music as, 38; of sexual powers, 1–5; spirit, 59, 60, 94, 114; unconsciousness during, 174; Vodou, 59–61. *See also* demon possession; Ezilis; Wailing Women Worldwide
power, 11, 130; Black Pentecostal women and, 3, 12, 14, 40–42; brokers, 62; in church, 14; demonic influence and, 151–52; disabling, 3; domains of, 177; among elite, 21;

power (*continued*)
emotional worship, 124; enabling, 3, 176; evaluating, 11; feeling versus having, 39; Maasai women and, 12–13, 177; material, 11; media, 11; of ordained/non-ordained, 23n8; Pentecostal performance of, 115; persuasive, 11; political, 12; of prayer, 19, 32, 115, 117, 119, 120, 136, 142, 166, 175–76, 185, 190; privilege and, 14; punitive, 12; secular modernity and, 11; semiotics of, in postcolonial societies, 71; spirit, 12, 20, 69; spiritual, 4, 11–21, 30, 32, 39, 42, 60–63, 75, 81–85, 104, 114, 117, 130, 133, 136, 152–54, 158, 160, 165–66, 174–77; spiritual and social, 177; states, religion, and, 4, 10–12, 20; technologies for accessing, 11; types of, 11–12, 14, 41, 177; visible, 14. *See also* agency; authority; charismatic churches; spiritual warfare

powerlessness: among women, 21

pragmatism, 190–93; African traditional religions and, 194; Alafia and, 192, 194

prayer, 166–76, 183; charismatic, 175–76; from deliverance, 119; Francisca Duncan-Williams and, 152, 159; and global deliverance, 119; God as lover in, 119; in Grenada, 109; infertility and, 181; intercessory, 19, 45, 61–62, 110, 115–17, 126–27; medical diagnoses directing, 140, 188; music, 12, 139; networks, 19, 109–23; as power, 19, 32, 115, 117, 119, 120, 136, 142, 166, 175–76, 185, 190; predestination and, 130, 141–42; *Seven Principles of*, 183; unanswered, 141; visible and vocal, 109; Vodou and, 55–57, 59; wailing as, 118–19, 126–27; warfare, 61, 115; warriors, 26, 44, 49, 53; women's role as, 14, 42, 119; Yoruba, 180. *See also* Doe Tetteh, Christie; Duncan-Williams, Francisca; Duncan-Williams, Nicholas; infertility; Wailing Women Worldwide

praying, 19, 67

preaching: COGIC women, 147n17; COOLJC, 136–37; Doe Tetteh's, 164, 179n11; female bodies, 94; geography of, 136; Jesus's, 145n5; Lawson, 132–33; racism and, 13; roots of, 135; women and, 147n17

pregnancy, 20–21, 80–85
Premack, Laura, 20–22, 180–96, 222
Prentiss, Henry, 132
Pritchard, Elizabeth A. 1–23, 39, 41–42, 222
Pro-Black movement, 40
prophecy: of Brazilians, 37–38; of Ethiopians, 37; of Isaiah, 37; power brokering through, 62; about pregnancy, 185
prosperity, 11, 20–21, 180; children as signifying, 21; definitions of, 180; gospel, 21, 68; material goods as, 21; in Nigeria, 18–19, 21; tithing and, 82; women's understandings of, 22. *See also* Neo-Pentecostalism; wealth

race: Blackness and, 15, 27, 41, 48–55, 104nn4–5; equality versus 15, 27; Haiti and, 15, 52; Pentecostals and, 13, 15, 23n13, 41, 48, 69; sin and, 13, 16; theology and, 13, 16, 48, 62, 112, 122. *See also* negro

racialization: Catholic, 49–50; Christian, 49; gender and, 57; of Haiti, 65; histories of, 48–49; versus physiognomy, 16. *See also* intersectionality theory

racial uplift, 16, 99–100

racism: Brazil and, 34; Christianity and, 53; in church, 39–40; in classical Greco-Roman civilization, 97, 104n4; colonial, 34, 55; discussions of, 29, 40; exorcism of, 23, 14; French and, 52–55, 64n4; indigenous peoples and, 53; mobilization and, 3; Pentecostals concern about, 41; as sin against God, 13, 50; singing and, 38; slave trade and, 105n4; structural, 104n4; systemic, 138

Radano, Ronald, 34
Rai, Amit, 7
rape: in Mozambique, 17, 72; slavery and, 99; white clothing and, 103
rap gospel music, 27–29, 32n2, 32n3, 32n6
rapture, 133
Rawlings, Jerry, 158, 160
Rawlings, Nana Konadu Agyeman, 158
religio-medical marketplace, 187, 190. *See also* Christ Apostolic Church
religious affiliation; CAC and, 189; data on

African Americans', 146; as fluid, 194; intent of, 6; Levitt on, 7; Mother Brown and, 93; pragmatism of, 194

"religious assemblages," 7; as structures of support, 10; unsettling boundaries, 9. *See also* Levitt, Peggy

Renamo (Resistência National Moçambicana), 72, 87n9; destruction of nation-state by, 72–73

reproduction, 82; of gender relations, 177; and politics, 193; separation of from state, 22, 194; sociocultural, 72; spirituality and, 12; women and cultural life, 73

respectability, 130, 134–35; gender and, 137; politics of, 135, 147n15

revival. *See* Spiritual Warfare movement

Rhema Ministries, 115

rhizomes, 7

Ricoeur, Paul, 145n5

ritualized actions, 133. *See also* Bell, Catherine M.

Robbins, Joel, 84, 146n11

Robertson, Pat, 45, 52

Robinson, Lizzie, 18, 19

runners (in church), 129–37

running (in church) 20, 130–31; fertility and, 164–65; healing and, 130, 134–37

Sackey, Brigid M., 157–58, 161, 178n8

saints (Holiness), 89, 144n4; caring acts of, 137–38; as commandment keepers, 94; Doctrinal Points of, 102; dress fashions of, 18, 90–95, 102–4; education of, 90; faith practices of, 139–45; female, 18, 90, 96; Great Migration and, 99; hair of women, 18; healing of, 20; holiness of, 90; Holiness Pentecostal, 144n3; Holy Spirit and, 95; male, 18; rapture and, 133; Sanctified church, 104n1; separation of, 95; vocal praise of, 129. *See also* Mother Brown

salvation, 11; Brazilian message of, 28; comfort of, 141; commandments and, 90; and demonic ancestral spirits, 52; ethnicity and, 46; expectation of, 20; for all, 125; identity through, 122; message entrusted to "negros," 34; North to South, 50; roles in, 15–16; status of in COOLJC, 133; stigma and, 122; transformation in dress and comportment after, 136

samba gospel music, 27–28, 42nn2–3

Satan. *See* Devil

Schüssler Fiorenza, Elisabeth, 145

Scott, Joan, 12

Scott, Shaunna, 32–33

Second Coming, 37, 133

secularity: religion as, 3, 6; understandings of, 56

segregation, 89, 99, 104n1, 147n15; *Brown v. Board of Education*, 89

self, 4, 156, 157; -accounts, 33; -affirmation, 157; -assurance, 34; bounded, 3; buffered, 3; charismatic women's, 156;; -confidence, 153; -denial, 157; -determining churches, 92–93;; -development, 21; enchanted, 3; -engaged, 22n1; gendered, 23; and God, 153; Holy Spirit and, 31; -image, 156; -overcoming, 11, 13; Pentecostals as, 22n1; premodern, 3; -presentation, 131, 134; -representation, 131; salvation and new, 136; "set apart," 22n1; women's, 76, 81–82

sex, 95, 156–57, 164, 173, 176; abusive, 173, 180; coercive, 168, 170, 173–75; Dambala and, 54; extramarital, 168; premarital, 122; racialization of, 16; as relationship, 157; rhetoric about, 157; women and, 68, 94, 156–57

sex education, 156; sermon on, 156–57, 178n2

sexism: systemic, 138

sexual: division of labor, 96; economy, 134–35; exploitation, 98–99; promiscuity, 153; provocation, 103; violence, 78

sexuality, 55–61; ambiguities of, 79; in Black church, 100, 105; Holiness-Pentecostal paradoxes of, 92, 135; hyper- and Blackness, 97, 99, 101, 105n5, 134; national identities and, 71; promiscuity in Neo-Pentecostalism, 153–54; sin and, 97

Sicilian Pentecostalism, 119

sin, 13, 22n1, 36, 54–55; accommodation to, 13; adultery as, 61; black skin and, 16, 105; body and, 95, 96, 103–4; Caribbean women and, 19–20; Eve and, 95; of idola-

sin (*continued*)
  try, 50; intercession for, 110, 117, 119; mediums and, 61; new birth and, 13; racism as, 13, 50–52, 54–55, 64n4; sanctification and, 101; set apart from, 22; sexuality and, 97; single mothers and, 122; song as exorcism of, 23n14; wailing and, 109, 127
singing, 20, 128–30; Black gospel, 23n14, 29–40, 42n2; Black identity through, 28; Black voices of, 34, 38; blues, 139; choice of, 141–42; comfort of, 143; conviction and, 139; for deceased, 130, 138; Devil and, 30–34; differences between male/female, 40–41, 42n3; eschatological tension of, 20; as exorcism, 23; God and, 36–38; as gratitude, 143; healing and, 56–57; identity and, 28–; as liberating, 37; men, 33–34; political views of, 41; as providing space, 38, 139, 143; purpose of, 39, 138; racism and, 38; as relating to God, 19; as restorative, 142; as search, 33; as spiritual battle, 29–31, 39; as spiritual power, 136; spirituals, 139; spontaneous, 130; suffering and, 35; survival and, 34–35; transformative power of, 139; weeping in, 35. *See also* Mother Reeves
slavery, 52; bodies and, 134–35; in Brazil, 27, 34, 69; empire and, 97; exorcism of, 23; freedom in God from, 57; French, 64; in Haiti, 51–52, 54, 57–58; Jezebel and, 60; marriage and, 122; music and, 9; in North America, 98–99; punishment for, 64n4; racism as preceding, 105n4; religious options and, 112–14; to Satan, 52; singing and, 35; teaching about, 40–41
slaves, 36; singing, 35–37
sleep: as death, 138, 141, 147n18; as sexual intercourse, 167–68, 172–73
social catapulting, 85
Solid Rock Chapel (Accra), 152, 162–64; attendance figures at, 168n9; laity in, 166–67
Soothill, Jane, 20–21, 151–79, 222
sounding bodies, 20, 118–43
sounds, of women, 19, 110, 112; God and, 19; singing, 19, 33; wailing, 19. *See also* wailing; Wailing Women Worldwide

Sowedo, Brother, 186
spirit: avenging, 76–78, 87n15; body rituals and, 81; egalitarian promise of, 13, 132–33; exorcising, 5, 17, 9, 81, 195; -filled performance, 8, 14, 62; Pentecostal understandings of, 5; war, 78
Spirit baptism, 132, 135, 151
Spirit possession, 59, 94, 98, 114, 174
spirits, ancestral. *See* ancestral spirits
spirits, struggle with, 17–18; living with, 81
spirit spouses, 55, 76–78, 80, 119; as ancestral spirits, 80; definitions of, 76; deliverance from, 80, 119; wealth and, 76, 78
spiritual: battle, 68–84; equality of believers, 154; gifts, as empowering women, 176; husband/*marido spiritual*, 68–69; malaise, 13; mapping, 44, 51–53; as supplemental texts, 20
spiritual patronage, 12, 159–60, 164–65. *See also* Doe Tetteh, Christie; Duncan-Williams, Francisca
spirituals, 8, 9, 100, 139
spiritual warfare, 2, 14–17, 59–61, 82–83; appropriation of, 68; in Brazil, 29–32; continuous, 84; gender and, 59, 85–86; gospel singers and, 33–34; in Haiti, 16, 44–64; interiorization of, 32; movement, 16; in Mozambique, 17, 68; music as, 29–31; in New Zealand, 33; in Nigeria, 14; singing as, 29–32; upward mobility and, 81–84, 86; violent national history and, 85
Spiritual Warfare Movement, 44, 49, 68, 86; definition of, 49. *See also* Third Wave evangelicalism; Wailing Women Worldwide
Spivak, Gayatri, 3
state: patronage, 20; separation from, 10–11. *See also* power
Stewart, Maria W., 13
storefront church, 17, 89–95, 111
submission (female), 21, 61, 63, 64n3, 95, 124, 132, 137, 154, 155; Christie Doe Tetteh on, 165; Francisca Duncan-Williams's, 160
suffering, 37–38; evil powers and, 81; as God's design, 36; singing, 35, 38–39, 41. *See also* Black rebellion

Taylor, Charles, 4–5, 10, 11
"Theo-geographies," 16, 47, 137. *See also* gendered: geography
"thingification": of Black persons, 110
Third Wave evangelicalism, 16, 44, 50, 63; definition of, 44; local leadership in, 51–52; names for, 64n1; prayer warriors in, 44, 49. *See also* spiritual warfare; Spiritual Warfare movement
Thompson, Alvin O., 105n4
tithing, 82–83; withholding, as power, 23n8
tongues: in Caribbean, 112; as characteristic of Pentecostalism, 2, 132, 151 (*see also* 195n2); in COOLJC, 136; in Ghana, 151; in Holiness Church, 102; in Nigeria, 195n2; ranking of, in WWW, 120; in Sanctified church, 102
touch: Christie Doe Tetteh and, 162, 165; Francisca Duncan-Williams's, 161; of Holy Ghost, 143; Jesus touching, 140; singing's capacity to, 36; woman, of Jesus, 96
Toulis, Nicole Rodriguez, 8, 14, 23n9
Toussaint, Gregory, 60
tradition, 87n20; as backward, 78, 84; banishing, 87n13; incorporation of, 97–98; revival of, 78
Tripp, Aili Mari, 71

Ugoala, Chinasa, 192–93
Umbanda, 69
uterine fibroids, 192

Van de Kamp, Linda, 17, 67–88, 222–23
victory: in Pentecostalism, 151
voice: bio-essentialization of, 38; God and, 38. *See also* singing
Vodou (Haitian), 16, 50, 54, 55, 61; possession, 59; spirits, 56–57; spiritual divorce from, 55–56

wages: egalitarianism and, 13; of Mozambique women, 86n5
Wagner, C. Peter, 16, 49, 51–53
Wagner Leadership Institute, 53. *See also* Wagner, C. Peter

wailing, 19, 109–27; as act of piety, 118; beginnings of, 115; as intercession, 19, 118–19, 121, 126; Jeremiah and, 109; as placating angry male God, 119; as power, 124; as prayer, 118, 120; relationship and, 19; as response to men's intransigence, 119; as softening stern God, 19; as superior to other practices, 120; as uniting ritual bond, 120; as weapon, 120
Wailing Women Worldwide (WWW), 19, 109–27; as act of piety, 118; African traditional religious practice and, 125; as army, 111, 120; beginnings of, 115–17; composition of, 126–27; as exclusionary, 126–27; as global prayer army, 117, 119–20; in global South, 126; as God's battle-axes, 120; Kingdom of God and, 127; leadership in, 110, 123–25, 127; marriage and, 121; missionary program of, 123–25, 127; personal and family priorities among, 122–23; prophecies of, 117; selectivity of, 126; as softening God's heart, 127; as soldiers, 120, 127; success of, 127; *Training Manual*, 115, 119, 121, 124; unobtrusiveness of, 124–25; as wives, 121; women's roles and, 124
war: Christ Apostolic Church and, 186–87; female spiritual strength and, 58; in Haiti, 58; kingdom and, 95; in Mozambique, 17, 67–87; rape and, 17. *See also* spiritual warfare
wealth, 180; evil and, 82; family and, 81–82, 85; health and, 2; marriage and, 75; Neo-Pentecostal churches and, 20; as peace, 192; Pentecostal churches and, 1; people as, 180; as power, 12; sharing, 85; spirits and, 76. *See also* alafia; spirit spouses
wedding: as cultural life, 73; in Haiti, 45–46; tent camp, 45–46, 54–55
weeping: Black voices as, 35; in singing, 35; Wailing Women Worldwide and, 118. *See also* wailing
Whitaker, Rosa, 161
Williams, Melvin, 101
witchcraft, 75, 76, 79, 164, 173–74; accusations of, 75, 180; Brazilians and, 79; deliverance from, 174; infertility and, 164, 180; spirit spouses and, 173; wealth and, 76

witches, 172, 176; pregnancy and, 185
womanizers, 181–83; pastors as, 183
women: anointing of, 132–33, 136, 167, 168; attitudes to, 71, 175; attitudes to in new and older Charismatic churches, 153, 166; Bible and, 19, 32, 88n22, 95, 109, 117, 118, 123–24, 143, 163; Bible Bands, 23n16; blood of, 132, 140, 184; bodies of, 5, 17, 18, 20, 32, 79–81, 91–104, 122–44, 182; clothing of, 18, 134; crucifixion and, 132; dress of, 17, 18, 56, 89, 91, 96, 134, 147n14, 16 (Muslims, COOLJC), 152; as exegetes, 20; as fighters, 31, 83, 87n22; leadership of, 32, 153; majority status of, 146n11; mourning, 19; in Mozambique, 72; in New Testament church, 132; Nigerian, 19–22, 109–21, 126, 185, 191–92; roles in churches, 32; sexual stereotypes of, 135; submission of, 63, 132; Yoruba, 190–91. *See also* anointing; Mother Brown; Wailing Women Worldwide; Women's Bible Bands
Women for Jesus fellowship, 152
Women In Action prayer meeting, 152
Women's Aglow Fellowship International, 112; leadership in, 126
Women's Bible Bands, 19, 23n16; literacy and, 23n16
Women's Conventions, 152–53
women's ordination: Haywood and, 132; Lawson and, 132
Word of Faith movement, 22n7
www. *See* Wailing Women Worldwide

Yuval-Davis, Nira, 71

www.ingramcontent.com/pod-product-compliance
Lightning Source LLC
Chambersburg PA
CBHW071816230426
43670CB00013B/2477